CULTURE, PEOPLE AND POWER

Culture, People and Power

India and the Globalized World

Edited by

Amitabh Mattoo
Heeraman Tiwari

Indian Council for Cultural Relations, New Delhi

SHIPRA

Rs. 750; US$ 37.50

ISBN: 978-81-7541-713-7

First Published in India in 2014

Culture, People and Power: India and the Globalized World

Published by:
SHIPRA PUBLICATIONS
H.O.: LG 18-19, Pankaj Central Market, Patparganj,
Delhi-110092, Tel: 91-11-2223 5152, 2223 6152
Br.Off.: 4617/18, Ansari Road, Darya Ganj,
New Delhi-110002, Tel: 9650028065, 9810522367
E-mail: info@shiprapublications.com
www.shiprapublications.com

सत्यमेव जयते

MEMBER OF PARLIAMENT
RAJYA SABHA
(UPPER HOUSE OF PARLIAMENT)

Dr. Karan Singh

PRESIDENT
INDIAN COUNCIL FOR
CULTURAL RELATIONS
(ICCR)

Message

I am pleased to introduce to the reader this ICCR volume on India's cultural heritage and intellectual power. The volume, *Culture, People and Power: India and the Globalized world,* is the result of an international seminar that the ICCR had organized in Delhi on the occasion of the 60th year of the founding of the ICCR. As I write this message for the volume today, I recall what I had written nearly two and a half decades ago (*Essays on Hinduism*, 1987:94): "India has always claimed to have a message for humanity. …If you go to Java or to Bali, or to Bangkok or Cambodia, you will see there the influence of Indian culture. … And we carried the message not through conquest, not through atomic bombs, not through force of arms, but through moral and spiritual power. Therefore, the claim that India has some message for the world is not simply chauvinism, it is based upon our achievements over the last three thousand years or more."

This was what India could achieve in the past. Today, in the changed dynamics and geo-strategic combinations of the globalized world, India's cultural and spiritual message is equally relevant and, perhaps, even more necessary. India has always shared its cultural and intellectual heritage with the world, and India's spiritual orientation makes it a natural friend of the world. If the story of Rāma, the message of the Buddha, the teachings of the *Bhagavadgītā* have inspired generations worldwide, it is because India's intellectual traditions and moral values carry a message for all humanity, and not only for India. Whether it was Kabir or Vivekanand, Sri Aurobindo or Mahatma Gandhi, all are rooted in these traditions and all have succeeded in inspiring the peoples of the world.

The contributors to this volume have discussed and analyzed various aspects of Indian culture and tradition, and argue how they are relevant to today's world, which is fast becoming a global village thanks to the advances made in the field of economy and technology. An institution like the ICCR provides a platform for the universe of Indian culture to be experienced and relished by the modern 'global village', and I am happy to note that this volume suitably adds to the Indian conception of universal humanism. I congratulate the editors and the staff at the ICCR for aiding and facilitating its publication.

Although economic prosperity and political freedom are necessary, true human happiness is difficult to realize without spiritual and cultural freedom and fulfilment. After all, the sole objective of economic freedom has to be human freedom, which as the ancient Indian culture teaches us, is not possible without spiritual freedom. The famous Indian economist and Nobel laureate, Amartya Sen, has made the value of human freedom fashionable by declaring it to be the preeminent goal of economic development: "The intrinsic importance of human freedom, in general, as the preeminent objective is strongly supplemented by the instrumental effectiveness of freedoms of particular kinds to promote freedoms of other kinds." (*Development As Freedom,* 1999:xii) That economic prosperity alone is not sufficient was the message given by the *Bṛhadāraṇyaka* sage Yājñavalkya: "Like the life of wealthy people, with money to be able to afford all the amenities, necessities of life will be your life, but there is no hope to attain absolute happiness and immortality through wealth alone." (*yathaivopakaraṇavatāṃ jīvitaṃ tathaiva te jīvitaṃ syād amṛtattvasya tu nā 'śāsti vittena.)*

(Karan Singh)
31st July, 2013

सत्यमेव जयते
SPECIAL SECRETARY
MINISTRY OF EXTERNAL AFFAIRS

Dr. Suresh K. Goel

DIRECTOR GENERAL
INDIAN COUNCIL FOR
CULTURAL RELATIONS
(ICCR)

Message

It is my great pleasure to present before you the volume, *Culture, People and Power: India and the Globalized World,* which is the result of the international seminar that the ICCR had organized in November 2010 to celebrate 60 years of Indian Council for Cultural Relations. This was also the occasion of the 122nd Birth Anniversary of Maulana Abul Kalam Azad, the founder of this unique organization. The President of the ICCR, Dr. Karan Singh, proposed the idea of holding an international seminar where eminent scholars from around the world were invited to discuss and debate on various aspect of India's cultural legacy and civilizational resilience in India's cultural and intellectual traditions. The past few decades have witnessed the resurgence of India in the field of economy, democratic values and culture. What is important, however, is that the growth of India's economic and political power has always been linked with its heritage and cultural traditions. The mission of the ICCR has been to complement India's link with the increasingly globalized world by developing India's cultural and civilizational heritage to develop collaborations and dialogue with different societies to achieve the vision of "*Vasudhaiva Kuṭuṃbakam*", the very basis of Indian philosophical thoughts and ICCR's works. If economic prosperity is necessary to keep the physical world healthy and strong, art and culture provide nourishment to the mind and the soul. India has over the millennia produced and sustained a very rich and diverse culture; it has also welcomed and absorbed cultural and political traditions of other civilizations with whom it has come into contact either through economic exchanges or by political relations. This elasticity and resilience has provided India with a unique position of its geo-strategic and economic power with which to influence the modern, globalized world.

The scholars who were invited to the seminar are all experts in the field of Indian culture, literature and politics; their contribution to the volume proves that. I congratulate and thank the editors of the volume, Amitabh Mattoo and Heeraman Tiwari, and the staff at the ICCR, led by Shri Sunil Mehdiretta, for bringing out the outcome of the seminar to the readers of the world.

(Suresh K. Goel)

Contents

PART III
ART AND CULTURE

Introduction

This volume is the fruit of an international seminar, *Indian Culture in a Globalized World,* organised by the *Indian Council for Cultural Relations* on its 60th anniversary in November 2010. This seminar was also dedicated to Maulana Abul Kalam Azad, one of the prominent leaders of India's freedom movement, a scholar-politician, and independent India's first education minister who in 1950 established the *Indian Council for Cultural Relations* with the aim to spreading and transmitting the multiplicity, the richness and the uniqueness of Indian culture to far away corners of the world. It is to celebrate this vision and sagacity of Maulana Azad that a large number of international and Indian scholars gathered in Delhi and held a very lively and rich discussions on the various aspects of Indian culture(s) and debated how India has contributed, and continues to do so, to the cultures of the world and how it has become even more relevant in the world today which is increasingly becoming interconnected, and semantically smaller, owing to the spread of modern technology and economic globalisation.

The papers in this volume discuss topics ranging from ancient Indian fine arts, religious beliefs, ethical nuances to the issues of contemporary sociopolitical debates, which together place India in a unique position in the globalised world. The papers here reflect what His Excellency Dr M. Hamid Ansari, the Vice President of India, delineated in his fine, inspiring opening address to the seminar, that the virtues of multiplicity in the ancient culture(s) of India has over the centuries, even millennia, kept its 'doors' unbolted through which the scented winds of various cultures rustled in only to be embraced, assimilated by the host. He said:

"Our subject today verges on the amorphous. It seeks elucidation and linkages of three concepts: globalization, culture, and Indian culture. While the first is commonly viewed solely as an economic phenomenon, the other two have been subjected to considerable philosophical and sociological analysis. All three tempt the uninitiated to wonder off in speculative labyrinth. Hence the need … to see things with the eye of reason", and the Indian culture, he suggested, has "a relevance to the globalising world of today. Being the confluence of ideas, values and tradition it cannot but be inherently syncretic. While maintaining the purity of individual traditions, …it accepts the authenticity of others and synthesizes them into newer and richer forms."[1] Dr Karan Singh, the Honourable President of ICCR and a profound scholar-politician, too, underscored the concept of 'Unity in diversity' in Indian culture, and to connect the thread of this concept he also invoked the ancient Vedic and Upaniṣadic pronouncements. Dr Karan Singh said: "Culture has been used in the broadest sense of the term as a 'way of life' which includes history, art, sculpture, dance, music, traditional and contemporary achievements, science and technology, perspective for future development and aspirations of our nations. Culture has no boundaries, and using it as a medium to interact with the masses has been the most effective and proven way to win hearts in this era of globalisation. Interacting through culture gives us a chance to interact and understand the great cultural heritage of the world."[2]

It is in this context that the papers of this volume become relevant to the India of today, i.e. a globalised India firmly keeping its feet in the ancient culture and wisdom bestowed by generations of philosophers, scholars and thinkers. Perhaps, it would have been easier in a volume like this to forgo the arrangements of the papers in a group or parts and allow them the freedom to speak for themselves. But we have tried to group them in three different parts, according to their respective themes and chronological proximity of the sources they discuss. Each part reflects the narratives and the subjects of the contributions. So, for example, in Part One, entitled *Power of Culture*, the papers highlight India's soft power in modern, globalized world. Dr Shashi Tharoor's paper discusses the soft power of India by analyzing how Indian culture has penetrated, in a very Indian way, into the lives of even those who know not much about India but relish things Indian. To illustrate a harmonious coexistence of various cultures in India, Tharoor employs wisdom and wit and culls the metaphor from India's cuisine culture to liken it to a Thali (or platter) rather than to a melting pot. Jean-Luc Racine in his paper suggests that soft power has always been the background sound of India, its vision and its signature. The construction of India's national image has been acquired through entrepreneurial zeal of its merchants and dissemination of its pacific ideas. Racine goes on to suggest that this image of India, 'connecting the present age of timeless civilizational legacy', has acquired even more relevance in the recent decades. David Cortright's paper reinforces this vision of India when he invokes the contribution and importance of Mahatma Gandhi in building not only the modern Indian nation but putting India at a global stage as the nation of inspiring hope among the people seeking social justice. Cortright analyses how Mahatma Gandhi's clever movement of civil rights through non-violent means has influence not only the many great leaders of the world — including the current President of USA, Barack Obama, who considers Mahatma Gandhi's ideas as his pool of inspiration in furthering the cause of global justice, — but has taught millions in many countries around the world how to achieve democratic and civil rights through non-violent protests. T.V. Paul considers India's culture, civilization, literature, philosophy, diplomacy and political organization as 'intangible indicators' of its soft power.

With its prosperity and globalization India needs also to pay attention to its knowledge industry by nurturing its intellectual resources to compete in an ever-increasing knowledge basket of the world as well as by promoting individual freedom; individual freedom has been a very important aspect of human civilization; the secret of success in individual development lies in nurturing freedom. Even the ancient Indian philosophical texts, viz. the *Upaniṣads,* have underlined the freedom of the self towards fulfilling the development of the self and of the world. The famous debate between sage Yājñavalkya and his wife, Maitreyī, in the *Bṛhadāraṇyaka Upaniṣad* illustrates this notion well. Maitreyī asks her husband, a great seer, how far will wealth (i.e. development) bring her what she wants? Will wealth substitute for their happiness, i.e. freedom? "If this whole earth, full of wealth, belongs to me, could I achieve deathless-ness or immortality?"[3] In other words, would wealth be able to afford us absolute happiness? Yājñavalkya's answer to this rather rhetorical question appears simple but, in fact, it is illustrative of the need for freedom in the process of development. For Yājñavalkya says: "No, like the life of wealthy people, with money to be able to afford all the amenities, necessities of life will be your life, but that there is no hope to attain deathlessness, immortality, through wealth."[4]

Part Two of the volume, entitled *People and Literature*, therefore, consists of essays which deal with India's People and Literature, where knowledge of India's past is discussed. Robert Goldman's paper highlights the relevance of the Indian epics, especially the *Rāmāyaṇa*, in India and in the vast Indian diaspora, its unending charm and values it instills among people. Johannes Bronkhorst discusses India's past by analyzing its Brahmanic tradition and suggests that, although like all traditions India's Brahmanic tradition does have a certain vision of the past, it is necessary to verify it historically and if required correct this vision to bring it to conformity with the present. For example one of the visions of the Brahmanic traditions is that it is old and unchanging; however, Bronkhorst believes that a close study of the ancient literature would encourage one to change this view, particularly when scrutinizing the contributions and interventions of the great figures like the Buddha. Patrick Olivelle discusses the dynamism of ancient Indian culture by pointing out how modern scholarship on ancient India is trapped in visions of the orientalists and colonial scholars and urges us to abandon the intellectual lenses provided by colonial scholarship; and to illustrate his point Olivelle analyses two central, defining categories of Indian civilization and Hinduism: *dharma* and *dvija*.

For cultural and intellectual health of any country it is important to hone and nurture literatures produced by languages of the land; and it is often alleged that in India with so many of its rich languages and vernaculars not adequate attention is paid to the literatures produced in these languages. Part Three, entitled *Art and Culture,* contains papers which deal with the issues of literature and fine arts and cultures of India. Muzaffar Ali, the famous Indian film director, advises how to bring about higher standards in Indian films to make them competitive in the world cinema. Sally Sutherland

Goldman traces the history of ancient Indian dramas which attracted the Western, European imagination. Sutherland Goldman talked about how themes and stories from Indian literature and culture have inspired many a theatre in both America and Europe from as early as the seventeenth and eighteenth centuries. To illustrate her point she picks up the example of Kālidāsa's great play, *Śakuntalā*, which was adopted and performed by great composers and directors in Europe and the USA. Muzaffar Alam's paper underlines the contribution of Mughal rulers in shaping the image of India before the world. Alam analyses the roles of Sufi Shaikhs in Indian cultural and social developments and suggests how the Sultans and Mughals of early medieval India quickly recognized the power of the Sufi concept of *wahdat-al wujud* ('Unity in Being') and adopted it in their sultanates and kingdoms to maintain peace and harmony in the diverse faiths of their subjects. Heeraman Tiwari's paper discusses the concept of identity and humanism in Classical Indian literature and philosophy drawing on the Sanskrit literary and philosophical texts.

The editors would like to thank all the contributors of the volume and to the President and the Director General of the ICCR for first organizing a wonderful seminar and then facilitating publication of its proceedings as a volume. We hope the readers will benefit from the works of the scholars and thinkers who have together made this volume possible. We would like to close by quoting here the famous lines of the seventh century Sanskrit poet and dramatist, Bhavabhūti, who said: 'One must always say and do what one has to say and do, there is no escaping criticism; there will always be people to challenge you, to question you.' (*sarvathā vyavahartavyaṃ kuto hy avacanīyatā*).

Amitabh Mattoo and Heeraman Tiwari

Notes

1. Inaugural Address by His Excellence Dr Hamid Ansari, the Vice President of the Republic of India, 11 November 2010.
2. The Address by Dr Karan Singh to the Inaugural Session of the Seminar, 11 November 2010.
3. *Bṛhdāraṇyaka Upaniṣad* 2.IV.2.
4. Ibid. 2.IV.2.

Part I
Power of Culture

1
The Soft Power of India

Shashi Tharoor

A panel of India culture may seem an odd place to use word "power", even if it is allied to the adjective "soft". And yet to speak of India's place in the world today there is no better template than its culture, which has become a source of attraction in the world transcending considerations of economic growth, military strength or population numbers. That is its "soft power".

The nation of soft power is relatively new in international discourse. The term was coined by Harvard's Joseph Nye to describe the extraordinary strengths of the United States that went well beyond American military dominance. Nye argued that "power is the ability to alter the behavior of others to get what you want, and there are three ways to do that" coercion (sticks), payments (carrots) and attraction (soft power). If you are able to attract others, you can economise on the sticks and carrots[1]. "Traditionally, power in world politics was seen in terms of military power: the side with the larger army was likely to win. But even in the past, this wasn't enough: after all, the US lost the Vietnam War, the Soviet Union was defeated in Afghanistan, and the US discovered in its first few years in Iraq the wisdom of Talleyrand's adage that the one thing you cannot do with a bayonet is to sit on it. Enter soft power – both as an alternative to hard power and as a complement to it. To quote Nye again: "the soft power of a country rests primarily on three resources: its culture (in places where it is attractive to others), its political values (when it lives up to them at home and abroad), and its foreign policies (when they are seen as legitimate and having moral authority.)"[2]

I would go slightly beyond this: a country's soft power, to me emerges from the world's perceptions of what that country is all about. The associations and attitudes conjured up in the global imagination by the mere mention of a country's name is often a more accurate gauge of its soft power than a dispassionate analysis of its foreign policies. In my view, hard power is exercised; soft power is evoked.

In his book *The Paradox of American Power* Nye took the analysis of soft power beyond the United States; other nations too, he suggested, could acquire it. In today's information era, he wrote, three types of countries are likely to gain soft power and so succeed: "those whose dominant cultures and ideals are closer to prevailing global norms (which now emphasize liberalism, pluralism, autonomy); those with the most access to multiple channels of communication and thus more influence over issues are framed; and those whose credibility is enhanced by their domestic and international performance."[3]

This is where India comes in. India's claim to a significant role in the world of the 21st century lie in the aspects and products of Indian society and culture that the world finds attractive. These assets may not directly persuade others to support India, but they go a long way toward enhancing India's intangible standing in the world's eye.

The roots of India's soft power run deep. India's is a civilization that, over millennia, has offered refuge and, more important, religious and cultural freedom, to Jews, Parsis, several varieties of Christians, and Muslims. Jews came to the south-western Indian coast centuries before Christ, with the destruction by the Babylonians of their First Temple, and they knew no persecution on Indian soil until the Portuguese arrived in the 16th century to inflict it. Christianity arrived on Indian soil with St. Thomas the Apostle ("Doubting Thomas"), who came to the Malabar Coast some time before 52 A.D. and was welcomed on shore, or so oral legend has it, by a flute – playing Jewish girl. He made many converts, so there are Indians today whose ancestors were Christian well before any Europeans discovered Christianity. In Kerala, where Islam came through traders, travellers, and missionaries rather than by the sword, the Zamorin of Calicut was so impressed by the seafaring skills of this community that he issued a decree obliging each fisherman's family to bring up one son as a Muslim to man his all –

Muslim navy! The India where the wail of the Muslim muezzin routinely blends with the chant of mantras at the Hindu temple, and where the tinkling of church bells accompanies the Sikh *gurudwara's* reading of the verses from the Guru Granth Sahib, is an India that fully embraces the world. Indeed the British historian E.P. Thompson wrote that this heritage of diversity is what makes India "perhaps the most important country for the future of the world. All the convergent influences of the world run through this society..... There is not a thought that is being thought in the West or East that is not active in some Indian mind."[4]

That Indian mind has been shaped by remarkably diverse forces: ancient Hindu tradition, myth and scripture; the impact of Islam and Christianity; and two centuries of British colonial rule. The result is unique. Though there are some who think and speak of India as a Hindu country, Indian civilization today is an evolved hybrid. We cannot speak of Indian culture today without *qawwali*, the poetry of Ghalib, or for that matter the game of cricket, our *de facto* national sport. When an Indian dons "national dress" for a formal event, he wears a variant of the sherwani, which did not exist before the Muslim invasions of India. When Indian Hindus voted recently in cynical and contrived competition to select the "new seven wonders" of the modern world, they voted for the Taj Mahal constructed by a Mughal king, not for Angkor Wat, the most magnificent architectural product of their religion. In the breadth (and not just the depth) of its cultural heritage lies some of India's soft power.

We are a land of rich diversities: I have observed in the past that we are all minorities in India. This land imposes no narrow conformities on its citizens: you can be many things and one thing. You can be a good Muslim, a good Keralite and a good Indian all at once. So the idea of India is of one land embracing many. It is the idea that a nation may endure differences of caste, creed, colour, culture, cuisine, conviction, costume and custom, and still rally around a democratic consensus. That consensus is around the simple principle that in a democracy you don't really need to agree – except on the ground rules of how you will disagree. Part of the reason for India's being respected in the world is that it has survived all the stresses and strains that have beset it, and that led so many to predict its imminent disintegration, by maintaining consensus on how to manage without consensus.

The world of the 21st century will increasingly be a world in which the use of hard power carries with it the odium of mass global public disapproval, whereas the blossoming of soft power, which lends itself more easily to the information era, will constitute a country's principal asset. Soft power is not about conquering others, but about being yourself. Increasingly, countries are judged by the soft-power elements they project onto the global consciousness, either deliberately (through the export of cultural products, the cultivation of foreign publics or even international propaganda) or unwittingly (through the ways in which they are perceived as a result of news stories about them in the global mass media). Soft power, in other words, is created partly by governments and partly despite governments; partly by deliberate action, partly by accident.

India produces various kinds of culture, notably including the films of Bollywood, now reaching ever-wider international audiences. The triumph of *Slumdog Millionaire* at the 2009 Oscars both reflects and reinforces this trend. Bollywood is bringing its brand of glitzy entertainment not just to the Indian diaspora in the US or UK but around the globe, to the screens of Syrians and Senegalese. A Senegalese friend told me of his illiterate mother who takes a bus to Dakar every month to watch a Bollywood film – she doesn't understand the Hindi dialogues and can't read the French subtitles, but these films are made to be understood despite such handicaps; she can still catch their spirit and understand the stories, and people like her look at India with stars in their eyes as a result. An Indian diplomat friend in Damascus a few years ago told me that the only publicly – displayed portraits in that city that were as big as those of then – President Hafez al – Assad were those of the Bollywood superstar Amitabh Bachchan. Indian art, classical music and dance have a similar effect. So does the work of Indian fashion designers, now striding across the world's catwalks. Indian cuisines, spreading around the world, raises our culture higher in people's reckoning; as the French have long known, the way to foreigners' hearts is through their palates. The proliferation of Indian restaurants around the world has been little short of astonishing. In England today, Indian curry houses employ more people than the iron and steel, coal and shipbuilding industries combined. (So the Empire can strike back.)

Globalization has both sparked and allayed many Indians' fears that economic liberalization will bring with it cultural imperialism of a particularly insidious kind – that "*Baywatch*" and burgers will supplant *Bharatnatyam* dances and *bhelpuri* snacks. Instead, India's recent experience with Western consumer products demonstrates that we can drink Coca-Cola without becoming coca-colonized. Indians will not become any less Indian if, in Mahatma Gandhi's metaphor, we open the doors and windows of our country and let foreign winds blow through our house – because Indians are strong enough not to be blown off their feet by these winds. Our popular culture has proved resilient enough to compete successfully with MTV and McDonald's. Besides, the strength of "Indianness" lies in its ability to absorb foreign influences and to transform them – by a peculiarly Indian Alchemy – into something that belongs naturally on the soil of India.

Indeed, from the export of Bollywood to bhangra dances, India has demonstrated that is a player in globalization, not merely a subject of it. India benefits from the future and the past – from the international appeal of its traditional practices (from ayurveda to yoga, both accelerating in popularity across the globe) and the transformed image of the country created by its thriving diaspora. Information Technology has made its own contribution to India's soft power. When Americans in Silicon Valley speak of the IITs (The Indian Institutes of Technology) with the same reverence they used to accord to MIT, and the Indianness of engineers and software developers is taken as synonymous with mathematical and scientific excellence, it is India that gains in respect. Sometimes this has unintended consequences. I met an Indian the other day, a history major like me, who told me of transiting through Schiphol Airport in Amsterdam and being accosted by an anxious European crying out "you're Indian"! You're Indian! Can you help me fix my laptop?" The old stereotype of Indians was that of snake-charmers and fakirs lying on beds of nails; now it is that every Indian must be a software guru or a computer geek.

In the information age, Joseph Nye has argued, it is often the side which has the better story that wins. India must remain the "land of the better story". As a society with a free press and a thriving mass media, with a people whose creative energies are daily encouraged to express themselves in a variety of appealing ways, India has an extraordinary ability to tell stories that are more persuasive and attractive than those of its rivals. This is not about propaganda; indeed, it will not work if it is directed from above, least of all by Government. But its impact, though intangible, can be huge.

To take one example: Afghanistan is clearly a crucial country for India's national security, as it is for the US's. President Obama has spoken of reinforcing American and NATO military capacity there. But the most interesting asset for India in Afghanistan doesn't come out of a military mission: it doesn't have one. It comes, instead, from one simple fact: till just about a year ago, you simply couldn't try to telephone an Afghan at 8:30 in the evening. Why? Because that was when the Indian TV soap opera "*Kyunki Saas Bhi Kabhi Bahu Thi*", dubbed into Dari, was telecast on Tolo TV, and no one wished to miss it. It was reportedly the most popular television show in Afghan history (at least until the onset of "Afghan Idol" last year), considered directly responsible for a spike in the sale of generator sets and even for absences from religious functions which clash with its broadcast times. (This has provoked visceral opposition to the show from the *mullahs,* who finally succeeded in their efforts to shut it down). But while it was on, "*Saas*" so thoroughly captured the public imagination in Afghanistan that, in this deeply conservative Islamic country where family problems are usually hidden behind the veil, it's an Indian TV show that has come to dominate society's discussion of family issues. I have read reports of wedding banquets being interrupted so that the guests could huddle around the television for half an hour, and even of an increase in crime at 8:30 pm because watchmen are sneaking a look at the TV rather than minding the store. One Reuters dispatch recounted how robbers in Mazar-i-Sharif stripped a vehicle of its wheels and mirrors recently during the telecast time and wrote on the car, in an allusion to the show's heroine, "Tulsi *Zindabad*" (long live Tulsi). That's soft power, and India does not have to thank the government or charge the taxpayer for its exercise. Instead, Indians too can simply say, "Tulsi *Zindabad.*"

Of course official government policy can also play a role. Pavan Varma, a former head of Indian Council for Cultural Relations (ICCR), has argued that "culturally India is a superpower" and that cultural diplomacy must be pursued for political ends. So India is highly visible at cultural shows around the world, and the ICCR is rather good at organizing Festivals of India in assorted foreign cities. That's good, but I'm not a fan of propaganda, which most people tend to see for what it is. I believe the message that really gets through is that of who we are, not what we want to show.

For soft power is not just what we can deliberately and consciously exhibit or put on display; it is rather how others see what we are, whether or not we are trying to show it to the world. To take a totally different example: Politically, the sight in May 2004 – after the world's largest exercise in democratic franchise (but then every Indian election is the world's largest exercise in democratic franchise!) of a leader of Roman Catholic background (Sonia Gandhi) making way for a Sikh (Manmohan Singh) to be sworn in as Prime Minister by a Muslim (President Abdul Kalam) – in a country 81% Hindu – caught the world's imagination and won its admiration. (This is not a Congress Minister's insight: I was travelling in the Gulf on behalf of the United Nations at the time, and the reactions of my Arab interlocutors to what had happened in India could not have been more gratifying).

So it is clear that If India wants to be a source of attraction to others, it must preserve the precious pluralism that is such a civilizational asset in our globalizing world. Our democracy, our thriving free media, our contentious civil society forums, our energetic human rights groups, and the repeated spectacle of our remarkable general elections, have all made of India a rare example of the successful management of diversity in the developing world. It adds to India's soft power when its non-governmental organizations actively defend human rights, promote environmentalism, fight injustice. It is a vital asset that the Indian press is free, lively, irreverent, and disdainful of sacred cows.

But every time there are reports of sectarian violence or a pogrom like the savagery in Gujarat in 2002, or a nativist attack like those by a fringe group in February on women drinking at a pub in Mangalore, India suffers a huge setback to our soft power. Soft power will not come from a narrow or restricted version of Indianness, confined to the sectarian prejudices of some of the self-appointed guardians of Indian culture ("*Bharatiya Sanskriti*"). It must instead proudly reflect the multi-religious identities of our people, our linguistic diversity, the myriad manifestations of our creative energies. India must maintain its true heritage in the eyes of the world.

And that will mean acknowledging that the central battle in contemporary Indian culture is that between those who, to borrow Walt Whitman's phrase, acknowledge that we are vast, we contain multitudes, and those who have presumptuously taken it upon themselves to define (in increasingly narrower terms) what is "truly" Indian. Pluralist India must, by definition, tolerate plural expressions of its many identities. To allow any self-appointed arbiters of Indian culture to impose their hypocrisy and double standards on the rest of us is to permit them to define Indianness down until it ceases to be Indian. To wield soft power, India must defend, assert and promote its culture of openness against the forces of intolerance and bigotry inside and outside the country.

To me, the essential strength of Indian Culture is that it is sustained by a larger idea of India – an Indian that safeguards the common space available to each identity, an India that celebrates diversity. If America is a melting-pot, then to me India is a *Thali,* a selection of sumptuous dishes in different bowls. Each tastes different, and does not necessarily mix with the next, but they belong together on the same plate, and they complement each other in making the meal a satisfying repast.

India's civilizational ethos has been an immeasurable asset for our country. It is essential that India does not allow the spectre of religious intolerance and political opportunism to undermine the soft power which is its greatest asset in the world of the 21st Century.

Notes and References

1. Nye, Joseph. *Soft Power: The Means to Success in World Politics*, New York, 2004.
2. Ibid.
3. Nye, Joseph. *The Paradox of American Power: Why the World's only Super Power can't Go it Alone*, New York: Oxford University Press, 2002.
4. Thompson, EP, 1977.

2
India's Soft Power: Culture and Beyond

Jean-Luc Racine

> "Soft power has always been part of India's legacy and we take pride that the message of India was spread beyond our region without recourse to arms. The 'empire of the monsoons', to use a convenient phrase, was built through trade, travel and the flow of ideas. The knowledge economy, in many ways, is embedded in our culture. The internet, for us, is an ally and not a threat. This soft power has gained in recent years with the demonstrated success of India's democratic polity. We are not just raising the living standards of a billion people and more, but doing so within a framework of liberal values and rule of law. The uniqueness of this effort is underlined by the diversity of ethnicities, languages and faiths that it encompasses. A globalised world must necessarily be a more pluralistic and rule-based one." –M.K. Narayanan, 2006.

India's self definition has for long been replete with visions of soft power, much before Joseph Nye coined this concept in 1990[1]. The construction of the national image, before and after Independence, put forward the fact that much of India's influence, particularly in South East Asia, has resulted from the entrepreneurship of her merchants and the dissemination, pacifically, of her ideas. The spread of Hindu concepts in arts and beliefs from Angkor to Bali, and the expansion of Buddhism to China, Japan and Korea are testimonies to the fact. The travels to India of Chinese monks Fa Xian (IVth century) or Yi Jing (VIIth century) illustrate, on the other way, ancient India's attractiveness. Much later, the *Travel to the West* became a classic of Chinese literature: it depicted the quest for Buddhist sutras ordered by Boddhisatva Guan Yin to monk Xuang Zang, who spent years in India in the VIIth century. Occasionally, during Indo-Chinese summits, this legacy of history is still recalled.[2]

While culture has always been a decisive dimension of India's soft power, the relevance of this issue has grown considerably with the emergence of the country during the last fifteen years or so. In this regard, the quote from M.K. Narayanan opening this paper expresses perfectly the way Indian decision-makers paint an image of emerging India connecting the present age of transition with a timeless civilisational legacy, and link cultural plurality and democratic polity to the capacity to diffuse to the world what is labelled as "the message of India". Soft power is thus explicitly recognised as a pre-existing tool—a part of Indian DNA, if I may say so—which has nevertheless to be cultivated for helping India to find her right place in the new global order. Significant is the fact that this assessment of India's soft power has been formulated by a National Security Adviser in an address delivered to the most noted global annual conference on security.[3] If culture is obviously a key element of soft power, one may believe that it could be relevant to look at culture in the broader framework defining (or limiting) soft power.

This is what I shall attempt in this contribution. Perhaps there is something personal behind this perspective. While I am today, as a scholar, focussing my research on the way India redefines herself and her role on the global chessboard, and on South Asian geopolitics, I have been active, under different capacities, in fields where soft power is deployed: as Director of the French Cultural Centre at Calcutta in the Seventies; as founder of the Social Sciences Department of the French Institute at Pondicherry in the Eighties; as Head, for the French side, of the Indo-French Programme of Cooperation in Social Sciences in the Nineties. The Fondation Maison des Sciences de l'Homme, to which I am still attached in Paris, has worked prominently since the late Sixties for a sustained dialogue between Indian scholars (and other scholars as well) and their French counterparts. I have been associated also with Indo-French bilateral cultural events, and with European Union-India initiatives, the most recent ones involving the Indian Council of World Affairs.

With this dual type of interests in mind, I would like to offer remarks on ICCR cultural diplomacy, before looking at the evolution of the image of India abroad. A case study will also be presented: the patterns of dissemination of Indian culture in France, as I have been able to observe it during the last thirty years or so. This being done, as soft power is not confined to its strict cultural dimension, I shall pay attention as well to other parameters which define it, particularly when they relate to other modes of expression, conveyed by medias, by the global movement of ideas, and by the broad perceptions circulating about India and Indian democracy. No need to say that this attempt will be sketchy—too sketchy perhaps.

The Quest for Global Reach : ICCR Cultural Diplomacy

For long, Western countries have developed their cultural and education policy abroad. The British Council, the Goethe-Institut (Max Müller Bhavan in India) and the Alliance française are well known around the world. In all these cases the main focus of the interaction with host countries is the teaching of the language, but it goes beyond that. The Alliance française, for instance, sets to itself three missions: (i) to provide French courses; (ii) to contribute to the dissemination of French and French speaking cultures (emphasis is given to plurality); (iii) to contribute to cultural diversity. It is worth noting that the Alliance was not the brainchild of the French government, although it receives quickly official support. L'Alliance française as such, which later on developed what is one of the largest cultural global network with more than 1000 centres, 450,000 students and 6 millions participants to cultural programmes, has been created in 1883, by a panel of private well know citizens including amongst others a high civil servant who has served also in diplomacy, Paul Cambon; a well known novelist, Jules Verne; a top scientist, Louis Pasteur; an academic publisher, Armand Colin, and an engineer of exceptional repute, Ferdinand de Lesseps, who had built the Suez Canal during the 1860s. The date 1883 is significant: just before, primary school in France has been declared free (1881), then compulsory (1882). The opening to the world, at a time of colonial expansion, was contemporary to the dissemination of universal primary education to all villages of the country.[4] In other words, there was a dialectical relation between deep transformation at home and projection of culture abroad.

The world is obviously quite different today, but in a way we recognise something comparable, if not similar, in the present situation: emerging India is transforming herself at home while projecting herself to the world. The creation of ICCR by Maulana Abul Kalam Azad in 1950 located the Council in the wide range of post-colonial initiatives taken for building free India on sound foundations. Sixty years later, the present expansion of the ICCR cultural centres abroad has to be understood in a context I would define as "post-post colonial". Till the end of the 1980s, India on a move was still largely defined by the post-colonial principles governing the construction of the newly independent State, as far as economy and diplomacy were concerned. From the Nineties, key decisions—the new turn of the economic policy in 1991 and the nuclear tests in 1998—have started to build up a new set of images and perceptions, which have defined the narrative of emerging India. Not that the Nehruvian core values are outdated, far from it, and they have to be preserved and enhanced for they are still the basis of a polity which contributes greatly to India's soft power. But after the difficult years of the 1980's, a new perception of India by herself, a new Indian vision of the world, and a new perception of India by the world have to a large extent defined what I call the "post-post colonial". Prime Minister Manmohan Singh, in a remarkable speech delivered at Oxford in 2005, expressed this vision in his own words: «As an Indian, I see a new sense of hope and purpose. This new optimism gives us Indians a new sense of self-confidence and it shapes our world-view today.»[5]

This new sense of confidence and the willingness to made India more visible abroad have given a strong impetus to ICCR's global policy, which has been clearly defined by its chairman Dr Karan Singh in a speech delivered in 2006 on cultural diplomacy. His argument is twofold. On the one hand, culture stands as the root of the nation, which believes in a spirit of give and take with the rest of the world: "Cultural diplomacy, of the more conscious and active kind, helps the spread of those aspects of our culture that we hold dear to our hearts, to our ways of living and thinking, which truly and essentially characterize us as a community and as a nation. We share our culture with others, we take what the others can offer". This "constructive interaction", could also stem from private initiative from individuals, NGOs and people to people networks able to sustain themselves outside the pale of the State power. On the other hand, this philosophy embedded in the age old concept of "vasudhaiva kuṭumbakam" ("the entire world is one single family") can and should also be actively implemented by the State apparatus, through its own diplomatic networks and through mandated but autonomous institutions dedicated to projecting Indian culture abroad: "The purpose of cultural diplomacy is to reinforce the strategic foreign policy objectives of the Government. Successful cultural diplomacy should be able to reach out, in a subtle yet effective manner, beyond the formal structures of Government to the larger opinion, key opinion makers, important segment of the media and private yet influential stakeholders in society".[6]

Looking at the present network of ICCR Centres abroad, I would venture a few observations, limited by the fact that information is not always easily available for all Centres. The twenty-four centres existing presently can be distributed in three or four categories, which can interestingly be related to India's perception of her realm of influence.

A first set is located in countries (eventually small countries) with a noticeable or a very large proportion of People of Indian Origin: Fiji (two centres), Guyana, Surinam, Trinidad & Tobago. Some of these Centres have been opened almost forty years ago, such as Georgetown and Suva, in 1972, or a bit later (Mauritius, 1987).

South Africa is a special case: the Durban centre can be related to the Indian diaspora, while the Johannesburg centre may materialise an other rationale, as South Africa is now an emerging country enjoying a special status in the circle of India's partners, in the trilateral IBSA (India, Brazil South Africa) set up in 2003, as well as in the new BASIC network (Brazil, Africa South, India China) established after the 2009 Copenhagen Summit on climate change.

A second category of centres illustrates the willingness of India to spread its cultural diplomacy in its immediate neighbourhood, in SAARC countries. If Pakistan is absent, Sri Lanka, Nepal, Bhutan and Afghanistan host now an Indian Cultural Centre. The Colombo centre has been opened in 1998—eight years after the withdrawal of the Indian Peace Keeping Force from Sri Lanka. The more recent openings express, so it seems, either political transitions in countries run at times by unstable regimes (Kabul and Kathmandu, 2007) or belated normalisation between neighbours (Dhaka, 2010).

A third category would fit with the concept of "extended neighbourhood" promoted by South Block during the 1990s. Interestingly, this concept reverberates what has been defined in 1950 as priority areas for ICCR. Maulana Abul Kalam Azad himself, in his address delivered for the inauguration of the Council in April 1950 stated that, while the Provisional Committee had decided to remove "all the territorial or geographical limitations on the activities of the Council", in order to establish "contacts between India and all other countries of the world whether in Asia or outside", a step by step approach was the need of the hour, and that two sections will be started first: "a Middle East and Turkey section, and a South and East Asian section".[7]

The Look East policy was slowly implemented on the cultural front. From the year of its political formulation in 1992, it took time for setting up centres in Thailand (2009) and Malaysia (2010), Indonesia being endowed with two centres (date unknown). Central Asia was more quickly approached after the collapse of USSR, as a centre was opened in Tashkent in 1995. Centres opened later on in Dushanbe, Tajikistan and Astana, Kazakhstan. As far as West Asia is concerned, the move is recent (Abu Dhabi, 2009) and the extended neighbourhood perspective is compounded by the presence of a large Indian diaspora.[8] Egypt is beyond the standard definition of extended neighbourhood, but a Centre has been opened in Cairo in 1982: too late for fitting in the non-alignment pattern of the Nehru years, but much earlier than most of the centres ICCR opened in countries deprived of a significant Indian diaspora.

The fourth and last category of centres is located in major cities of leading countries. Centres have been established in Moscow in 1989, in London in 1992, in Berlin in 1994, in Tokyo in 2009.

This geographical tour would be incomplete if the time factor were not taken into account. While the number of ICCR centres abroad has been limited for long, a policy of considerable expansion has been engaged during the past few years. One third of the existing centres have been open after year 2000 and, to quote the ICCR website, other centres "in the pipeline" include Thimpu, Mexico City, Sao Paulo, Dar-es-Salaam, Budapest, Yangoon, Paris, Washington, Hanoi, Lagos, Prague, Singapore, Rome and Kuwait. An interesting list indeed, with addresses SAARC (Bhutan), the extended neighbourhood (Vietnam, Singapore, Myanmar, Kuwait), major European countries (France, Italy) including in Eastern

Europe (Czech Republic and Hungary), the U.S. and, last but not least, key partners for a South-South dialogue in Africa (Nigeria, Tanzania) and, in a continent untouched so far, Brazil and Mexico. As far as China is concerned, besides cultural festivals across the two countries[9] and other events in several large cities, the ICCR contributes to the activities of the Culture and Information Wing of the Indian Embassy in Beijing : this could be developed into a full-fledged ICCR Centre in the future.

In addition, one should keep in mind that ICCR does not confine itself to running and expanding the network of its centres abroad. For long, cultural activities related to literature, music, dance, fine arts have been funded in countries deprived of cultural centres. Indian festivals abroad and foreign festivals in India are regularly organised. Some sixty teaching chairs have been established in foreign universities across the world, half of them in countries deprived for the time being of cultural centres (Canada, France, U.S.A., China, and many others), and scholarships are provided to foreign students from more than seventy countries under the "general scheme", in addition to what is offered through the special schemes for Commonwealth countries (54 scholarships) and for African countries (135). In this context, Afghanistan deserves a specific attention, not only because India is one of the largest providers of funds for reconstruction with more than one billion US$ committed, but also because hundreds of Afghan students are registered in Indian universities, most of them with scholarships.

If soft power is a part of ICCR agenda, government soft power policy is not limited to cultural activities, as testify two recent projects selected by the Government of India in 2005 and 2006 respectively: the SAARC University and the Nalanda University. The first one, as its name implies, is bound to attract students from the eight SAARC countries. It opened on a modest basis, with 50 students, on the JNU campus in 2010, and is bound to shift in 2014 to its own New Delhi premises with a goal of attracting on due time 7000 students, half of them Indians. Masters are for the time proposed in Development economics and Computer application: the focus is clear. Nalanda University is quite different. It aims at reviving the glory of the past, when Buddhism prospered in one of the most ancient places of higher learning which attracted scholars from far away, from the fifth century CE onwards, in what is today

Bihar. With Nobel laureate Amartya Sen leading the Mentor Group in charge of implementing the project, and with sixteen countries interested with it (including Japan and China) Nalanda has already attracted the attention of The Economist.[10] Public diplomacy was also on the forefront when President Pratibha Patil inaugurated in Henan province of China, in May 2010, an Indian style temple at the White Horse monastery in Luoyang where two Indian monks having translated Buddhist sutras in Chinese have been buried in the 1st century A.D. This was a major event of the Festival of India in China.

Civil Society : The Quintessential Soft Power

Whatever the role of the State could be, soft power escapes from any government monopoly. The Government of India itself recognized it, when it decided to pay attention to the Indian diaspora after decades of benign neglect. Appointed in 2000 by the Ministry of External Affairs, the High Level Committee on the India Diaspora released its report in December 2001 (it included a chapter on culture). The first "Day of Indian diaspora", Pravasi Bharatiya Divas, has been celebrated in 2003, and from this day onward, on every January 9th (the day of arrival of mahatma Gandhi in South Africa) noted members of the Indian diaspora are honoured by the Government of India, which in 2004 set up a new Ministry, first named Ministry of Non-Resident Indians, and quickly renamed Ministry of Overseas Indian Affairs. This upgrading of "Non Resident Indians", and the feeling that "Peoples of Indian Origin" might also contribute positively to the image of India abroad put an official seal on a fact already well recognised. The Indian diaspora in the U.S., in this context, is obviously playing a specially important role, which goes beyond culture.

For instance, the US-India Business Council, established in 1975, contributed strongly to develop new perceptions about India in America. The connexion between American experts on India and Indian (or Indian-born) analysts explains as well why U.S. leading think tanks started from the 1990s to release reports calling for a redefinition of US South Asia policy, and for India's upgrading on Foggy Bottom and the White House agendas. The mix of soft power, economic interest, strategic thinking, diplomatic negotiations and political will have reshaped the relationship between what

Dennis Kux and Daniel Moynihan labelled in the early Nineties "Estranged Democracies".[11] Later on, the US India Political Action Committee (UNINPAC) opened office in Washington in 2002 with a clear goal: «to impact policy on issues of concern to the Indian-American community in a non-fragmented manner». The Committee is proud to mention on its website : «One of the most significant events in USINPAC's history was its success in impacting the passage into law of the US-India civilian nuclear cooperation agreement in 2008. USINPAC had been at the forefront of advocating and lobbying the US Congress and Indian policy-makers right since the deal's inception in 2005».[12]

Shashi Tharoor, commenting upon Joseph Nye, the Harvard professor who theoricised soft power in relation to the future of America[13], put it that way : "It is not the side with the bigger army, but the side with the better story, that wins", arguing that "India is already the land with the better story".[14] I do not know if India has the best story to tell, but her grand narrative, which was a bit hesitant during the difficult 1980s after being brilliant during Nehru's times, is certainly a very good story, which is consistently improving, despite weaknesses and recurrent black spots. For the time being, let us recognize that India's image has greatly improved during the last couple of decades.

It is something of a cliché to recall it, but it is true that the image of India has been for long offering antithetic characters. On the one hand, there was a time when European intellectuals—or at least some of them—saw in India one of the greatest sources of human thinking, one of the main nodes of intellect on the map of world civilisations. This perception went beyond the image of India as a land of spirituality: philosophers and thinkers were engaged in the discovery of India much before Jawaharlal Nehru published his well known book in 1946. During most of the XIX century, European scholars carried on a tradition opened with the establishment of the Asiatic Society in Calcutta in 1784, translated fundamental Indian texts—scriptures and shastras—and commented upon what the Indian great tradition had brought to the world. Wilhem Halbfass has well documented this relationship located in the global history of philosophy.[15] But later on, as French essayist Roger-Pol Droit noted during the Eighties, India's image suffered a setback, and except in the circles of Indianists and Indophiles, India was largely "forgotten" by Western philosophers who entered in "amnesia".[16] More broadly and in a very different field, Katherine Mayo's Mother India, published in 1927, contributed to disseminate a very negative perception of the country, Gandhi dismissing her book as "a drain inspector report".[17] However, and as usual, nothing is just black or white. Tagore had received the Nobel Prize in 1913 after Gitanjali has been translated into French with the help of a leading French author, André Gide (Gide will himself get the Nobel Prize in 1947), and another noted French novelist and thinker, Romain Rolland (Nobel Prize 1915), during the same Twenties painted in black by Mayo, contributed to build a totally different image of India through four books: Gandhi (1924), L'Inde vivante (India alive, 1929), La vie de Ramakrishna (1929), La vie de Vivekananda (1930).

To cut a long story short, this dual perspective held ground for long, after Independence as well. In 1957, Satyajit Ray received the Golden Lion at Venice for Aparajito, and the year before Tibor Mende had published in French its Conversations avec Nehru, but at that time the prevalent image of India was already changing: the concept of "third world" appeared in France in 1952. Loaded with wide expectations after the Bandung Summit in 1955, it lost pretty quickly the dynamic connotation enthused in the Non Aligned Movement, and soon prevailed the concept of underdevelopment. The Sixties told us the same dual story, in a way: M.S. Subbulaksmi's concert at the U.N. in 1966 and Ravi Shankar opening his school in California in 1967 promoted the image of India's cultural sophistication to different types of audiences, but these years were also those of the food crisis in Bihar. Calcutta, the city of Indian Renaissance in the XIX century, became painted more often as the city of the destitute than as the City of joy of Lapierre's fame. The Nobel Peace prize given to Mother Teresa in 1979 added to this image abroad, albeit the founder of the Missionaries of Charity was greatly celebrated in India (and elsewhere) before and after her death.

Another image of Indianness was to appear soon, through an exceptional writer: Salman Rushdie, distinguished for Midnight's Children in 1981. The topic of the book, focussed largely on post-colonial India, the creativity of the style, the strength of the narrative, the impact it had—putting Indian literature in diaspora on the global map, far away from Naipaul's distant relation with the country of his ancestors—opened a new era. In a way, Rushdie's success and notoriety anticipated in the cultural field the success other Indians in diaspora met with, decades later, in the field of enterprises, be they computer wizards in California or steel tycoon Lakshmi Mittal.[18] By that time, India's soft power had decidedly become multifaceted. Sustained for long by the success of Indian writers, musicians and artists abroad, India's soft power was to be boosted during the Nineties by the emergence of a new type of Indian entrepreneurs meeting with global reach, in the field of information technology first—the success story of TCS, Infosys and Wipro is too well known for being commented again—but in other fields as well: biotechnology, and also manufacturing, with Tata conglomerate buying Tetley Tea in 2000, then Jaguar and Land Rover in 2008. Indian companies acquiring some of the most prestigious brands associated with the epitome of British way of life had a symbolic value lost to none: soft power is not necessarily opposed to the hard power of money…

India's cultural soft power had acquired since a couple of decades an additional dimension going beyond literature. While distinguished Indian scholars had for long occupied positions of prestige in British Universities (Sarvepalli Radakrishnan, long before becoming President, had held the Spalding Chair of Eastern Religions and Ethics at Oxford University from 1936 to 1952, the best known names being today, as far as Great Britain is concerned, Lord Meghnad Desai and Lord Bikhu Parekh), a new development occurred with noted scholars entering in numbers Ivy League Universities in America. This trend was not resulting only from individual life stories. It testified—and still testifies—to the fecundity of Indian scholars of humanities and social sciences. Subaltern studies, for instance, made history in India before becoming one of the parameters of post-colonial studies in U.S. campuses, and disseminating amongst African and Latin American intellectuals. The list of distinguished Indian scholars (or scholars of Indian origin) having made a noted contribution to global thinking, and having offered that way an acute illustration of India's soft power is too long for being offered here.[19] What should be noted is that the Indian experience of these intellectuals in diaspora contributed decisively to their way to address general issues: India is thus, often explicitly but sometimes discreetly, reincorporated in the analysis of the world past and present—foreign experts on India playing their role as well in this process of universalisation of the sources of knowledge.

Amartya Sen is obviously the most emblematic figure amongst all these Indian intellectuals abroad, for at least three reasons. First, the type of welfare economics he has propounded has a strong humanistic dimension, which contrasts with the more technical expertise of many other Nobel laureates from his profession. Second, he is more than an economist, as testify the Lamont professorship of Economics and Philosophy he holds at Harvard, as well as a number of his books, from *Development as Freedom* to *The Argumentative Indian* and *The Idea of Justice.* Third, celebrated the world over, Sen remains faithful to India where he comes every year, and where he is actively engaged in the field of ideas and action. Due to his family background and his connection with Shantiniketan and because of his focus on welfare economics and justice, Amartya Sen, a global citizen, is also of very distinguished heir of an Indian tradition of permanent regeneration of the idea of India that Tagore and Nehru have both, in their own way, illustrated.

Mention should be made as well of the success in business met by those Indians or PIO who got to the top. Laskhmi Mittal is emblematic here, but he is not alone in the coveted world of top chief executives: Indra Nooyi, at the helm of Pepsi Cola, is perhaps the best known today, but dozens of names could be given in each field of activity, U.S. politics and medias included. All this has an impact on the perceptions of India, and on the decision to invest in India and to build partnership with Indian companies.

A French Case Study: Past, Present and Future

For assessing the evolution of India's soft power, France offers an interesting case study. France lost India to the British in the Eighteenth century, and kept only five small settlements in India till 1962: her relationship with India cannot of course compare with Britain's special status, or with the attractiveness of America. How Indian culture, how Indian image have been disseminated in a country asserting strongly a non-English language background? Historically, the French encounter with India was not just a matter of trade and power. It went also beyond the case of brilliant French military officers serving Indian royal families. A number of scholars, sometimes missionaries such as Coeurdoux (the Jesuit pillaged by the better known abbé Dubois who published, in London in 1816 and in Paris in 1825, one of the first detailed

Western accounts of Indian beliefs and society), sometimes not (as Anquetil-Duperron), devoted their life to the study of Indian classics, and the first European chair of Sanskrit was established in Paris in 1814. The long story of Indo-French cultural encounters all along the nineteenth century and the first half of the twentieth century and Indian influence on literature, opera, art and intellectual life is well documented[20]. Paris' attractiveness on young Indian artists in the 1950s is a matter of history as well, with a distinguished generation of great painters who either came back to India after years in Paris (Paritosh Sen, Akbar Padamsee, Francis de Souza) or stayed in France, as S.H. Raza did after marrying a French artist.

However, the continuation (and, indeed, expansion) of the French tradition of Indian studies, and the permanence of interest were largely confined to a small elite of connaisseurs, besides those interested with Indian spirituality, which have easy access to the relevant literature produced by general publishers or by specialised publishing houses, and to organisations dedicated to various facets of Hindu (or Buddhist) philosophy. The Vedanta tradition of the Ramakrishna Centre established in 1948 in an ashram 30 km East of Paris deserves a special mention here. It traces its history to an association, "The Friends of Indian Thought", established by academic scholars in the Thirties.

Till the Seventies and the Eighties, Indian culture was mostly accessible in Paris through circles specialized on "the Orient." For long, attending concerts by Indian musicians or enjoying bharatanatyam recitals would bring you to the Musée Guimet auditorium, or to Mandapa, an association dedicated to Indian music and dance, for discovering kathakali, odissi or kudiyattam. Today, noted concerts and recitals, advertised in the metro corridors, are commonplace at the large Théâtre de la Ville, a stone throw from Notre Dame, programming artists from all great world cultures. While films festivals present creative cinema, Bollywood inspires the Indian popular show "Bharati", coming year after year, as the Red Army choirs were doing forty years ago…

For acceding in translation from original languages to Indian classics or pre-Independence Indian novels (Tagore excepted), you had thirty years ago to buy books published either by small specialised publishers (the Presses Orientalistes de France, for Bankim Chandra Chatterjee for instance) or by UNESCO in its series of « representative works » (for Surdas and Kabir). Then, a new trend appeared. If a couple of M.K. Narayan's books have been published in French in the Sixties, most of the translations appeared in the Eighties and Nineties. Small general publishers started publishing Indian writers, and the movement gained momentum. Today, after precursors such as Philippe Picquier, who made a name by publishing mostly Asian authors, all major French publishers of literature have Indian novelists on their catalogue: Gallimard, Le Seuil, Buchet Chastel, Albin Michel, Actes Sud, to quote only a few. Besides the best known authors (Salman Rushdie, Vikram Seth, Arundhati Roy, Amitav Ghosh…), writers from all generations such as Mahasweta Devi, Raj Kamal Jha, Amit Chaudhuri, Tarun Tejpal, Upamanyu Chatterjee, amongst many others, are accessible in French, and new names such as Alka Saraogi, Chetan Bhagat and Aravind Adiga are now quickly translated. Sure enough, most translations are from English writing authors, a good number of them from the diaspora, but translations from Indian languages are developing (Nirmal Verma, Vaikom Mohammad Basheer, Krishna Baldev Vaid, U.N. Ananthamurthy, Mashudevan Nair…). Besides contemporary novelists, classics have now entered the highly sophisticated sanctum sanctorum of the French publishing scene: the *Bibliothèque de la Pléiade*. Somadeva's *Kathāsaritsāgara* in 1996, then Vālmīki's *Rāmāyaṇa* in 1999, followed by an anthology of Sanskrit theatre (Bhāsa, Kālidāsa, Śūdraka and others) in 2006, the *Mahābhārata* being available in an abridged two volumes pocket edition. The literary scene is thus complex, and rich.

Less visible perhaps, but as significant is the rise of French translations of Indian intellectuals and essayists. The Maison des Sciences de l'Homme was pretty alone when it published, for an academic readership, T.N. Madan in 1990 and Sukhamoy Chakravarty in 1994,—Sudhir Kakar translated by private publishers since the Eighties being a noted exception. Today, general publishers offer in translation, to quote just a few names, essays from Amartya Sen, Shashi Tharoor, Sunil Khilnani, Rajmohan Gandhi, Ashis Nandy, Arundhati Roy, Pavan Varma, Narendra Yadav, Partha Chatterjee and Dipesh Chakrabarty—the list is not comprehensive. India's economic growth helps also to translate into French Indian analysts of "India Unbound" such as Gurcharan Das.

India's emergence is also acknowledged in the press. Since a decade or so, no year passes without a news magazines publishing an Indian cover story. This does not always translate into big business: Indo-French trade and investments are far from negligible and they quickly expand, but they remain below their potential. The debate on outsourcing jobs abroad is not particularly focussed on India. TV channels and radio stations call experts on South Asia more often for commenting upon disturbing events in Pakistan than for analysing Indian dynamics, except during major elections or in times of trouble, such as Mumbai terrorist attacks or Kashmir riots for instance. Independent websites specialised on Indian culture or on Indian news have also appeared during the past few years.

On a more cultural field, mention should be made of exceptional exhibitions (on Gupta art in Paris, in 2007) and of months-long festivals held from time to time. The latest of these initiatives patronized by governments but involving civil society was *Namaste France*, co-organised by ICCR with "Cultures France" agency in 2010, which followed *Bonjour India* festival held a few months earlier in India: dozens of events of all types were organised in several cities across both the countries.

This expanding visibility of India raises a stimulating question: what will the ICCR cultural centre offer when it will open in Paris? You may attend in Paris, as in all great European cities, Hindi courses, yoga classes, Indian film festivals, music concerts, dance recitals. Musée Guimet cultural activities, focussed on the various facets of Asia's culture, offers frequent Indian events, as does also the Maison des Cultures du Monde. Open to world cultures, the Musée du Quai Branly has presented in 2010 a noted exhibition "Other Indian Masters", dedicated to Adivasi art, while the Pompidou Centre is planning for 2011 an innovative exhibition on the present Indian avant-garde. Modest in size, independent associations such as the Association France Union Indienne (AFUI), established in 1956, organise lectures, debates, book releases. The strength of the ICCR Centre, besides its funding and its unparalleled contacts with all facets of Indian culture, will be its capacity to offer continuous activities (the Nehru Centre in London offered no less than 25 events in October 2010). The Parisian public will be interested to discover which conception of culture will preside over the Centre programmes—in fact which conception of soft power will prevail when are at stake, so it seems, the understanding by emotion and sensitivity, but also by reason and intellect of what is India today, of which idea(s) of India are entertained, of which India's vision—or competing visions—of the present world is. "The Argumentative Indian", as illustrated by Amartya Sen in his series of essays collected in 2005 on Indian history, culture and identity, would be a wonderful addition to regular programmes.

From Soft Power to Smart Power

For concluding this tentative overview of Indian soft power, I would like to locate culture and ideas in a larger framework, and connect them to other facets of present Indian dynamics. If cultural diplomacy is a must, it cannot be the only tool of influence. To quote again Shashi Tharoor : « The message that really gets through is that of who we are, not what we want to show. For soft power is not just what we can deliberately and consciously exhibit or put on display; it is rather how others see what we are, whether or not we are trying to show it to the world ».[21]

How others see India is the result of an intricate process, besides the fact that everyone does not see the same India—or for that matter the same China. The Chinese case is significant in this regard, for China uses soft power in her own way. The success of the 2008 Olympic games held in Shanghai—the showcase of China's innovation and modernity—is a case in point (particularly when contrasted with the controversies attached to India's Commonwealth Games in 2010). Quite different of course is the Chinese image related to the fate of dissidents attracting international attention such as Nobel Peace Prize Liu Xiaobo, only to the displeasure of Beijing cracking down on the signatories of Charter 08. Does this weaken the rise of China? The negative image of authoritarian regime does not prevent millions of students from learning Chinese language in Western schools in order to address the world of to-morrow. The strength of the Chinese economy, now ranked third behind the European Union and the U.S., holds the key to China's power and China's prestige, and enables Beijing to develop its network of Confucius Institutes (an interesting name, indeed) at an unmatched pace: since the opening of the first institute in 2004 more than 200 centres have been opened in more than 35 countries on five continents (14 in France already), most of them in partnership with local Universities (one in India only, at JNU). For the Confucius Institutes are not full-fledged cultural centres. Under the aegis of the Office of Chinese Language Council International, they are basically supporting the dissemination of the Chinese language. This being said, remember what was, thirty years ago, the expanse of USSR's soft power, Moscow's systematic policy of attracting students from Third World countries, and the impressive dissemination of Russian literature (and propaganda) in all the most important Indian languages, including through book fairs in district towns. Here again, beyond the cultivation of soft power, the important point was what USSR really was...

Soft power relies upon the strength of ideas, whatever their field of application, not just on what is usually defined as culture. "A country's soft power rests upon the attractiveness of its culture, the appeal of its domestic political and social values, and the style and substance of its foreign policies", says Joseph Nye.[22] Indeed, but the list of attributes is not complete. What about the economic dimension of power, in substance as well as in style? What about the capacity of innovation? What about other parameters defining power? In her confirmation hearing at the U.S. Senate, Hillary Clinton, then Secretary of State designate, made a point in defining what was the new mantra of the Obama administration: smart power[23]. « We must use what has been called smart power, the full range of tools at our disposal—diplomatic, economic, military, political, legal, and cultural—picking the right tool or combination of tools for each situation. With smart power, diplomacy will be the vanguard of our foreign policy. This is not a radical idea. The Ancient Roman poet Terence declared that 'In every endeavour, the seemly course for wise men is to try persuasion first'».[24]

Smart power is not just the combination of hard and soft power in a winning strategy. It is something subtler, more intricate, which finds its relevance in the field of ideas supposed to change the world for the better, if only step-by-step. However, this international relevance cannot be expanded in a vacuum. What happens at home remains the base of genuine power, soft or smart, for the capacity to impact on the world is on the long run the exemplariness of the combine between values and action. In a seminal paper on the evolution of India's soft power, from Gandhi onwards, Jacques Hymans called recently for going beyond Nye's implication that soft power is efficient when it meets with the "universality" of the "ideal liberal state", arguing also that soft vulnerability, sometimes the unintended consequence of soft power, could also pave the way to real power, if properly used: "soft vulnerability is the fate of seeing others doing what you don't want on the basis of how they see you [...]. Soft power may be latent in soft vulnerability, [...] soft vulnerability may be latent in apparent soft power".[25] In a global information age, everything is now a parameter in the definition of a country image: its successes as well as its shortcomings or its failures, its initiatives or the lack of them; its way to combine the sense of national interest with common goods and global security.

This is where the debates in India on what is the Indian nation, on what is the essence of the Indian civilisation, provide the key for the future of India's smart power, and also the basis for the dissemination of India's soft power. Countries' whose grand narrative defining the ideological basis of their emergence in tune with the complexities of the global chessboard will be the best equipped for improving their image, and their status. I join again Shashi Tharoor here, when he suggests that India's greatness lies in what she is—an "evolved hybrid" of bound together diversities, who has developed her democratic credentials "by maintaining consensus on how to manage without consensus".[26] The recognition of diversity and the capacity to evolve consensus, at minima if necessary, are not opposed to the hard power real-politik. Indeed, they contribute to its acceptability in a world where "global consciousness" will become more and more a cardinal parameter. The "Rediscovery of India", to quote Meghnad Desai, an India "re-imagined" would say Nandan Nilekani,[27] prepares the future, but cannot be disconnected from the best of the past. "Whose India? Which India?" The final questions formulated by Lord Desai echo those raised by the founding fathers of the nation, who had themselves, before the concept of soft power was coined, linked the fate of India—"the ancient, the eternal and the ever-new"—to her openness to the world. Read again *Young India,* June 1st, 1921: "I want the cultures of all lands to be blown about my house as freely as possible...". Read again *Harijan*, May 9, 1936 : "No culture can live if it attempts to be exclusive". Hear again Nehru redeeming his pledge "to the service of India and her people and to the still larger cause of humanity", on August 14, 1947. The "tryst with destiny" is not just a part of India's history. It is also a part of Indian culture, and as such an ever-lively part of the world heritage.

Notes and References

1. Joseph Nye. *Born to Lead: The Changing Nature of American Power*, New York, Basic Books, 1990
2. See for example § 29 in the Joint Declaration by the Republic of India and the People's Republic of China, signed on 23 November 2006, during the visit to India of President Hu Jintao. http://www.pib.nic.in/newsite/erelease. aspx?relid=22168.
3. «Asia's Global Foreign Policy and Security Interest», speech by Mr. M.K. Narayanan, National Security Adviser, at the 42th Munich Conference on Security Policy, February 5, 2006.
4. By comparison, the Goethe-Institut has been established as we know it in 1951. It defines its goals as follows: "Acting on behalf of the Federal Republic of Germany Goethe-Institut promotes various issues of foreign cultural and educational policy. According to its statute, the three principal objectives of the institute are: i) to promote the study of the German language abroad; ii) to encourage international cultural cooperation; iii) to convey an all-round image of Germany by providing information on its culture, society and politics". http://www.goethe.de/uun/org/enindex.htm
5. Address by Prime Minister Dr. Manmohan Singh at Oxford University in Acceptance of an Honorary Degree from Oxford University on July 8, 2005. http://www.hinduonnet.com/thehindu/nic/0046/pmspeech.htm
6. Address by Dr. Karan Singh, President, Indian Council for Cultural Relations, to the Association of Indian Diplomats, March 22, 2006.

   http://www.karansingh.com/index.php?action=politics&subaction=poly_a ddress
7. Address at the Inauguration of the Indian Council for Cultural Relations, April 9, 1950 in: Speeches of Maulana Azad, 1947-1955, New Delhi, Ministry of Information and Broadcasting, Publications Division, 1956, pp. 132-134.
8. An Indian cultural centre exists as well at Doha, under the patronage of the Indian Embassy, but not under ICCR aegis.
9. The Festival of India in China and the Festival of China in India have been inaugurated in their respective host country in April 2010.
10. « Ivory Pagodas. An ancient pan-Asian University might yet open again », The Economist, September 2nd, 2010. http://www.economist.com /node/16953200
11. Dennis H. Kux & Daniel P. Monihan: *India and The United States: Estranged Democracies 1941-1991*, National Defence University Press, Washington D.C., 1993.
12. http://www.usinpac.com. See the History column.
13. Joseph S. Nye: *Soft Power: The Means to Success in World Politics, Public Affairs*, New York, 2004. In an op-ed of the Boston Globe introducing the concept of « smart power », Nye wrote: « In traditional

international conflicts, the side with the stronger military force tended to win. In today's information age, it is often the party with the stronger story that wins." In "Mideast, the Goal is 'Smart Power'", Boston Globe, August 18, 2006.

14. Shashi Tharoor : « India's soft power », *Taipeh Times*, 7 January 2008. http://www.taipeitimes.com/News/editorials/print/2008/01/07/2003396110
15. Wilhelm Halbfass: *Indien und Europe. Perspektiven ihre geistigen Begegnung*, Schwabe Verlag, Basel, 1981. Indian edition: *India and Europe: An Essay in Philosphical Understanding*. Motilal Banarsidass, Delhi, 1990
16. Roger-Pol Droit : L'oubli de l'Inde. Une amnésie philosophique, Paris, Presses Universitaires de France, 1989 [latest updated edition : 2004]
17. On Mother India and on comments the book drew, see Amardeep Singh : http://www.lehigh.edu/~amsp/2006/02/teaching-journal-katherine-mayos.html
18. This is not to forget the merits of scientists of Indian origin who got the Nobel Prize in Medicine (Hargobind Khorana in 1968), in Physics (Subrahmanya Chandrasekhar in 1983) or in Chemistry (Venkatraman Ramakrishna in 2009), decades after Chandrasekhra Venkata Raman was distinguished in 1930. The post Independence laureates were celebrated in India as bringing glory to their country of origin, although they had become U.S. citizens, but the impact of these laureates on India's image cannot compete with the aura of Tagore, Mother Teresa, and, closer to us, Amartya Sen.
19. See on that point Jackie Assayag and Véronique Beneï (eds): *At Home in Diaspora. South Asian Scholars and the West*, Indiana University Press, Bloomington & Permanent Black, New Delhi, 2003.
20. See Samuel Berthet: Cultural Dynamics and Strategies of the Indian Elites 1870-1947. *Indo-French Relations during the Raj*. New Delhi, Manohar, 2006 and Roland Lardinois : L'invention de l'Inde. Entre ésotérisme et science, Paris, CNRS Editions, 2007.
21. Shashi Tharoor: « India Strategic Power: 'Soft' » Global Brief, May 13, 2009 http://globalbrief.ca/blog/2009/05/13/soft-is-the-word/
22. Joseph N. Nye: « Soft power matters in Asia », Japan Times, December 5, 2005 http://belfercenter.ksg.harvard.edu/publication/1486/ soft_power_matters_in_asia.html
23. See the report of CSIS Commission on Smart Power, Centre for Strategic and International Studies, Washington D.C., 2007. Joseph N. Nye and Richard L. Armitage co-chaired the Committee. media.csis.org/smartpower/ 071105_CSIS_Smart_Power_Report.pdf
24. « Transcript of Hillary Clinton's Confirmation Hearing », U.S. Senate, January 13, 2009. http://www.cfr.org/us-election-2008/transcript-hillary-clintons-confirmation-hearing/p18225

25. Jacques E. C. Hymans: « India soft power and vulnerability », India Review, vol. 8, n°3., 2009, pp. 234-265. Quotes p. 259.
26. Shashi Tharoor, op. cit., Global Brief, 2009.
27. Meghnad Desai: *The Rediscovery of India*, Allen Lane, New Delhi, 2009; Nandan Nilekani: *Imagining India. Ideas for the New Century*, Allen Lane, New Delhi, 2008.

3
Gandhi's Global Influence

David Cortright

Gandhi has unparalleled global influence and relevance for our time and perhaps for all time. A powerful testament to this impact was expressed in the opening words of President Barack Obama's historic address to the Indian parliament in November 2010: "I might not be standing here before you as President of the United States, had it not been for Gandhi and the message he shared with America and the world."[1]

This was not just a casual or gratuitous remark by an eloquent orator. It was a heartfelt statement by a President with a special fondness for and appreciation of Gandhi. Obama has long admired Gandhi's role as a pioneer and inspiration in the cause of social justice. He kept a photo of Gandhi next to that of Dr. Martin Luther King Jr. in his office when he served as a member of the U.S. Senate. In September 2009, Obama was asked by a school girl in Virginia, "If you could have dinner with any person, living or dead, who would that be?" The president replied that it would be Gandhi. It would probably be a "very small meal," he joked, since Gandhi ate so little, but he was serious in describing Gandhi as a "real hero of mine."[2] Many other people around the world similarly regard Gandhi as a hero and continue to respect his historic achievements and his development of the methods of mass nonviolent social resistance.

I think it is safe to say that Gandhi is India's greatest cultural messenger. No other person of Indian heritage is better known or has had a more profound influence on contemporary global thinking. Even today, more than 60 years after his death, his message resonates loudly and convincingly to hundreds of millions of people on every continent. Photos and statues of Gandhi abound in many countries, especially in the offices of organizations working for justice and peace. The nonviolent social action methods he pioneered have been used with increasing frequency in numerous struggles all over the world in recent decades. His legacy and method were a direct influence on the resisters who brought down the Mubarak dictatorship in Egypt.

Gandhi's Gifts to America

Gandhi has exerted a significant influence on my own country, although he never visited our shores. He has inspired generations of social reformers and political leaders. African Americans have been particularly influenced by Gandhi. They were keenly interested in and impressed as soon as word of Gandhi's accomplishments arrived in the Americas around the time of World War I. The great intellectual W.E. Du Bois wrote presciently in 1922 that Gandhi's methods of mass noncooperation could be used to liberate black Americans.[3] By the time Martin Luther King Jr. entered the stage of history in the 1950s, knowledge of Gandhi's methods and achievements was already widespread in the African American community. Gandhi's philosophy and method provided an essential guide for the Civil Rights Movement. King was impressed especially by Gandhi's ability to achieve freedom for the people of India without stirring hatred and rancor among his British adversaries. King understood that African Americans would have to do likewise, and that nonviolent methods of struggle would allow them to live in harmony with their white brothers and sisters in the post-segregationist society they sought to create. Gandhi's religiously inspired nonviolent philosophy helped King better understand the social meaning of the commandment to love at the heart of his own Christian belief system:

> Gandhi was probably the first person in history to lift the love ethic of Jesus above mere interaction between individuals to a powerful and effective social force on a large scale. Love for Gandhi was a potent instrument for social and collective transformation. It was in this Gandhian emphasis on love and nonviolence that I discovered the method for social reform that I had been seeking for so many months.[4]

Gandhi also deeply influenced Cesar Chavez, who founded the United Farm Workers Union and played an important role in lifting the condition of America's poorest and most exploited workers. Chavez spoke of his great admiration for this "little half naked man without a gun," a person of color like himself who could stand up to race prejudice and overcome the power of a great empire.[5] Chavez found many things to admire in Gandhi: his success in winning Indian independence, his uncompromising commitment to nonviolence, his use of the boycott, and his fasting. He found similarities between his own efforts to overcome racial prejudice and poverty and Gandhi's attempts to empower the downtrodden. In Gandhi Chavez found a leader who could inspire poor people to challenge the rich and powerful, a formula of obvious relevance to oppressed migrant workers facing wealthy land owners.

In the United States a growing number of communities have erected memorials to the Mahatma. In New York's Union Square, on the Embarcadero pier in San Francisco, at the Indian embassy in Washington DC, statues of Gandhi pay tribute to his greatness. In numerous colleges and universities, including my own University of Notre Dame, courses are taught on the philosophy and methods of Gandhi. I teach such a course. Similar accounts of the influence of Gandhi could be told in many other countries.

Following Gandhi

In 2006 the popular movie *Lage Raho Munna Bhai* popularized the idea of *Gandhigiri*, "doing a Gandhi." In the film Gandhi appears to the likeable Mumbai gangster and urges him to tell the truth and do the right thing. Munna Bhai and his sidekick ask themselves, "what would Gandhi do?" as they hilariously attempt to extricate themselves from the complications created by their bumbling deceits. The movie won praise from many, including Prime Minister Manmohan Singh, and for a time prompted many to ask that same question.[6] What does it mean to follow Gandhi? The Bollywood version of 'doing a Gandhi' narrows the Mahatma's message to simply telling the truth. This is important but barely scratches the surface of Gandhi's profound meaning, and completely ignores the broad social and political implications of his ideas and example.

Throughout the world many people extol Gandhi's greatness, but few grasp the deeper meaning and revolutionary significance of his nonviolent philosophy and method. In India his image is on the currency but his spirit is mostly absent in the land. "Doing a Gandhi" involves much more than personal honesty. Gandhi-doing has broad social and political implications. It involves a fundamental transformation of our approach to the world, culturally, socially and politically. Gandhi's thinking was deeply radical in the best sense. He went to the root of problems to address the basic structures of social, economic and political oppression. He sought to change all aspects of individual and social life. He overturned outdated hierarchies and shattered outmoded assumptions. He altered our way of being and doing in the world.

Gandhi was deeply informed and well educated, but he was not an intellectual. He did not write for academic journals or publish books for academic presses. He was quintessentially a man of action. My message is my life, he often said. His writings were voluminous, 100 volumes, but his strongest statements came through the actions he undertook personally and in the actions of the millions he inspired and organized. He is most remembered for his courageous and successful campaigns against colonial rule in India and against racial injustice in South Africa. His actions and words opened new possibilities for achieving human progress. In this paper I explore some of Gandhi's core principles and consider their relevance to the most demanding political and cultural challenges of our time, including the struggle against terrorism and violent extremism.

Gandhi's core message was nonviolence, ahimsa, the refusal to injure another. He espoused tolerance and respect for all persons, especially the most marginalized and oppressed. How urgently world culture needs to absorb these values today. Gandhi emphasized the necessity of breaking the cycle of violence. By refusing to extend the chain of vengeance, he insisted, we create new possibilities for social improvement. Hate and violence only create more hate and violence. It is necessary to step outside that vicious cycle. We get rid of the enemy by getting rid of enmity. Hatred by its nature leads to destruction, but love creates and builds new relationships and new possibilities. Nonviolence transforms with redemptive power.

Gandhian nonviolence is often equated with pacifism, but this is a misperception. Gandhi developed the nonviolent method as a means of fighting for justice, not as a solution to the problem of war. His theory transcends the narrow limits of absolute pacifism. He fought tenaciously against political oppression, but he did so with nonviolence, which he considered the mightiest weapon on earth. Gandhi developed his method as a third way, between war and quiescence. His perspective was that of Camus, who wrote that we must be neither victim nor executioner. We must resist injustice and oppression, but we must find methods of resistance that do not create new forms of violence and oppression.

Gandhi showed the power and effectiveness of nonviolence through the success of India's freedom movement. His colleagues adopted his methods because they considered them the most effective way of achieving their political goals. Few fully accepted Gandhi's philosophy of pure nonviolence, but they all understood the social power of the mass noncooperation techniques Gandhi developed. As Jawaharlal Nehru wrote, we "accepted that method ... not only as the right method but as the most effective one for our purpose."[7] The same has been true for nonviolent freedom fighters in struggles across the world. Nonviolent methods are applied widely today and are increasingly recognized as "a force more powerful," the surest path to justice and political freedom, whatever one's religious or secular persuasion.[8]

Transforming the World

Gandhi's demonstration of the power of nonviolence is surely one of India's greatest gifts to the world. Gandhi's strategic insights have been adapted and applied in literally hundreds of struggles for justice and freedom in dozens of countries. The amplification of Gandhi's message and influence has benefited greatly from the strategic analysis of his methods by the American scholar Gene Sharp, author of the classic three-volume work, *The Politics of Nonviolent Action*. Sharp has published dozens of books and pamphlets outlining the strategy and tactics of Gandhi's method. Sharp's works have been published in many languages and have provided the basis for training and education programs on nonviolent action in dozens of countries. Sharp's emphasis on the practical dimensions of Gandhian nonviolence is embodied in the work of the International Center on Nonviolent Conflict based in Washington, DC, and in similar education and training centers on nonviolence in other countries.

Political realists dismiss nonviolence as naïve and unworkable. Tyrants and terrorists only understand the message of violence, we are told. Nonviolence has been tried and found wanting. Writer and nonviolent activist Barbara Deming argued to the contrary. "It has not been tried. We have hardly begun to try [nonviolence]. The people who dismiss it … do not understand what it could be."[9] Gandhi said at the end of his life that the "technique of unconquerable nonviolence of the strong has not been discovered as yet."[10] Organized nonviolence is a new and still undeveloped method of achieving political change. Only during the 20th century, with Gandhi's disobedience campaigns in South Africa and India, did mass nonviolent action begin to emerge as a viable means of social change. It is a method still "in the process of invention," wrote Deming. While examples of nonviolent action can be found throughout history, as Sharp documents, only in the last century has nonviolent action made significant contributions to political change.[11] In recent decades the Gandhian method of strategic nonviolent action has been applied and enlarged upon with increasing frequency in a growing number of countries.

Examples of major nonviolent successes are many. Perhaps the most dramatic was the nonviolent transformation of Central and Eastern Europe in the late 1980s, the "velvet revolution" that swept away communist dictatorship without firing a shot and ended the Soviet Union. The "people power" movement of the Philippines ended the dictatorship of Ferdinand Marcos in 1986. Nonviolent resistance was decisive in the latter stages of the South African freedom movement, helping to end the hated apartheid regime. Nonviolent movements swept through Latin America in the 1980s and 90s, ending military dictatorship in Chile and democratizing governments throughout the continent. Nonviolent power inspired the Serbian youth group *Otpor*, Resistance, which sparked the movement to overthrow Slobodan Milosevic in 2000. Nonviolent methods were applied in the Rose, Orange and Tulip "revolutions" of Georgia, Ukraine, and Kyrgyzstan in 2003-5. Mass civil disobedience in Nepal overthrew the monarchy in April 2006 and laid the basis for the creation of a democratic republic. The Gandhian nonviolent method has brought about significant political change and social transformation on every continent.

The Gandhian method does not always work, of course. Examples of failure exist, including the Tiananmen Square massacre of 1989, the isolation and collapse of the Kosovar nonviolent resistance struggle in the early 1990s, and the so far unsuccessful Burmese democracy movement. Countless attempts to achieve justice and resist occupation in the Palestinian Occupied Territories have failed so far to alter the structures of oppression.

The overall record of success is nonetheless impressive. Walter Wink wrote, "Never before have citizens actualized this potential in such overwhelming numbers or to such stunning effect. And yet 'people power' is still in its infancy!"[12] Nonviolent resistance offers a third way, distinct from war and inaction, for addressing the challenges of injustice. The alternative to war is not surrender or appeasement, but the fight for justice through nonviolent action. The choice is not between accepting oppression and using violence. Nonviolent resistance offers a different option.

Gandhi on the Nile

The recent democratic uprising that brought down the Mubarak dictatorship in Egypt stands as one of history's most dramatic expressions of "people power." The people's victory in Egypt was preceded by the downfall of the Ben Ali regime in Tunisia and has inspired movements for freedom and democracy throughout the Arab world and beyond. Never before have people in the region mobilized in such vast numbers to shake off the chains of autocracy. The protests have touched off a massive wave of social ferment shaking the foundations of Middle East and global politics. Organizers of the Cairo protests claim an "historic achievement that has not happened since the time of the pharaohs."[13] Whether the transitions can live up to such hype and succeed in creating genuinely democratic societies remains to be seen, but the demonstrated power of nonviolent action is undeniable.

Conventional wisdom assumes that nonviolent action can work only in societies that are lawful and democratic, but the revolutions in Egypt and Tunisia show that civil resistance can succeed even in highly oppressive systems, against ruthless regimes that did not hesitate to kill and torture their opponents. During the protests, hundreds of demonstrators were killed, most at the hands of security forces and pro-Mubarak thugs, yet people continued to pour into the streets day after day to demand their freedom. The victory of the protestors was virtually total, and was all the more amazing because it was so swift and seemingly spontaneous.

Or was it? It turns out that the Egyptian movement had elements of Gandhian inspiration. Some of the youth leaders who initiated the unarmed revolutions in Egypt and Tunisia were encouraged by classic teachings on nonviolent strategy and tactics. One of the groups that sparked the protests was the April 6 Youth Movement, which adopted the methods and style of *Otpor* in Serbia and traveled to Belgrade to receive training in unarmed resistance methods. Some of the activists were trained at the Academy of Change in Qatar, which promotes ideas drawn from the work of Gene Sharp.[14] The linkage to Gandhian methods was evident in all of this. Although contemporary urban resistance techniques are very different from those used by Gandhi and King, they employ some of the core principles that are key to the success of Gandhian nonviolence.

The first is the principle of mass. We know from all other examples of successful nonviolent resistance that size matters. Gandhi always emphasized the need to mobilize the masses. Much of his success in India derived from his ability to transform the Congress from a debating society of merchants and lawyers into a mass fighting organization with millions of followers in all regions, classes and castes. To achieve success, he argued, protestors must mobilize very large numbers of people and must be able to sustain mass action for weeks or even months if necessary. In Egypt the movement to overthrow Mubarak mobilized hundreds of thousands of people on an almost daily basis despite repression and attacks by pro-government goon squads. When Mubarak tried to coopt the movement and then refused to step down, the protestors mobilized even greater numbers. As the protests grew larger they spread to other political groupings and social sectors. The Muslim Brotherhood did not start the movement but joined the protests and provided important organizational capacity. Trade unions also entered the fray, adding energy and potency in the final days.

A second factor is nonviolent discipline. The people taking to the streets in Cairo and other cities faced repression with remarkable restraint and courage, refusing to be provoked into over-reaction. The organizers constantly emphasized the need to remain peaceful. Those who had participated in workshops or read the Arab translations of Gene Sharp's work knew that violence on the part of the movement would be contrary to the strategy of effective resistance. Gandhi, King, and other pioneers of social transformation emphasized the necessity of absolute nonviolent discipline, not merely as a moral choice (it's the right thing to do) but as a practical requirement for winning the sympathy of bystanders and encouraging loyalty shifts within the military and police (it works).

A third factor was the movement's successful efforts to encourage loyalty shifts within the military. The resisters in Egypt were remarkably effective at reassuring and ultimately gaining the support of the military. They scrupulously avoided violent or confrontational tactics that might force the armed forces to choose sides against them. Protest organizers urged demonstrators to "hug a soldier," to show that the struggle was against the dictatorship not the military. They brought food for the soldiers and tried to win their friendship. On the eve of the "million-man march" on February 1 the armed forces declared they would not use force against "our great people." This was a decisive breakthrough for the movement. It was followed 10 days later by the military's break with Mubarak and demand for his resignation.

The challenges ahead for Egypt and the region are daunting, but the democratic revolutions have opened the way to a freer future and have taught an indelible lesson in the ability of nonviolent means to change the course of history. Gandhi's presence looms over the mass protests of the Arab world, although his name is seldom invoked. The methods he pioneered have taken root in a region that was previously least free but that is now struggling to assert the right of people to overthrow dictatorship and achieve self determination.

A Force More Powerful

Gandhi's methods have the benefit of being superior morally and politically. They are right and also more effective. George Orwell was no greater admirer of Gandhi, and he reviled pacifism, but he recognized the unique strength and importance of Gandhi's new method. "Gandhi's attitude was not that of most Western pacifists," he wrote. "Satyagraha ... was a sort of nonviolent warfare, a way of defeating the enemy without hurting him and without feeling or arousing hatred."[15] Gandhi would have corrected Orwell to say that the goal is not defeating the adversary but achieving reconciliation and political accommodation, but otherwise he would have agreed with Orwell's description. Gandhi introduced a revolutionary new form of political struggle into history. He offered a more effective way of fighting against injustice, one that achieves success without resorting to violence and without stirring the intense passions of hatred and revenge that usually accompany armed struggle and that often lead to further rounds of violence.

Recent empirical studies confirm the superiority of nonviolent action as a method of achieving significant social change. A study published in 2008 in *International Security* reviewed 323 historical examples of resistance campaigns over a span of more than one hundred years to determine whether violent or nonviolent methods work better in achieving political change.[16] Each case involved an intensive conflict, sometimes lasting several years, in which major sociopolitical movements struggled to gain specific concessions from government adversaries. The study by Maria J. Stephan and Erica Chenoweth employed the most rigorous scholarly methods to examine systematically the strategic impact of violent and nonviolent methods of political struggle. The results decisively validated the greater effectiveness of nonviolent action. The findings show that nonviolent methods were twice as effective as violent means in achieving success in major resistance campaigns. In the cases examined, nonviolent means were successful 53 per cent of the time, compared to a 26 per cent success rate when violence was employed.

The key factor in explaining this result, according to Stephan and Chenoweth, is that nonviolent campaigns are better able to withstand the repression that inevitably confronts major resistance campaigns, and may even turn such repression to their advantage. When the adversary violently represses a disciplined nonviolent campaign, the nonviolent resisters may benefit politically. Chavez identified this as the "strange chemistry" of nonviolent action. Whenever the adversary commits an unjust act against nonviolent protesters, said Chavez, "we get tenfold paid back in benefits."[17] Deming described this as the "special genius" of nonviolent action.[18] Unjustified repression against disciplined nonviolent action can spark a sympathetic reaction among third parties and in the ranks of the adversary. This may spark loyalty shifts and increase support for the nonviolent campaigners, while undermining the legitimacy of the adversary. The influential theologian Reinhold

Niebuhr wrote that excessive brutality against nonviolent action "robs the opponent of the moral conceit" that identifies his interest with the larger good of society. He describes this as the "most important of all the imponderables in a social struggle."[19] The willingness of nonviolent campaigners to risk and accept repression without retaliation is fundamental to the political success of the Gandhian method. It alters political dynamics and tips the balance of sympathy and political support against the adversary and toward the nonviolent movement.

Loyalty shifts are a key mechanism of nonviolent change, according to Stephan and Chenoweth, occurring in more than half the successful nonviolent campaigns studied.[20] Hierarchical power systems depend upon the obedience and loyalty of followers. When that loyalty falters, the oppressive power of the command system begins to erode. Resistance movements that generate disaffection in the ranks of the opponent greatly increase their chances of political success. This was a key to the success of the unarmed revolution in Egypt, and it has been evident in many other historic campaigns. In East Germany in 1989 soldiers of the communist regime refused to fire upon candlelight protestors in Leipzig, which opened the door to further massive protests and the fall of the Berlin Wall. During the military coup in Moscow in 1991, Boris Yeltsin famously climbed aboard a tank and urged soldiers not to attack their own people. During the overthrow of Slobodan Milosevic in Serbia and the Orange Revolution in Ukraine resistance leaders negotiated with and reassured senior commanders and thereby kept the military on the sidelines. This ability to encourage loyalty shifts in the military is essential to the political power of nonviolent revolution.

A Force for Freedom

Nonviolent action is not only more effective than armed struggle in achieving social change, it is also more likely to expand opportunities for democracy and political freedom. Nonviolent resistance methods are superior to violent means both quantitatively and qualitatively. This is the conclusion of an important study conducted in 2005 by Freedom House, the U.S.-based organization dedicated to promoting human rights and political liberty. The Freedom House researchers examined 67 political transitions in recent decades, many in previously closed or authoritarian governments. They evaluated the regimes resulting from these political transitions according to the standard Freedom House ratings of free, partly free or not free. The study found that nonviolent civic resistance was a driving factor in 50 of the 67 transitions. In those 50 cases nearly all the resulting regimes (92 percent) were more democratic.[21] Nonviolent movements were three times more likely than armed struggles to produce sustainable freedom.

The key variable in achieving greater democracy was identified as the presence of a 'people power' effect—a bottom-up nonviolent resistance movement. "The stronger and more cohesive the nonviolent civic coalition," the study concluded, "the deeper the transformation in the direction of freedom and democracy." The presence of a robust civic coalition has a statistically significant effect on increasing the level of freedom.[22]

Nonviolent movements create more freedom and democracy because they are by their very nature free and democratic. They are mass-based, participatory expressions of free will with broad popular support. In Poland the power of Solidarity flowed from the ten million members it represented and the support it received from virtually the entire industrial working class and indeed most of society. The same was true of the United Democratic Front in South Africa. With the backing of churches, trade unions and countless community organizations, the UDC and the African National Congress were able to mobilize millions and could rightly claim to speak for the majority population.

In an armed struggle, by contrast, the resistance is carried out by a smaller, specialized cadre of fighters. An armed struggle must operate according to military discipline, and its success may depend on the rigidity and impregnability of its command structure. In the heat of battle there is no room for debate or dissent. Armed movements are less able to accommodate factions and may turn on themselves in violent purges. Most of the armed revolutions of the 20th century produced repressive and dictatorial regimes. Those who win by the gun tend to rule by the gun.

An expansion of democracy reflects the very essence of nonviolence. As Jonathan Schell has observed, nonviolence is inseparably linked to democracy. The spread of democracy extends the arena of human affairs in which political disputes are resolved without violence. Democracy embodies free expression, political cooperation and mutual accommodation of interests. Nonviolence "is written into liberalism's genetic code," wrote Schell. "In this basic respect, the long march of liberal democracy is a 'peace movement'—possibly the most important and successful of them all."[23]

Gandhi against Bin Laden

The principles of Gandhian nonviolence are applicable to international policy. They provide guidance for dealing with even the most intractable dilemmas of global security, including the crisis of insurgency and terrorism in Afghanistan and Pakistan. Although the lineage to Gandhi on policy issues is indirect, since he never held office and did not say much about international affairs, his general emphasis on the value of nonviolent means of addressing political problems is highly relevant. Nonviolent strategies offer hope for more just solutions even in the most seemingly intractable disputes. Gandhi can teach us much about how to counter bin Laden.

The success of the unarmed revolution in Egypt has dealt a blow to violent extremists. The demonstrated power of nonviolent resistance in the heart of the Arab and Muslim world undermines the central narrative of al-Qaida. Bin Laden and Ayman Al Zawahiri claim that terrorist violence is necessary to bring down autocratic governments in the Arab world and beyond. But in Egypt and Tunisia people ended tyranny through nonviolent means, not bombings and assassinations. Mohamed ElBaradei has suggested that a successful outcome of the nonviolent transition in Egypt may help to undermine the appeal of al-Qaida and "could be the best medicine to get rid of radicalism."[24] If nonviolent methods can lead to a peaceful, pluralistic transition, this nullifies the al-Qaida narrative.

It was in Mubarak's jails that Al Zawahiri was tortured and seared with the hatred that led him to join Bin Laden and become Al Qaeda's senior commander. The dream of overthrowing his tormentors now has been achieved, not through mass killing as he imagined but through nonviolent action. The significance of this ironic twist will not be lost on would-be recruits, who can now see a different and more successful path toward ending oppression, in contrast to the utter failure of Al Qaeda to achieve anything but the killing of countless fellow Muslims.

The opening of democratic political space may be the best antidote to terrorism. It provides alternatives for those who might otherwise be tempted by the lure of militancy. It gives aggrieved people legitimate outlets for addressing political demands, making it less likely they will turn toward violent extremism.

Empirical evidence indicates that the use of military force is not an effective means of countering terrorist organizations. A 2008 RAND Corporation study, How Terrorist Groups End, shows that terrorist groups usually end through political processes and effective law enforcement, not the use of military force. An examination of 268 terrorist organizations that ended during a period of nearly forty years found that the primary factors accounting for their demise were participation in political processes (43 per cent) and effective policing (40 per cent). Military force accounted for the end of terrorist groups in only 7 percent of the cases examined. Terrorist groups end most often when they adopt nonviolent means and join a political process, or when local law enforcement agencies arrest key members. Policing works better than war because law enforcement officials are rooted in local communities, and they can gain the knowledge and trust of local residents that enables them to penetrate terrorist networks.[25] Political bargaining and accommodation are most common when terrorist groups have localized rather than global objectives, as is the case with Taliban insurgents in Afghanistan.

The United States and its NATO allies would be more successful in Afghanistan if they adopted civilian rather than military methods. Preventing terrorist attacks is a legitimate purpose, but war is the wrong means. The presence of foreign military forces in Afghanistan is the problem, not the solution. It fuels armed resistance and generates support for extremist groups. U.S. military attacks in the region inevitably kill innocent civilians and validate Al Qaeda's warped image of America waging war on Islam. Opinion polls have shown more than 70 per cent of the population in Pakistan believing that American policy is directed against Islam.[26] As long as such attitudes prevail, there will be no end of would-be recruits willing to blow themselves up to kill Americans and their allies.

Washington and its allies could exert enormous positive leverage in Afghanistan, not by escalating the war but by offering to reduce their military presence in return for local cooperation in isolating Al Qaeda and preventing global terrorist strikes. Most Taliban fighters are motivated by the desire to remove foreign forces from their communities, which suggests that they might be amenable to negotiation if that goal can be met. As Western nations disengage militarily, they should greatly increase their support for economic development and democratic governance. The focus should be on supporting civil society and the millions of Pakistanis and Afghans, especially women, who reject the intolerance of the Taliban and aspire to a life of greater freedom and opportunity. Providing support for human rights, social development, and democratic governance will be more effective over the long run in generating hope for a better future and reducing support for violent extremism.

I am not suggesting in these pages that nonviolent means are always successful. Gandhian methods of policy are not appropriate for every setting. When governments confront extreme threats of mass violence, the use of limited force is sometimes necessary. Pacifist theologians acknowledge that police action is ethically superior to war as a means of protecting the innocent. In Afghanistan, where extremist groups have terrorized reformers and destroyed schools for girls, security protections will be needed for those who attempt to create a better life for their communities. These contingencies are not a justification for policies of war and military occupation, however. They do not alter the moral and political superiority of nonviolent means of achieving political change.

Conclusion

If Gandhi is India's greatest cultural messenger to the world, it must be admitted that few people in India or other nations grasp the revolutionary significance of his nonviolent philosophy and method. Even those in the Arab world who increasingly use nonviolent methods to achieve political change have little awareness of the deeper meaning of Gandhian nonviolence. Theirs is mostly a pragmatic choice of favoring nonviolent methods as the most effective means of confronting heavily armed repressive adversaries. In much of the world, and in India itself, most people are ignorant of or indifferent to Gandhi's philosophy. The challenges of 'doing a Gandhi' are profound. They require a break with conventional thinking about the nature of political power and social change. Many find it easier to admire Gandhi's greatness in general rather than follow his specific teachings on nonviolence. Yet his ideas and methods are gradually taking hold, even if their provenance is not always acknowledged, as the power of nonviolence becomes increasingly relevant and necessary to the struggle for human freedom.

Notes and References

1. Barack Obama, "Remarks by the President to the Joint Session of the Indian Parliament in New Delhi, India" (speech, New Delhi, India, 8 November 2010), http://www.whitehouse.gov/the-press-office/2010/11/08/remarks-president-joint-session-indian-parliament-new-delhi-india (accessed 17 April 2011).
2. "Obama says he would like to have dinner with Mahatma Gandhi," The Times of India, 9 September 2009, http://articles.timesofindia.indiatimes.com/2009-09-09/us/28071380_1_obama-wakefield-high-school-mahatma-gandhi (accessed 17 April 2011).
3. Sudarsham Kapur, *Raising Up a Prophet: The African-American Encounter with Gandhi*, New Delhi: Oxford University Press, 1993, 37.
4. Martin Luther King, Jr., *Stride toward Freedom*, New York, Harper & Brothers, 1958, 97.
5. Martin Luther King, Jr., *Strength to Love*, New York: Harper & Row, 1963, 138.
6. Prime Minister's Office, Government of India, "Prime Minister Manmohan Singh's Speech at Satyagraha Centenary Commemoration" (Kingsmead Stadium, Durban, South Africa, 1 October 2006), http://pmindia.nic.in/visits/content.asp?id=123 (accessed 27 April 2007).
7. Jawaharlal Nehru, *Toward Freedom: The Autobiography of Jawaharlal Nehru*, New York: John Day, 1941, 80.
8. Peter Ackerman and Jack Duvall, *A Force More Powerful: A Century of Nonviolent Conflict*, New York: Palgrave, 2000.
9. Barbara Deming, "On Revolution and Equilibrium," in *Revolution & Equilibrium*, New York: Grossman, 1971, 199.
10. Quoted in Judith M. Brown, *Gandhi: Prisoner of Hope*, New Haven, CT: Yale University Press, 1989, 375.
11. See in particular Gene Sharp, The Politics of Nonviolent Action, Boston, MA: Porter Sargent, 1973 and Waging Nonviolent Struggle: 20th Century Practice and 21st Century Potential, Boston, MA: Porter Sargent, 2005.
12. Walter Wink, *Engaging the Powers: Discernment and Resistance*, Minneapolis, MN: Fortress, 1992, 252.

13. David D. Kirkpatrick, "Egypt Army Sets 6-Month Blueprint, But Future Role is Unclear," February 14, 2011, at http://www.nytimes.com/2011/02/15/world/middleeast/15egypt.html
14. David D. Kirkpatrick and David E. Sanger, "A Tunisian-Egyptian Link That Shook Arab History," *The New York Times*, February 13, 2011, at http://www.nytimes.com/2011/02/14/world/middleeast/14egypt-tunisia-protests.html
15. George Orwell, "Reflections on Gandhi," in *A Collection of Essays* (New York: Harcourt Brace, 1946), 177.
16. Maria J. Stephan and Erica Chenoweth, "Why Civil Resistance Works: The Strategic Logic of Nonviolent Conflict," *International Security* 33, no. 1 (Summer 2008): 20.
17. Quoted in Susan Ferris and Ricardo Sandoval, The Flight in the Fields: Cesar Chavez and the Farmworkers Movement, ed. Diana Hembree, New York: Harcourt Brace, 1997, 114.
18. Deming, "On Revolution and Equilibrium," 211.
19. Niebuhr, Moral Man and Immoral Society, 250.
20. Stephan and Chenoweth, "Why Civil Resistance Works," 21.
21. Adrian Karatnycky and Peter Ackerman, "How Freedom is Won: From Civic Resistance to Durable Democracy," *International Journal of Not-for-Profit Law* 7, no. 3 (June 2005): 50.
22. Adrian Karatnycky and Peter Ackerman, "How Freedom is Won: From Civic Resistance to Durable Democracy," *International Journal of Not-for-Profit Law* 7, no. 3 (June 2005), 51.
23. Jonathan Schell, *The Unconquerable World: Power, Nonviolence, and the Will of the People*, New York: Metropolitan Books, 2003, 236, 240.
24. Quoted in Roger Cohen, "From 9/11 to 2/11," *New York Times*, 13 February 2011, A23.
25. Seth G. Jones and Martin C. Libicki, *How Terrorist Groups End: Lessons for Countering al Qa'ida*, Santa Monica, CA: RAND Corporation, 2008, xiii–xiv, 42-43.
26. Steven Kull et al., "Public Opinion in the Islamic World on Terrorism, al Qaeda, and U.S. Policies", Program on International Policy Attitudes, University of Maryland, 25 February 2009, 11, http://www.worldpublic opinion.org/pipa/pdf/feb09/STARTII_Feb09_rpt.pdf (accessed 23 March 2009).

4
India's Soft Power in a Globalized World

T.V. Paul[1]

Soft power-based on intangible indicators such as culture, civilization, literature, philosophy, institutional involvement, diplomacy, political organization, and state capacity—has emerged as an important factor in the globalizing world for a country seeking higher status and influence. India, with its unique cultural and civilizational strengths has a great opportunity to become a global leader in the area of soft power. The key ingredients of India's soft power resources are its multi-ethnic culture, peace generating, syncretic civilizational values (including religious and philosophical ideals), and unique art forms and literature. More importantly, the key cultural and institutional values that contemporary India possesses have great promise for managing multi-ethnic societies, especially in the developing world. These arise from four institutional structures that India's first Prime Minister Jawaharlal Nehru helped establish in India: democracy, secularism, federalism, and the 3-language formula. As the 21st century advances, India is slowly making use of its soft power assets, assisted by the increasing attention it is being paid by the global media and the scholarly world.

This chapter will focus on some of these elements of India's present and putative soft power assets while underscoring the need for greater hard power resources in order to harness soft power more effectively as a country relying on soft power alone cannot achieve a global leadership role or higher status. I argue soft power without hard power is a chimera and that they should not be seen in oppositional terms, especially for an aspiring global power. It will conclude by arguing for increased use of global communication networks and seeking the assistance of the extensive Indian diaspora for channeling and disseminating India's soft power assets. However, harnessing soft power resources effectively would require India to become a more equitable and efficient society, and a global economic power, a state whose society transforms into a more egalitarian value system and an economy that commands a major share of the global wealth, especially global trade and investment.

What is Soft Power?

Scholars have categorized power resources as 'hard' and 'soft.' Hard power sources include: military, economic, demographic, and technological assets. Soft power resources consist of: culture, arts, literature, philosophy, civilizational values, global-institutional involvement, diplomacy, political organization, and state capacity (see Nayar and Paul, 2003). As defined by Joseph Nye, soft power "is the ability to get what you want through attraction rather than coercion or payments. It arises from the attractiveness of a country's culture, political ideals, and policies. When our policies are seen as legitimate in the eyes of others, our soft power is enhanced" (Nye, 2004: x).[2] It is affecting the preferences of others in congruence with the influencing party's preferences as the latter has something valuable to offer as well as worth emulating. However, the possession of soft power resources does not automatically make a country powerful in the world stage. It is when power assets are translated into influencing the behavior of other states then one can say power is materialized. The translation of assets into influence requires well-calibrated national strategies that assess and reassess one's abilities in the changing global context and make timely policy adaptations. The current era of deepened globalization offers a powerful window of opportunity for emerging powers such as India to actualize their soft power resources more effectively.

A key question in this context arises: Can soft power resources alone make a country powerful? Does a nation need hard power resources to harness soft power resources effectively? Contrary to some assertions, I argue that soft power resources alone will not bring power or status to a country. It is the confluence of hard and soft power resources that make a country powerful and bring it leadership role and status in the global arena with an enduring footing. A country relying solely on soft power without hard power assets can be exposed easily as happened to India in 1962 when China inflicted a humiliating military defeat, tarnishing India's hard won soft power position in the world, especially among other developing countries. By the early 1960s, India had shown that epochal changes like freedom of a country from colonialism can be achieved largely through non-violent means, the Afro-Asian states can be organized as a cushioning force in world politics in the midst of an intense Cold War rivalry among the great powers, and that democracy can be established in a large, poor, under-developed and multi-ethnic country. India had also shown under Nehru's leadership that diplomacy has much power and that despite limited hard power resources, it could be used in global institutional forums for mediating conflict among the major powers to some extent. Yet, all these came crashing down in the Himalayas as the military conflict with China exposed the limitations of India's soft power, making Nehru's active global engagement a casualty in that process. Despite these pitfalls, soft power can still bring reputation, credibility and legitimacy to a state's power position in the global system if it is developed and exercised in conjunction with hard power resources.

As India's hard power capabilities, especially in the economic and military realms have accelerated following its economic liberalization since 1991, and it has made increasing efforts to acquire a global power status, it is high time to revisit the value of soft power resources as tools of grand strategy and foreign policy for this emerging power.[3] What soft power does is that it gives legitimacy and credibility to a state's leadership role in the world, and more effectiveness to the exercise and wielding of its hard power resources. Legitimacy of power implies that other states accept the power of a country as rightful and worthy of recognizing through formal and informal mechanisms which may include assigning additional leadership roles in global institutions. In many ways soft power falls under the category of means of 'social creativity' to achieve prestige and status by promoting new norms or a developmental model, in contrast to 'social competition' which attempts to attain preeminence through competitive or coercive means. It is also useful for staking out "a distinctive position without directly challenging" the dominant powers in the international system (Larson and Shevchenko, 2010). Joseph Nye argues: "countries that are well-placed in terms of soft-power do better. The countries that are likely to gain soft power in an information age are: 1. Those whose dominant culture and ideas are closer to prevailing global norms (which now emphasize liberalism, pluralism, and autonomy); 2. Those with the most access to multiple channels of communication and thus more influence over how issues are framed; and 3. Those whose credibility is enhanced by their domestic and international performance" (Nye, 2002: 70). Nye also contends that "soft power of a country rests on three resources: its culture (in places where it is attractive to others), its political values (when it lives up to them at home and abroad), and its foreign policies (when they are seen as legitimate and having moral authority)" (Nye, 2004:11). How do these factors apply to the Indian case?

India's Soft Power Assets

India has tremendous assets in the soft power area, yet to be fully harnessed effectively. What are they? Its multi-ethnic culture, peace generating civilizational values (including religious and philosophical ideals), and the unique art forms and literatures are perhaps the core of this soft power asset mix. More importantly, key values and institutions that contemporary India possesses have great promise for managing multi-ethnic societies, especially in the developing world. These arise largely from four institutional structures that first Prime Minister Jawaharlal Nehru helped to establish in India: democracy, secularism, federalism, and the 3-language formula. First I will deal with India's deep multi-ethnic culture and its grand civilizational assets and their potential in producing and projecting soft power.

Culture and Soft Power

The unique culture of a country can be a soft power asset or a currency of attraction and influence. "Culture is a set of values and practices that create meaning for a society. It has many manifestations. It is common to distinguish between high culture such as literature, art, and education, which appeals to elites, and popular culture, which focuses on mass entertainment" (Nye,

2004:11). Culture is what gives sustenance to a civilization and the latter is defined by the uniqueness and idiosyncrasies of a culture. Both civilization and culture refer to the "values, norms, institutions, and modes of thinking to which successive generations in a given society have attached primary importance" (Bozeman, 1975, 1, quoted in Huntington, 1996, 41).

The unique art, dance, architecture, cuisine, literature and languages of India are all part of its composite culture and civilizational offerings to the world and are therefore, soft power assets. These assets can bring global influence if they are accepted as valuable and worthy of emulation by different societies in the world.

- India's traditional and modern ***art*** have slowly become internationally accepted as powerful assets. Visitors to any major art museums in the world where Asian art is exhibited will see India's contributions in this regard. However, the most salient forms of Indian *art* or *architecture* that is not properly marketed internationally is the traditional facades of Indian buildings. Even in domestic building structures within India, traditional architectural forms are often missing while concrete jungles are coming up in all urban centers. A visitor to Bali, Indonesia, is astounded by the beauty of the intricate architecture and art forms which originated from ancient India. Today, Indian artists are slowly making headway in the global scene in auctions and exhibitions, although much more can be attained in this area.
- Indian ***cuisine*** has already made tremendous impact globally as evident in countries like UK where it has now become the most preferred international food. Here again, the cuisine that is most popular is North Indian. Other cuisines from the South (e.g. Kerala) could be globally branded as Thai cuisine is today. The cuisine of India's different regions could be made popular through sustained campaigns by India's government agencies and private corporations. One avenue to do so is holding food festivals and establishment of global food chains similar to what US companies like McDonalds and Kentucky Fried Chicken have done. A key element in this regard for marketing is the

vegetarian cuisine consumed by a majority of the Indian population. Globally, more and more people are adopting vegetarian diets as a way to avoid many of the modern day diseases like cancer and heart ailments. The problem here is a dearth of sustained appreciation campaign for vegetarian food and branding of India's offerings in the cuisine area. Traditional Indian medicines like *Ayurveda* similarly require global branding, and have the potential to become a very valuable alternative medicine for certain ailments. However, the lack of strict regulations has generated fake Ayurvedic doctors and medicines, some involving arsenic materials.

- The ***literature*** of India in the English language has become global, especially those written by Indian expatriate authors. In fact many of the leading authors in English literature today are of Indian origin and their themes are related to India or Indian diaspora. The list is long and it includes: Salman Rushdie, Arundhati Roy, Abraham Verghese, Rohinton Mistry, Vikram Seth, Amitav Ghosh, Aravind Adiga, Kiran Desai, and V.S. Naipaul. A similar attempt to brand locally produced vernacular language Indian literature could be undertaken. In this area, the Latin American countries have made major global impact. High quality translations and dissemination of literary works into the global market place by developing collaborations with major publishing houses and literary agents are essential for this purpose.
- The ***apparel designs*** and ***fashions*** of India have tremendous soft power potential. Clothing is an area where India could excel given the colorfulness and variety of brands India can offer. Fusion is the key to make Indian attires global brands. Indian companies have to design clothes in conjunction with global leaders in this area and market them through shows and media presentations and encourage global chains to purchase them.
- The different art forms such as classical and modern-day ***dancing*** could be made global brands. Take the case of *Bharatanayam, Kathak, Kuchipudy, Kathkali* and *Mohiniyattam,* the prominent classical dance forms of India. These are unique art forms that many foreigners

initially find difficult to appreciate, but with some simplifications they could be made globally more attractive. Leading Western artists such as Beatles, Michael Jackson, Madonna, and Shakira have adopted elements of Indian dances or music in their performances and their idea of fusion hold much promise for globalizing Indian dance forms.

- The ***Music*** of India has a particular soothing and peace generating characteristic. More upbeat dance and music forms such as the *Bhangra* are now popular in many wedding parties and other festivities in North America and other English speaking countries. I believe a substantial number of Indian musical traditions such as *Hindustani, Karnatik*, instrumental (especially using flute, tabala and sarong), Ghazals, all have great potential to be marketed and exposed on a global scale. Eminent figures like Pandit Ravi Shankar have done much to popularize Indian instrumental music in the West since the 1960s. Once again adaptations including fusions are needed to make them attractive to the 21st century global audience. In this area, India holds more promise than the music and dance forms of China or for that matter, any other developing country.
- ***Films*** from India have already made a major mark in the global arena. Bollywood produces the largest number of films by any country and is now increasingly viewed as second to Hollywood in terms of global reach. These movies are known for entertainment and as such they have made major impact in Asia, Middle East and Africa, and slowly spreading to the Western countries. Here again quantity versus quality is a major problem. Indian films often lack realism and if entertaining themes are developed with a realistic portrayal of story lines they could make powerful inroads into global film industry. Foreign collaboration would help as proven by the success of the movie, 'Slumdog Millionaire.' Many other Bollywood movies could have achieved similar prominence. Take the case of the movie 'My Name is Khan.' Even though that movie was a commercial success it could have made much more global appeal had it shown a more realistic portrayal of the main characters. The film, 'Lagaan,' despite some

incredible elements in it, made a major mark and won an Oscar nomination as it projects the tender feelings and struggles of the characters and the political saga of Colonial India in an artistic way. Proper marketing is necessary for Bollywood to make a global impact beyond its exiting strongholds in Asia, Middle East, and Africa.

Civilizational Route to Soft power

Civilizations and their inherent cultures are the core of much soft power in modern and ancient times. Empires that left lasting impressions are those with civilizations. In today's world, such imperial civilizations are hard to establish and it is the multi-cultural and pluralistic civilizations that are most valued in a globalized era, as people from different ethnic and religious backgrounds have to live together even if they do not share all key attributes and values on what constitute the goals and ends in social life. States Katzenstein:

The power of a civilization depends on the practices that promote or diminish its magnetism. Such magnetisms reflect creativity, typically shaped by rival positions and disagreements that command attention. Competing schools of thought that are in vigorous debate and disagreement thus are crucial to civilizational prestige. Civilizations are marked by dialogue, debate, and disagreement that generate intellectual and artistic tension. In their engagement of the world, both attraction and propagation characterize zones of civilizational prestige that are composed of multiple, competing networks and distant connections. Such zones attract students and visitors of different kinds, some from very far away. Conversely, zones of high prestige also send out teachers and missionaries, both to civilizational peripheries and other civilizations. Zones of prestige are not free-standing and monolithic. Diversity and active debate among rival positions spur creativity and stymie uniformity of opinion (Katzenstein, 2010, 18).

The multi-dimensional ***civilizational*** assets of India have great actual and potential soft power significance. What are the strengths of the Indian civilization? Foremost is the unique peace generating ethos inherent in Hinduism, Buddhism and other minority religions like Islam, Jainism, Sikhism, and Christianity as practiced in India. In many respects, India is one of the most enduring 'grand' or 'mega' civilizations of the world, which has contributed immensely to many fields: religion, philosophy, art, literature, science and mathematics for over three millennia (see, Basham, 1975). India has an immense tradition of intellectual 'dialogue' and skepticism and a tradition of "accepted heterodoxy" including atheists and religionists (Sen, 2005, xii). Three world religions emanated from India—Hinduism, Buddhism and Sikhism—in addition to the smaller religion, Jainism. Christianity reached Indian shores in AD 52 (believed to be with the arrival of St. Thomas in Kerala) even before it was acceptable in Europe, while persecuted religious minorities such as Zoroastrians, Jews, and Baha'is found India receiving them with open arms. While Islam in the North arrived largely through invading Muslim rulers and latter day conversions, in the South and beyond, it came via Arab traders and its spread has been largely through peaceful means. What is unique about this religious mix is their relative peaceful co-existence, despite some significant aberrations during the reign of the Mughal ruler, Aurangzeb, and since the 1930s, especially before and after the partition of the sub-continent in 1947.

The minority religions, even foreign-originated ones like Islam and Christianity, have developed eclectic forms of ideas in conjunction with Indian ideals, largely emanating from Buddhism and Hinduism. The peace-generating ideals were promoted by India's ancient and modern heroes, four of whom are most prominent: Lord Buddha, Asoka the Great, Akbar the Great, and Mahatma Gandhi; all of whom are remembered for instilling peaceful values in India and beyond. The impressive spread of Buddhism from India to other countries in South Asia, China to Japan in East Asia, and to Southeast Asia and beyond was accomplished through peaceful means. Buddha's teachings even without reference to God reached millions over the millennia and this feat may well be ancient India's greatest soft power diffusion and contribution to world peace. States Nehru: Buddha's "message was one of universal benevolence, of love for all. For, 'never in this world does hatred cease by hatred; hatred ceases by love.' And 'let a man overcome anger by kindness, evil by good' (1989:128). Even within religions, medieval India produced movements like *Bhakti* (Devotion) and *Sufism*, known for their peaceful eclectic ideas and practices (Madan, 1989). Similar to Buddhism, Jainism also brought many ideals of peace. What is unique about the Indian civilization is that it received and naturalized diverse cultural forms. "The metaphor of a 'composite civilization' captures the many religions, starting with Hinduism but continuing with Islam and Christianity, which found a home in India and suggests that all are acceptable" (Rudolph, 2010, 148). States Tharoor (2007, 8): In India "everything exists in countless variants. There is no single standard, no fixed stereotype and no 'one way.' This pluralism is acknowledged in the way India arranges its own affairs: all groups, faiths, tastes, and ideologies survive and contend for their place in the sun."

Since India's independence, violence generating behavior has come from fringe elements of these religions, yet they contain powerful strings of harmony and peace in a deeper and sustainable manner. Some modern-day meditation gurus like Deepak Chopra and Maharshi Mahesh Yogi have articulated the elements of this peace, but it is not fully used as a soft power resource by India. The deeper meanings of yoga and meditation arise from the spiritual level of India's civilizational offerings to the world and these need to be articulated further.

The biggest manifestation of the multi-cultural and multi-ethnic soft power asset is the simple fact that India contains almost the same population as Africa and the Middle East combined, and more varieties of religions and cultures than any other nation-state in the world. Although a very non-egalitarian society, India has a mechanism for social order much more peace-generating that many other civilizations. The democratic and secular values since independence have helped in this area tremendously. On a per capita basis, there is also much less crime and violence in India although this may be changing. However, when extremist elements, be they left-wing or right-wing, try to undermine that harmony India and its soft power suffer. Rapid peaceful social and economic change and social engineering may be necessary to quell much of the extremist violence. The exclusivist civilizational ideas propounded by extremist religious parties or groups, be it Hindutva or Islamic fundamentalism, can hurt India's soft power as such ideas have little attraction for outsiders who are not members of a given religion or ethnic group. They simply generate 'in-group', 'out-group' mentalities and violence among diverse communities.

Scholars have increasingly talked of India emerging (or resuming) its role as a bridge-building civilization. Kishore

Mahbubani argues that one example of that is Bollywood movies which are watched equally passionately by both Hindus and Muslims, the latter in many Asian and Middle Eastern and African countries. Some of Bollywood's leading actors and actresses are Muslims, a feat hard to find in Hollywood which also often depicts other cultures as inferior or in oppositional terms. "At a time many Westerners are convinced that the West cannot co-exist in peace with the Islamic world, they should study how India has been able to accommodate so many civilizations—including Hindu, Buddhist, Islamic and Christian cultures–and how most of them have lived in peace with each other for most of its history" (Mahbubani, 2008:173). He contends: "The Indian capacity for engaging other cultures and civilizations may well define India's role in the relations between the West and the East. It could perform one particular task: to convincing the leading minds in the West that they should stop seeing themselves as safe guardians and custodians of one leading civilization, but as guardians and custodians of human civilizations" (Mahbubani, 2008, 173). This may well be needed as Europe with its fortress mentality and unwillingness to accept multiculturalism and China with its uniquely ethnic nationalism and authoritarian system emerge as counter civilizational positions in a world simultaneously containing much intolerance preached by fundamentalist religious groups such as al-Qaeda and the Taliban. Can India emerge as a bridge-builder, showing that exclusivist agendas are values of yesteryears, that the future belongs to multi-cultural and multi-civilizational paths, each trying to accept and understand in a composite culture that could result from the intensified globalization of universal values, which are not to be confined to Western values or ideas or Eastern approaches as typified by China as well as Islamic countries?

Political and Economic Systems and Soft Power

The ***political system*** of a country can be a source of soft power. In India's case, these arise from four institutional structures: democracy, secularism, federalism, and the 3-language formula. These institutional ideas also derive from India as an inclusive civilization, despite some deep hierarchical issues arising from the caste system and corruption among the political elite.

- Despite all its pitfalls and messiness, Indian ***democracy*** has sustained and it is a wonder for many social science theorists leading some to brand it as "Indian exceptionalism" (meaning non-replicable!). Since its independence in 1947, democracy has brought power transfers non-violently (barring some elections-related violence) in India and an imperfect, yet important democratic model for the governance of a multi-ethnic and multi-religious society.
- Similarly, India's ***secularism*** has become strong (despite occasional aberrations like the Gujarat and Ayodhya episodes). Tangible evidence is the growing percentage of minority populations in India – be they Muslim, Christians or Sikhs, versus minority populations in India's South Asian neighbors, especially, Pakistan and Bangladesh, and their allegiance to the Indian nation. The secular values are also evident in the growing integration of the Muslim population in India and their low participation in global Jihadist organizations like al Qaeda. At least in the past two federal elections, the Indian electorate refused to vote into power the BJP which contains elements of Hindu nationalism. The growing pragmatism of the Indian electorate was visible in these elections. The ***federal*** set up of the Indian constitution has allowed the provincial governments to function reasonably autonomously and in some cases more effectively than in others.
- India's 2 plus 1 ***language*** policy (Hindi, English plus local language) has brought tremendous peace in this area, an issue that still bedevils even advanced countries like Canada, US, and Spain.

These political models can be improved and adapted to emerging states in Africa and Asia, including India's South Asian neighbors that are plagued by ethnic violence arising from intolerance towards minority groups. In this regard China has a major weakness as it is an authoritarian system and hence not a model for 21st century states in terms of political organization.[4] Beijing's ethnic integration strategies in Tibet and Xinxiang are highly coercive and disregard local customs and values.

However, India's asset in this regard is also its bane. The Indian state is a ***soft*** or a *strong/weak state*, exhibiting some strengths, while showing many signs of a weak state (Paul, 2010). The reason why India's political system has not received the credit it deserves is because of its chaotic nature and the inefficiency of the Indian state at every level—central, state, municipal/village—to deliver public services efficiently and effectively. The Indian private sector has largely been more effective at least in areas where they have been allowed to operate, such as aviation and wireless telephone services.

The Indian ***economic*** successes can also be a great soft power asset. It is incredible to many outside observers how India could sustain 6-9 per cent average economic growth rate during the past two decades with all the inefficiencies that the Indian system generates (Luce, 2007). It clearly shows India's entrepreneurial genius, if freed, could make this a model for the 21st century economic growth. India shows that a developing country can rapidly grow and does not need the Chinese or East Asian top-down and mercantile model for economic growth. In the words of White House economic advisor, Larry Summers, the world will soon focus on what he terms the 'Mumbai consensus' described as: "a developing state driven not by mercantilist capitalism or exports but a people-centric focus on growing levels of consumption based globally" (Bajaj, 2010). According to Morgan Stanley, India by 2013-15 will become the fastest growing economy in the world helped by its demographic dividend, continuing structural reforms and globalization (Ahya and Gupta, 2010).

However, the big weakness here is the rampant inequalities and distributional injustices as well as the corruption that the Indian system generates which takes away some of the kudos that it deserves. The continuing appalling conditions of the workers, extreme poverty in rural and urban centers, extant child labor, poor treatment of women and wide-spread caste discrimination, and a general lack of public hygiene all affect the way India is perceived by outsiders despite its economic and political successes. There is immense violence in the Naxal infested areas and in recent years there have been a high number of suicides by indebted farmers. India has also great difficulty dealing with insurgencies in Kashmir and the Northeast and often resorts to highhanded methods which create blows to India's image and soft power. The rapid economic growth is also yet to be seen in urban planning and infrastructure development. For instance, Indian road builders have a dearth of understanding of the need for building proper footpaths and crosswalks for pedestrians. Managing and controlling pollution and waste is another major weakness of India. Indian schools should offer compulsory education on hygiene and waste disposal while clean lavatories need to be set up in all urban and rural centers of India. More importantly, if India can find a meaningful manner of peaceful wealth redistribution and solution to the problems I listed above, it will be able to offer a powerful economic and developmental model, as the East Asian NICs did in the 1970s and 1980s. In addition to raw economic numbers, India has to pay much more attention to quality of life and human index parameters while making an all out effort to lift up the millions of people from abject poverty and destitution.

Diplomacy as Soft Power

Diplomacy has two key dimensions that can be soft power assets. The first is the actual diplomatic practices and policies shown by governmental diplomatic representatives through their activism in global institutional forums and foreign capitals. The second dimension is **public diplomacy** which relies on the distribution of information and cultural programs overseas aimed at improving the prestige and image of a country. They are also means to counter negative stereotypes and propaganda often generated by opponents or others who do so out of lack of knowledge or specific prejudices they carry. In this sense, diplomacy is also a tool for soft power enhancement. The US government (USGAO, 2004) describes public diplomacy goals are "to increase the understanding of American values, policies and initiatives and to counter anti-American sentiment and misinformation about the United States around the world. This includes reaching beyond foreign governments to promote better appreciation of the United States abroad, greater receptivity to US policies among foreign publics, and sustained access and influence in important sectors of foreign societies."

A caveat here is that if public diplomacy is undertaken overzealously it could become sheer propaganda and that other countries would start resenting it. While America has been the most successful country in public diplomacy in the contemporary era, it has also generated reactions that have diminished its soft power assets, because of the actual foreign policy that the US has pursued in places like the Middle East and the Persian Gulf. It should be noted that the messenger also matters for diplomacy as much as the message, and how the message is presented to the rest of the world. In this regard, President Barack Obama's arrival has made a major difference compared to his predecessor George W. Bush for the presentation and appreciation of America's public diplomacy and soft power itself.

India pursued diplomacy quite successfully until the 1960s as a soft power asset. By organizing the newly emerging Afro-Asian states and by leading their cause at the UN, supporting and promoting peace-keeping operations, and offering mediation during major power conflicts such as in Korea, Nehru's India received more influence in the global arena than its hard power warranted. This changed dramatically as China, the other emergent power, viewed Indian activism as affecting its position in Asia and engaged in a punitive military action, which exposed India's inability to withstand a powerful military challenge. Since the 1960s India has lowered diplomacy as a tool of soft power although activism continued in specific venues such as the UN forums. In the post Cold War globalized world, India once again, has begun using its diplomacy more effectively, be it at the UN, G-20, BRICS, WTO, global climate talks or engagement with the EU and the ASEAN states. There is increased confidence and pragmatism in India's global diplomacy and engagement (Raja Mohan, 2003). It also comes out of a realization among the Indian elite that its hard power resources are growing substantially and that if the present trends continue within a few decades India may overtake many of the other countries in the world, except China and the United States in gross economic terms. Today India is also viewed in many Asian capitals "as a predictable, stabilizing, cooperative and attractive rising power," and it is marked by a "lack of apprehension about India's rise," unlike China's (Lee, 2010). This general lack of worry about India's rise may have much to do with India's soft power assets. However, China appears to have many successes in soft power area as well through its diplomatic engagement and economic developmental policies with its neighbors, especially the ASEAN states, as well as Africa and Latin America. Furthermore, with its economic success, Chinese languages and China studies are becoming more popular world over, a feat India is yet to replicate.

A major weakness of India's public diplomacy is the attitude and behavioral dispositions of India's political and bureaucratic elite and how they are perceived abroad. A country needs good spokespeople who are articulate and have great media presence to capitalize on its public diplomacy efforts. Indian political class (barring a few exceptions) does not have good public presence or ability to speak to a global audience. This goes for the Indian bureaucracy and diplomatic class as well. India needs to pay attention to creating individual spokespeople who can exhibit the qualities that are necessary for selling India's soft power assets abroad. Moreover, India has to use its human talent from corporations (especially globalized ones), media, scholars, artists and writers in bringing forth its soft power assets to the world's attention. In some cases, it is the globally powerful media persons, scholars and artists from other countries who can accomplish this for India. Thomas Freedman of the New York Times is a prominent example, whose writings have done quite a bit of publicity for India's soft power assets. This may also mean bringing these scholars and media people to India through exchange programs and visits on a regular basis as the US does.

Knowledge and Ideas as Soft Power

The discussion so far has showed that India has much soft power assets, and yet some are not utilized, or are constrained by countervailing factors. In the last two decades or so, India's soft power assets have become recognized globally more than ever before. The two major reasons for this are India's rapid economic growth and the globalization of the media with the arrival of new information technologies. Knowledge, especially, scientific knowledge, has both hard and soft power values. India's success in harnessing information and electronic technologies have shown that the ancient Vedic adage 'knowledge is wealth' is finally coming to fruition (Das, 2002: 325). In order to fully harness this asset India needs to set up knowledge generating research intensive universities and open up its educational institutions for international students and foreign scholarly collaborations. The biggest ambassadors of America's soft power have been the thousands of foreign students who studied in the US since the 1940s and who carry American ideals of freedom and entrepreneurship back to their home countries and to the global arena. India has a number of teaching institutions, some of high quality, but others seem to lag behind. India needs to build educational institutions of higher learning of world standards and develop cutting edge research and publications and produce innovative ideas in all key disciplines including social sciences. These universities could attract top talent, especially from the Indian diaspora which is untapped now. The global focus in education could be a major source of soft power for India unlike most other developing countries. Social science disciplines such as International Relations and Economics should receive higher prominence in India similar to the Chinese approaches to these disciplines. The International Relations discipline especially is very weak in India for a variety of structural and cultural reasons, including governmental attitudes (Paul, 2010; Mattoo, 2010).

The Role of Diaspora in Soft Power

One critical source of soft power dissemination is the diaspora. India is well-endowed in this area. Despite earlier skepticism of the value of the diaspora, today Indian expatriates have emerged as a key source of disseminating India's culture, values and other soft power assets in the global arena. Many of the Indian arts, music, and dances are kept alive in these diaspora communities. Second and third generation Indians increasingly are yearning for knowledge and understanding of their roots. Many are returning to India for employment purposes. This trend is likely to continue as the advanced industrialized countries suffer possible economic downturn for a long period of time. However, in order to fully tap this resource, India needs to court the young second generation diaspora and those approaching retirement who may have the wealth and time to promote Indian ideals (Kapur, 2003:447).

In order to use the diaspora most effectively, India needs more creative ideas and policies. The Indian government's 'pravasi' (non-resident Indian) policies of the past few years have made some progress, but it is still way below the threshold of what India can achieve. Establishing Indian research institutions/centers and university research chairs abroad that are more amalgams of contemporary studies and cultural studies would help. The current India programs in many Western universities are too focused on ancient history or religious aspects devoid of contemporary issues such as political economy and foreign policy. Diaspora children should have easy ways to study and work in India. Barring a few scientific and technological institutions, Indian universities remain a weak asset as the scholarship and teaching methods they generate are sub-par in terms of global standards. They do not yet appear in any of the university ranking lists in the top few hundreds. Foreign collaboration might help in improving higher education standards, but the key is internal innovation and modernization.

India's Soft Power in a Globalizing World: Some Conclusions

The major question is can India offer a model for global governance and ideas for peace and order different from Western liberal ideas or the Chinese authoritarian ideas? In this regard China has indeed made some contribution through its "peaceful rise" strategy. However the question arises, peaceful rise for what? What are the normative and economic and political ideas that China will bring to the table to make the world a better place? Can these compete with Western liberal ideas such as democracy, rule of law, freedom and multilateralism based on global institutions? Can India offer ideas of peace and unity based on its eclectic civilizational/cultural ethos and mores? Inclusiveness, interdependence and unity in diversity are essential for the world, as without these values, the 21st century will see many more conflicts, of both internal and external varieties. The rapid rise of new powers like China and India may generate conflict with the declining powers or between the newly emerging powers themselves. Can India's soft power assets be utilized to prevent massive internal upheavals and aggressive nationalism that such power transition conflicts can generate, as in the case of the European state system for over 500 years? Can India act as a 'bridging power' of the West and East? I believe it can and a first thing to do is develop a national strategy with this goal in mind. New ideas from India for a peaceful global order are very essential here.

India has to make use of advanced information technology and modern media to fully realize its soft power potential. Those countries that can harness information technology to their advantage will have the most significant ability to project soft power in the 21st century. This would mean India emerging as a media center and developing alternative media forms, including internet-based platforms and specialized television channels meant for a global audience. However, when a country is exposed to global communication networks, it is also showing its weaknesses. How a country performs, and organizes its public space and how its citizens behave and are treated are all visible to the rest of the world. Countries like China have a major advantage here as it can control the flow of information whereas India is an open book. Hence, India's asset in this regard becomes its bane.

The highly negative media publicity of the 2010 Delhi Commonwealth Games showed that Western as well as local media are ready to jump on India to show its weaknesses. Although much of it was warranted, the same Western media failed to show adequately the highly successful opening ceremony and the pageantry that it produced or the fairly successful conduct of the games. This example also illustrates that soft power is not competition free and that other countries that view the rising power as a challenge may attempt wittingly or unwittingly to undermine it. India can develop a network like al-Jazeera and offer global coverage more effectively and dispassionately. India needs institutions like America's National Endowment for Democracy and a number of information and cultural centers abroad similar to overseas American, British and French centers, apart from the usual diplomatic missions. It needs to establish fellowships and visiting scholarships for a variety of disciplines and areas where India can identify its soft power assets and select candidates on the basis of merit.

Similar to the proposed Confucian institutes China has been setting up, India can possibly establish Institutions for inter-civilizational and inter-religious dialogue, spread of non-violent and multicultural engagement and the dissemination of ideas of democracy, secularism and freedom, and the achievement of sustainable economic development. One concrete idea I propose is the setting up of "India Multiculturalism Centers" in key cities of the world bringing together Indian/Eastern and Western scholars and thinkers to discuss core developmental and socio-political issues. These centers can deal with issues of multiculturalism and secularism along with global equity and justice. One caution here is guarding against giving monopoly of such institutions to leftist- or rightist-oriented scholars or government appointed ex-diplomats/military personnel who sometimes prevent independent thinking and free exchange of ideas.

Avenues such as international scholarly, artistic, youth

exchanges, opening of cultural and educational centers, exhibitions, books and periodical exchanges, all can contribute to soft power dissemination. Institutions like ICCR are already doing some of these. Indian tourism department's 'Incredible India' advertisements have shown India's ability to design and execute a well-crafted campaign. "The Buddha circuit tours" are great programs that need to be advertised further. This author recently visited some such Buddhist centers in Bihar but found places like Bodh Gaya lacking decent hotel facilities and a clean environment. A sustained campaign for soft power needs deeper understanding of India in foreign countries and the removal of lingering negative perceptions among opinion-makers and intellectuals. Setting up of research chairs and research institutes on modern India in core disciplines such as history, political science, economics, business (and not purely in humanities) and encouraging foreign universities to offer more courses and program on India would help. Here Indian government could actively court the wealthy diaspora in countries like the US, Canada, and the UK that seems more interested in building temples and mosques than research centers. Indian universities and research institutions should attract large numbers of foreign students and scholars. Removal of archaic visa rules and bureaucratic restrictions will be absolutely necessary for this purpose. In addition, exchange students and faculty should be offered world class clean facilities as people make opinions on the basis of their living conditions in a foreign country. A major source of soft power dissemination are ordinary tourists whose numbers have grown in the Indian case, despite the fact that tourist facilities in India are still very uneven and clean, cheap hotels are difficult to find in major cities. Indian workers seem to lack basic skills as evident in their inability to keep lavatories clean in the newly built world class airports in Delhi and Mumbai. Specialized tourist programs like visiting religious and pilgrim centers are offered in India, especially the Buddhist centers, but these are not widely known.

The universal values of the Indian culture are the assets that need to be brought out more cogently and powerfully. Intensified globalization has offered India with its deep civilization and culture a window of opportunity to actualize its soft power resources more effectively. Institutions like ICCR can be great vehicles in this pursuit. Global perceptions change slowly and they would only happen if India's internal performance and economic advancement continue unabated. During the past decade India has made major strides in economic growth, but without much progress in distribution of the wealth and proper regulatory mechanisms to prevent large-scale corruption. Soft power assets should form a major part of India's grand strategy to emerge as a peace-loving global power, but they are not replacements for hard power resources, as the former cannot be sustained too long without the latter. They both should be developed in tandem.

Bibliography

Ahya, Chetan and Tanvee Gupta. "India and China: New Tigers of Asia: part III. Morgan Stanley Report August 13, 2010 <http://www.scribd.com/doc/36081710/Morgan-Stanley-India-and-China-New-Tigers-of-Asia-Part-III-20100813>

Bajaj, Vikas. "In Mumbai, Advisor to Obama Extols India's Economic Model," *The New York Times*, October 16, 2010.

Basham, A.L., ed., *A Cultural History of India* (Oxford: Oxford University Press, 1975).

Bozeman, Ada B. "Civilizations under Stress," *Virginia Quarterly Review* 51 (Winter 1975), 1-18.

Bell, Daniel A., "Developing China's Soft Power," *The New York Times*, September 24, 2010, 6.

Das, Gurcharan. *India Unbound* (New York: Anchor Books, 2002).

Debroy, Bibek. "India's Soft Power and Cultural Influnce," in Tan Tai Yong, ed., *Challenges of Economic Growth, Inequality and Conflict in South Asia*, Singapore, World Scientific, 2010: 107-126.

Huntington, Samuel P. *The Clash of Civilizations and the Remakign of World Order* (New York: Simon 7 Schuster, 1996).

Hymans, Jacques E. "India's Soft Power and Vulneability," *India Review* 8, no.3. July-September 2009:234-65.

Kapur, Devesh, "Indian Diaspora as a Strategic Asset," *Economic and Political Weekly*, February 1, 2003: 445-48.

Katzenstein, Peter J. "A World of Plural and Pluralist Civilizations: Multiple Actors, Traditions and Practices," in Katzenstein (ed)., *Civilizations in World Politics: Plural and Pluralist Perspectives, (*London: Routledge, 2010), 1-40.

Larson, Deborah Welch and Alexei Shevchenko, "Status, identity and Rising Powers," Book manuscript in progress, UCLA, October 2010.

Lee, John. "India's Edge over China: Soft Power," *Bloomberg Business Week Insight*, June 17, 2010.

Luce, Edward. *In Spite of the Gods: The Strange Rise of Modern India* (New York: Doubleday, 2007).

Madhan, T.N. "Religion in India," *Daedalus* 118(4), Fall 1989:115-146.

Mahbubani, Kishore, The New Asian Hemisphere: The Irresistible Shift of Global Power to the East (New York: Public Affairs, 2008).

Mattoo, Amitabh. "The State of International Studies in India," *International Studies*, 46 (1-2), 2010, 37-48.

Nayar, Baldev Raj and T.V. Paul, *India in the World Order: Searching for Major Power Status* (Cambridge: Cambridge University Press, 2003).

Nehru, Jawaharlal. *The Discovery of India*, 8th impression (New Delhi: Oxford University Press, 1989).

Nye, Joseph S. "The Information Revolution and American Soft Power," *Asia-Pacific Review* 9(1), 2002:60-76.

——. Soft Power: The Means to Success in World Politics (New York: Pacific Affairs, 2004).

Paul, T.V. ed., *South Asia's Weak State: Understanding the Regional Insecurity Predicament* (Stanford: Stanford University Press, 2010).

——. "Integrating International Relations Studies in India to Global Scholarship," *International Studies*, 46 (1-2), 2010, 129-45.

Raja Mohan, C. Crossing the Rubicon (New York: Palgrave-Macmillan, 2003).

Rudolph, Susanne Hoeber. "Four Variants of Indian Civilization," in Katzenstin ed. *Civilizations in World Politics*, pp.137-56.

Sen, Amartya. *The Argumentative Indian* (New York: Farrar, Straus and Giroux, 2005).

Tharoor, Shashi. *The Elephant, The Tiger and the Cell Phone* (New York: Arcade Publishing, 2007).

U.S. Government Accountability Office Report, U.S. Public Diplomacy, GAO-05-323, Washington D.C. April 2005.

Wagner, Christian. "From Hard Power to Soft Power? Ideas, Interaction, Institutions, and Images in India's South Asia Policy," Heidelberg Papers in *South Asian and Comparative Politics*, No.26, South Asia Institute, University of Heidelberg, March 2005.

Notes and References

1. An earlier version of this chapter was Presented at the Seminar on "Indian Culture in a Globalized World," on the Occasion of the 60th Anniversary of the Indian Council for Cultural Relations (ICCR), New Delhi, November 11-12, 2010. I thank the organizers of the conference, especially Professor Amitabh Mattoo of the Jawaharlal Nehru University and Rekha Chakravarti and Mahesh Shankar for their research assistance.
2. States Nye: "Seduction is always more effective than coercion, and many values like democracy, human rights, and individual opportunities are deeply seductive… But attraction can turn to repulsion if we act in an arrogant manner and destroy the real meaning of our deeper values" (Nye, 2004:x).
3. For different perspectives on India's soft power see Wagner, 2005; Hymans, 2009; Debroy, 2010.
4. A recent article argued for China promoting its Confucian values such as meritocracy and harmony globally as a way out of its sot power deficit (Bell, 2010).

Part II
People and Literature

5
Indian Themes, Indian Values: The *Rāmāyaṇa* and the Civilization of Southern Asia and Beyond

R.P. Goldman

Āji āmi tāre dekhi lābo
Bhārater je mahimā
Tyāg kori āshiācche apon aṁganseemā
Arghyo dibo tāre
Bhārat bahire taba dwāre

This day I will bear witness to the glory of Bhārat
Which came, leaving behind the boundaries of its own land.
I will do it all honor here beyond Bhārat at your very door.
Siam, Rabindranath Tagore (1911)[1]

Tagore penned these lines in the fall of 1927 after returning from a journey of several months through Southeast Asia where he was much impressed at the way in which the local cultures had beautifully adapted and made their own representations of the *Rāmāyaṇa* and *Mahābhārata.* Indeed he undertook this "pilgrimage", he wrote to a friend "to see the signs of India's entry into the universal".[2]

The past decades have witnessed much talk about globalization in various contexts of our contemporary world. But, as Gurudev reminds us, globalization is by no means exclusively a modern phenomenon. At several salient moments in history from antiquity to the present forms of globalization, that is the spread of regional cultures across vast, if not fully global, geographical areas, has taken place and led to the formation of new and enduring forms of cultural, social, political moral and spiritual integration.

One important moment in the history of globalization can be seen in the spread of seminal features of pre-modern Indian civilization across Southern Asia and into West, Central, and East Asia as well.

What is remarkable about the waves of cultural globalization emanating from India in antiquity is that they were not spread by military campaigns or imperial expansion as was the case, for example, in the wide reach of administrative structures along with civic and religious ideologies throughout the Roman Empire, or the expansion of Greek philosophical thought through the conquests of Alexander and his successors.

Instead, Indian concepts and forms of social, political, aesthetic and spiritual thought appear to have spread widely throughout southern Asia during the first millennium CE though mechanisms of what we have come to call, in Joseph S. Nye's famous and influential phrase, "soft power."[3] The mechanisms through which this phenomenon took place were surely numerous and varied and are not fully understood. But perhaps the most striking and important of these mechanisms involved the circulation of both Hindu and Buddhist texts that encoded critical values of the civilization of ancient Indian, along with the interpreters of these values, the *brāhmaṇas* and *bhikṣus* who travelled throughout the region along with merchants and traders. In short, it can be argued that the first globalization of Indian civilization was, in its essence a literary, cultural and spiritual one.

Interestingly, the spread of Indian concepts of the ideal forms of social, political and religious life, is short of *dharma*, took place in two directions and in the form of two rather different sets of texts carried, it would appear, by different groups.

One set of texts which moved generally from India to the west and whose contents were translated and assimilated by peoples of the Middle East, Southern and Western Europe, was most likely carried by merchants along the caravan and sea routes, was that dealing with everyday political and social relations, in other words with how to survive and prosper in a complex and potentially dangerous world. This type of text is principally representative or what we would call *nīti* or wisdom about how to negotiate various forms of social and political interaction and most characteristically took the form of animal fables and folk tales designed to provide people, notably kings ands their courtiers, with survival manuals for daily life. This genre of literature, best exemplified by the *Pañcatantra* and various other emboxed collections of stories, established itself, through its numerous literary offspring as the form *par excellence* of education made palatable as entertainment and can be seen as the source of texts such as the Arabic, Persian, Syriac and Hebrew tale collections of the Middle East, and European versions in Latin, German, Old Spanish, French and English to name a few while the originally Indic form of stories emboxed one within the other and all surrounded by a large framing narrative can be seen reflected in the Thousand and One Nights, the works of Boccaccio, Chaucer and numerous other writers east and west. These tale collections similarly migrated east to Southeast Asia, China etc, along with brahmans, Buddhists and others.

But the history of these tales and of their diffusion has been fairly intensively studied and is well known.[4] Today I would like to talk about another class of texts that were, and continue to be, critical elements in the spread of the central early Indian concepts and norms concerning culture, politics, religion and society. The texts I have in mind are the great ancient Sanskrit epic poems, the *Rāmāyaṇa* and the *Mahābhārata.* As space is limited and the subject is vast I will confine my remarks chiefly to the former work, which I believe has had the greater influence of the two.

Before, however, talking about the epic poems as instruments of early globalization, it would be well for us to reflect that, first and foremost, and important function of the poems was to diffuse critical elements of Vedic civilization to social spheres in India itself that were, in antiquity, either excluded from or restricted in their direct access to the Vedic texts themselves. In couching many of the core ideas and values of the Vedas in the form of gripping epic narratives of love and war, of grand heroes and heroines as well as towering villains and demonesses, of curses and boons and the amazing feats of gods, *rākṣasas,* men and *vānaras,* the epic poets, Vālmīki and Vyāsa created works fit for performance in all literary, artistic and dramatic media.

As is well known, the diffusion of critical elements of India's culture throughout southern Asia and beyond has left a very palpable legacy of traditions, institutions and monuments throughout the region. These take the form of inscriptions, place names temples, literary and performative texts, and religious, social and political systems.

Today I would like to argue that the monumental ancient Sanskrit poem, the *Rāmāyaṇa* of Vālmīki along with the innumerable and varied later renderings of the Rāmacarita that it directly or indirectly inspired, was one of the principal instruments of this striking and still poorly understood phenomenon.

Like a very few highly culturally influential texts of antiquity, such works as the *Holy Bible,* the *Holy Quran,* and the corpora of Buddhist canonical works, the *Rāmāyaṇa* has transcended barriers of language, region, and culture to become central to the social, political, and religious formations of a vast spectrum of nations and civilizations from ancient times to the present day. Unlike those texts, however—and in this it is virtually unique—it has ensconced itself at the heart of many different religious cultures, first, no doubt Hinduism in all of its rich and complex diversity, but also in the traditions of Jainism, Buddhism, Sikhism, and even Islam, as well as in a number of tribal religions across a vast and populous swathe of territory extending from Iran in the west to Bali and the Philippines in the east and from Tibet and Mongolia in the north to Sri Lanka in the south. Elements of the *Rāmāyaṇa* are also to be found in many of the cultural artifacts of East Asia as well; but to detail all of these is beyond the scope of the present inquiry.

During a history that stretches back more than two millennia, the central tale of the sorely tested but unshakably righteous, Prince Rāma and his faithful, though long suffering, wife Sītā has been represented in an extraordinary variety of forms, in virtually all of the languages and artistic idioms of South and Southeast Asia as monumental epics, poetic and dramatic works, purāṇic narrative, religious tracts and sermons, temple sculpture, court painting, folktales, dance forms, novels, cinema, and television serializations to name but a few.

It is the purpose of the present paper to highlight and investigate some of the salient issues in this history and in the history of *Rāmāyaṇa* scholarship and to offer some suggestions as to why this remarkable story been able uniquely to transcend so many linguistic, religious, and cultural boundaries to become one of the most defining and unifying elements of the cultures of Southern Asia.

Although it is little known in the West beyond a limited circle of scholars of South and Southeast Asian Studies and the diverse émigré communities from Southern Asia, it can easily be argued that the *Rāmāyaṇa* —viewed broadly as the sum of its innumerable textual, artistic, and performative representations—is in many ways and for many millions of people in dozens of countries the greatest story ever told.

In the present paper I hope to shed some modest light on the fascination this tale has exercised over so many people in so many countries for so many centuries including the distinguished participants in the ICCR's Seminar on "Indian Culture in a Globalized World," some of whom, like myself, have devoted many decades of their lives to the study of the rich culture of traditional India.

[To begin, let me say that, although this, like many points in the evolving field of Sanskrit epic studies, is still a matter of debate, I believe that directly or indirectly, one of the principal sources and inspiration for the unparalleled trans-regional cultural efflorescence of Indian culture and civilization throughout Southern Asia is the monumental Sanskrit epic poem attributed to the legendary Indian poet-seer whom we know by the odd name of Vālmīki, "The Son of The Anthill." Since, moreover, I believe that Vālmīki's immortal work is the direct or indirect source of all the innumerable subsequent versions of the Rāmakathā I should like to begin with a brief traditional *hommage* to the First Poet.

कूजन्तं राम रामेति मधुरं मधुराक्षरम् ।
आरुह्य कविताशाखां वन्दे वाल्मीकिकोकिलम् ॥
वाल्मीकेर्मुनिसिंहस्य कवितावनचारिणः ।
शृण्वन्रामकथानादं को न याति परां गतिम् ॥
यः पिबन्सततं रामचरितामृतसागरम् ।
अतृप्तस्तं मुनिं वन्दे प्राचेतसमकल्मषम् ॥[5]

I pay homage to the cuckoo, Vālmīki who, having ascended the tree of poetry, perches there sweetly warbling the sweet song, "Rāma, Rāma!" For who, having once heard the tale of Rāma, in the form of the mighty roar of Vālmīki, the lion among sages who ranges the woodlands of poetry, would not attain the highest bliss? So I make my obeisance to that blameless sage Prācetasa, who drinks incessantly from the ocean of the nectar of the tale of Rāma, and yet is never sated.

The art critic Holland Cotter began his review in *The New York Times* of the 1999 "International Asian Art Fair," (an annual New York event since 1996) with the following comment: "'Asia' doesn't exist and it never has. It isn't a place or a culture; it's a geopolitical fiction, a patchwork of people, climates and languages stitched together lightly, and only here and there, by the bright thread of Buddhism."[6]

Although Cotter's remark is subject to a number of serious criticisms, it does raise a number of theoretical as well as practical difficulties in considering how or even if to conceptualize "Asia" as a distinctive cultural area.

One way to open, perhaps, a small window onto the issues raised by the question of the extent to which there truly exists any form of trans-national Asian cultural identity, I believe, is to explore some of the reasons for the extraordinary spread and popularity of one of the region's most characteristic and enduring cultural phenomena, the virtually unique spectrum of literary, performative, plastic, and religious artifacts that we call collectively the *Rāmāyaṇa*.

I would like to focus on some aspects of the trans-cultural success of Vālmīki's *Rāmāyaṇa* and its innumerable subsequent variations. In so doing I will attempt to touch upon some of the seminal features of this great work and to evaluate them as possible causes for two phenomena. The first of these is the unparalleled ease with which the *Rāmāyaṇa* lent itself to a myriad of adaptations to root itself in so many of the different cultures of India and Southeast Asia.[7] The second is a corresponding lack of similar success in penetrating the cultures and languages of ancient and medieval Europe while other corpora of early Sanskrit and Middle Indic narratives appear, as I mentioned earlier, to have readily spread to and naturalized themselves throughout the Middle East, the Mediterranean and Western Europe.

The *Rāmāyaṇa* attributed to Vālmīki was probably composed around the middle of the first millennium BCE. Despite the fact that (at least until the era of the modern South Asian Diaspora and the attendant exposure of western audiences to a variety of Asian performing arts) the story had remained largely unknown to all but a tiny scholarly community in the West, the *Rāmāyaṇa* and its numerous re-tellings in one form or another have, since that time, become, to a greater or lesser degree, part of the cultural heritage of virtually all regions of Asia. Indeed, in this the *Rāmāyaṇa* in its most broadly conceived form may be rivaled only by Cotter's "bright thread of Buddhism" in all of its regional and sectarian diversity. In fact the two cultural phenomena, Buddhism and the *Rāmāyaṇa*, are to at least some extent interconnected and shared much of the same geographical range in the pre-modern world.

Let us consider some of the particular features of Vālmīki's *Rāmāyaṇa* as well as some other versions of the Rāma story, that have enabled it to travel so freely and widely across geographic, linguistic, ethnic, class, and religious barriers to become, in many respects as close to being a pan-Asian text as we can identify, while at the same time failing to penetrate deeply the cultures of the West. In order to do this I will begin by talking briefly about the epic poem of Vālmīki in particular and then move on to a discussion of some of its central concerns which have enabled the Rāma legend to become "naturalized' as it were in a dazzling variety of religious, linguistic, and social milieus in India as well as in far-flung regions of the Asian continent and its neighboring archipelago.

If educated Westerners know anything at all of the *Rāmāyaṇa*, they would generally recognize it as an epic poem held in high esteem as a religious text of Hinduism. Some who follow international news might be aware that it has been placed in recent decades at the center of the politics of religious nationalism in India. Indeed to read a discussion of the life and times of Rāma today one has to go no farther than one's daily newspaper.[8] Others with a bit more specialized interest in South Asian culture or religion would additionally be aware that it is one of the primary early literary sources for the specifically Vaiṣṇava theological motif of the *avatāra.* This is the periodic "descent" into history and the world on the part of the supreme divinity, the Lord Viṣṇu, in one form or another in order to reestablish the dominance of *dharma,* righteousness over *adharma,* evil, which has been subverted through the agency of a powerful, demonic figure. Through the acquisition of a divine boon of some kind this figure, has managed to tip the moral balance of the universe in favor of *adharma,* that is unrighteousness, social disharmony, and the general subversion of religious norms. This doctrine of the *avatāra* is perhaps best known and most succinctly stated in its often-quoted formulation from the *Bhagavad Gītā:*

यदा यदा हि धर्मस्य ग्लानिर्भवति भारत ।
अभ्युत्थानमधर्मस्य तदात्मानं सृजाम्यहम् ।।
परित्राणाय साधूनां विनाशाय च दुष्कृताम्।
धर्मसंस्थापनार्थाय संभवामि युगे युगे।।[9]

"Whenever righteousness declines, O Bhārata, and unrighteousness is rampant, I project myself into the world. It is for the protection of the virtuous and the destruction of the wicked—that is for the re-establishment of righteousness—that I take birth age after age."

People with such a sense of what the *Rāmāyaṇa* is, are, of course, quite correct as far as their information goes. For without a doubt the representation of Rāma as an incarnation of the supreme Godhead come to earth in human form to rid the world of the monstrous Rāvaṇa and his demonic legions is the central theme of the epic in its most widely known versions in Hindu India. This theme is absolutely central to the Sanskrit poem of Vālmīki, and of numerous influential devotional retellings of the tale, notably such popular works as the 16th century Avadhī Hindi *Rāmcaritmānas* of the poet-saint Tulsī Dās as well as countless other literary and folk versions in the many languages of the Indian subcontinent.

But the *Rāmāyaṇa* in India is by no means popular only among the adherents of the various forms of Hinduism. The tale and the figure of its hero were of considerable importance to the followers of ancient India's two great, surviving non-Hindu religious traditions, Buddhism and Jainism. Moreover, this is so despite the fact that both of those religions deny the divinity or salvific power of Rāma or indeed any of the Vaiṣṇava *avatāras* even if the Vaiṣṇavas will later not hesitate to accept both the Buddha and the Jaina Tīrthaṁkara Ṛṣabhanātha as *avatāras* themselves[10].

The Rāmakathā was adapted early on by the Buddhist authors in whose works its various parts come to figure significantly especially in the important collection of Jātaka tales which provide a transmigrational biography of the previous lives of the Buddha. One of these tales, the *Dasarathajātaka,* recounts a version of the epic story that completely excises the epic's central *avatāric* narrative of the rapacious demon king, his abduction of Sītā, and Rāma's central feat, the demon's destruction. The tale focuses instead on its hero Rāma Paṇḍita's legendary self-control as an example of this cardinal Buddhist virtue. In another, the *Sāmajātaka,* the *Ayodhyākaṇḍa* episode in which the banishment of Rāma is attributed to a curse laid upon his father for having, in his youth, accidentally slain the son of a blind ascetic couple is reworked with a different cast of characters. In the first of these stories the hero of the *Rāmāyaṇa* is represented as merely one of the numerous earlier incarnations of the Buddha the person destined to one day attain enlightenment. Moreover, Vālmīki's poem was known to and admired by the first century CE Buddhist poet Aśvaghoṣa who not only alludes to the *Rāmāyaṇa's* representation of Vālmīki as the First Poet but also clearly uses his poem as the model for his poetic biography of the Buddha, the *Buddhacarita.*[11]

Jain authors have been especially fascinated with the story of Rāma, regarding him not, of course, as an incarnation of Godhead, but as one of the sixty-three *śalākāpuruṣas,* or exemplary Jain laymen and so have made him the hero of numerous Jain *Rāmāyaṇas* in both Sanskrit and Prakrit.[12] The Jain texts generally refer to the hero as Padma or, in Prakṛt, Pauma as in Vimalasūri's noteworthy version dating to the first half of the first millennium CE, the *Paumacariya.* Here even the celebrated martial character of the epic warrior hero, the scourge of the demonic *rākṣasas* must give way before the profound Jain adherence to the principle of *ahiṃsā,* or non-injury to living beings. Thus the Hindu *avatāra's* central and most defining feat, the killing of his ten-headed nemesis, Rāvaṇa, is, in Jaina versions of the tale, assigned to his loyal younger brother Lakṣmaṇa who, unavoidably, must expiate the negative *karma* incurred thereby, for his actions.

In these and similar ways, the Rāma story came in time, with numerous shifts of emphasis and religious and philosophical orientation to dominate the folk, literary, and religious literatures of virtually very one of India's numerous languages and regions. Similarly it comes to be one of the single most commonly represented and influential themes in the plastic and performing arts from temple friezes and courtly miniature paintings to elaborate folk and dance dramas and contemporary film and video.

But the spread and cultural saturation of the Rāma story was by no means confined to the Indian subcontinent. As is well known to students of the cultures of Southeast Asia it has achieved a position of productive cultural centrality in virtually all of the countries of this far-flung and highly diverse region.[13] In Burma, from at least the 11th century CE dramatic, prose and poetic courtly version of the story extol Rāma as an idealized *bodhisattva.* Similarly in Buddhist Thailand, the *Rāmakien,* the principal Thai version of the epic, becomes the foundational text of the Ayutthayan dynasty (1409-1767), which named its dynasts as well as its capital in keeping with the epic in yet another example of the close identification of Southern Asian monarchs with Rāma and the cult of divine kingship that owes much to the Rāma legend. In Thai at least six or seven poetic or dramatic versions of the story, many of which are attributed to the various King Rāmas, are widely known and performed. In Laos the *Phra Lak Phra Lam,* the *Lava Rāmāyaṇa* and the *Khvāy Thuarāphī* give eloquent testimony to the localization and naturalization (to use Sachchidandand Sahai's phrase)[14] of the epic in a variety of milieus. In Old Javanese we have the *Rāmāyaṇa Kakāwin,* while in Islamic Malaysia and Indonesia, as is well known, the Rāma story in the form of texts such as the *Hikayat Seri Rāma,* the *Cerita Mahārāja Rawana,* the widespread and diverse styles of *wayang* or shadow puppet theater, and the temple sculptures of such complexes as Prambanan is found.[15] These have established the story of Rāma—there regarded as the model of an ideal Islamic prince—as one of the region's principal cultural artifacts and acculturative devices. The *Rāmāyaṇa* tradition is, as noted, well attested in Burma with the performance tradition of the *Yāma-pwe*[16] and has deeply saturated traditional Cambodian culture in a wide variety of forms including various literary renderings of the Rāma story, known as *Rāmakerti* from around the 16th century CE and the famous reliefs at Angkor Wat. In Sri Lankā the literary rendering of the story attributed to the sixth century CE monarch Kumāradāsa, the *Jānakīharaṇa,* is thought to be the earliest Sanskrit work to have been composed on that island. Even as far as the Philippines we find texts such as the *Maharadia Lawana,* discovered and studied by Juan Francisco, current among the Maranao ethnic group from perhaps the 17th century which have kept the story, derived no doubt from Malay sources, alive.[17]

The diffusion and influence of the *Rāmāyaṇa* has also spread in a variety of ways to West Asia, Central Asia and East Asia and this too is part of the wider tale of the globalization of Indian culture. But time will not permit me here to discuss this aspect of the epic's history in detail.

This extraordinary spread of the Rāma story with all of its innumerable local variations and its naturalization in the many cultures where it found a home is fairly well known. What needs to be explored is the question of what it is about the *Rāmāyaṇa* in all of its many variations that has made it so appealing throughout the immense distances and diversity of Asia and yet seemingly so alien to the peoples of neighboring regions. Why, for example, do we not find Greek or Roman or Arabic *Rāmāyaṇas?* The Greeks had significant cultural, military and political relations with India at least from the time of Alexander while the Hellenistic successor kingdoms of the Indian northwest persisted for centuries after his time. There is ample evidence of artistic and even philosophical-religious exchange between the culture of India and that of Greece whose people famously appreciated a good epic tale of love and war. The Romans maintained lively commercial relationships with India in the first centuries CE and exotic eastern religions such as Mithraism and Christianity became powerful forces in Imperial Rome. The Arabs too established close trading relationships with India across the Arabian Sea and were among the bearers of the elaborate story and fable literature of Hindustan that spread so widely and productively throughout the Middle East and Europe. But in none of these cultural traditions do we find anything that can realistically be called a direct representation in literature, religion or art of any known version of the *Rāmāyaṇa*.

Why is this? The diversity of the manifestations of the *Rāmāyaṇa* in Asia would appear to suggest that there are certain features of the older versions of the story that can be ruled out as reasons for its appeal to some cultures and its lack of appeal to others. For example we can with some certainty rule out linguistic affinity. This old Indo-Aryan saga spread widely and easily across many major linguistic families including Indo-Aryan, Dravidian, Munda, Tibeto-Burmese, Altaic, Malay-Indonesian to name a few. The same can be said of some hypothetical boundaries of literary genres. The Indian and Southeast Asian cultural universes are particularly fond of long epic poetic narratives while those of East Asia are stereotypically said not to favor this genre. Yet the tale has spread widely in a variety of genres through many parts of East Asia while it appears to have made no impression on the epic-friendly cultures of the Near East and Mediterranean world. Religion, too, must be discarded as an exclusive index of the epic's spread.

Although it is doubtless true that the Rāma story has spread to most the countries stitched together, in Cotter's phrase, by the "bright thread of Buddhism," and that, moreover the medium for this spread was, especially in East Asia, Buddhist texts, the story has become enormously popular amongst non-Buddhist groups including Hindus, Jains, Christians, Muslims, Parsis and Sikhs in India. Similarly, it emerged as one of the premier cultural artifacts of the Islamic peoples of insular and peninsular Southeast Asia and the Buddhist cultures of the mainland.

With this as a background, let me turn to a brief discussion of some of the critical elements in Vālmīki's elaborate rendition of the *Rāmāyaṇa* into some 50,000 lines of epic Sanskrit verse. For, as I noted above, it is this text that first fixes the basic outlines of the story and may well be source, directly or indirectly for all other versions.

The immense success of the Vālmīki *Rāmāyaṇa* and its perennial power to inspire re-workings in mainstream Hindu (particularly Vaiṣṇava) India derives, I believe, from its influence, at varying periods, in four critical areas of life: the religious, the aesthetic, the political, and the social.

The first two of these, although immensely important in establishing the prestige of the story and accounting for its diffusion in many contexts in India, are not, in my opinion, the principal factors in the spread of the story to other parts of Asia. I have also discussed them elsewhere and so will touch upon them only briefly in the present context.

As noted above, for Vālmīki, Tulsī Dās and dozens of authors of *Rāmāyaṇa* variants as well as for hundreds of millions of Hindus who know and love their poems, the epic hero Rama is a manifestation of God on earth. This factor, however, is of little or no importance to the authors and audiences of Jain, Buddhist, and Islamic versions of the tale except insofar as the resonance of its hero as an extraordinary and exemplary man or the equivalent of a *bodhisattva* may be seen as having originally recommended the story to wider, non-Hindu audiences.

The aesthetic component in the prestige and popularity of Vālmīki and the monumental epic poem ascribed to him is absolutely unique within the realm of Sanskrit poetry and poetics and such of the vernacular tradition that allude to the poet's legendary role as the originator of the genre of poetry. For if the poet and his poem have not been regarded universally as the best that the tradition has to offer, there is nearly unanimous agreement that they are, respectively the First Poet and the First Poem. The epic, as it has come down to us, is provided with prologue *(upodghāta)* in the form of a celebrated meta-poetical narrative which tells how the sage, moving through a sequence of transformative personal experiences, the first edifying, the second emotive, and the third inspirational, is able to fuse them into the production of a new medium of expression, the poetic. This characterization of Vālmīki as the First Poet or *Ādikavi* and his *Rāmāyaṇa* as the First Poem or *Ādikāvya* appears to have gained an acceptance that was both early and widespread so that, as noted above, at least as early as the era of the celebrated Buddhist poet Aśaghoṣa in the first or second century CE poets and rhetoricians writing in Sanskrit and non-Sanskritic traditions alike will offer conventional forms of homage to Vālmīki as standing at the head of the lineage of poets.

Clearly the accomplishment of Vālmīki is one that the literary culture of traditional India regards as foundational although, since the episode has received little detailed analysis from this perspective, it is not easy to say in exactly what ways the *Rāmāyaṇa* was seen to be sharply differentiated from the textual milieu (the genre of *itihāsa-purāṇa)* out of which it emerged. Nonetheless it seems clear, both from the *Rāmāyaṇa's* own *upodghāta* or preface and later discussions of the events it describes, that the creation of true *kāvya* is possible only when there is an equal blending of the didactic (content) and the aesthetic (form) and the whole is imbued with a sublimated form of powerful emotionality *(rasa)*. The *upodghāta* also seems to give great importance to the fact that the literary product thus engendered gains something of its claim to the title "poetry" through the very fact that it is performable and appreciable by performers and audiences other than the poet whose own, unsublimated, emotions originally triggered its production.

There is thus no doubt that part of the great prestige Vālmīki and his creation have enjoyed in India derives from the idea that his work is divinely inspired and constitutes the first manifestation of the genre of poetry in the world. This is clear from the attention paid to him and his work in the copious Sanskrit literature on poetics and in later poetry and drama as well. Moreover the crucial performative aspect of the poem and must have had a significant influence on the numerous renditions of its story in the folk theatre, dance drama and puppet theater traditions of India and Southeast Asia.

Moreover, the particular representation of kingship that is put forward in the *Rāmāyaṇa* tradition as inaugurated by Vālmīki has had a considerable influence on the pre-modern and perhaps later ideology of governance across Southern Asia. For on this level the story presents in one of its most dramatic and widely popular forms the early Indic notion of the divinity of the king. Here the epic and *dharmaśdstra* representation of the king as a *bhumyāṃ devaḥ,* a god on earth—who may be viewed as a composite of the *lokapālas,* the divine world guardians—takes on a specifically Vaisnava coloration in the homology of the *avatāra* and the monarch who literally establishes God's kingdom on earth. Vālmīki thus, for the first time posits in the 11,000 year reign of King Rāma, the model of the millenarian heaven on earth that, in later times comes to be known as the Rāmarājya, a concept that has gained significant political traction in modern and contemporary India since at least the time of Gandhi who saw it as a model for an ideal state.[18]

This particular construction of the king as a god on earth resonated widely across pre-modern South and Southeast Asia to the point where by the medieval period many Hindu monarchs invested heavily in the construction of Rāma temples in many parts of India. It can also be seen in the traditional representation of sovereignty in pre-modern Java, Cambodia, and other areas of Southeast Asia. In pre-modern Thailand in particular, a central ruling dynasty modeled itself closely upon the figure and history of Rāma, naming its capital Ayutthaya and its successive dynasts after the epic hero, Rāma I, Rāma II and so on.

Finally and perhaps most importantly there is what I would call the social or the socio-didactic element in most versions of the *Rāmāyaṇa* from the time of Vālmīki onwards. It is this, I would argue, that has become the most globalized feature of his poem. That is to say it is the one, which, in its innumerable local variations, has most fully accounted for the spread and popularity of the Rāma legend as a bearer of Indic culture through so much of Asia.

In fact, Vālmīki's stated source, a brief oral narrative of Rāma's career, related to him by the divine seer Nārada makes no explicit reference to theology or indeed to any cosmic or even "national" mission of its hero. It is instead the story of an ideal prince, endowed with all the virtues of an Aryan aristocrat of the Vedic age. Rāma willingly foregoes his royal inheritance in deference to a vow of his father and cheerfully accepts a life of banishment and penury rather than assert his own claims against his society's powerful imperatives of filial deference, truthfulness *(satya),* and righteousness *(dharma).* In exile, he suffers the agony of the abduction of his beloved wife, but exhibits exemplary fortitude and perseverance, mounting a successful military campaign to recover her and punish her abductors. Finally, he returns to his native land, regains his birthright, and rules wisely as a righteous emperor, maintaining ritual order and social harmony throughout his vast realm through his exemplary conduct and his sagacious governance. In order for him to achieve this *summum bonum,* he must once again prove to the world his valuation of austere conformance to the social and political code by painfully abandoning his beloved queen, yet again sacrificing his personal happiness on the altar of public duty. There is no fairy tale ending in Vālmīki's epic as it has come down to us.

What Nārada's tale gives us and Vālmīki and later authors, reciters and performers embellish and enrich is the classical and never superseded idealized representation of the normative and idealized Asian personality, powerful, lovable and learned, capable of commanding nations and contesting even the gods, but always ready to renounce his own interests and desires in favor of those of the social and ritual order. Rāma is above all a prodigy of self-control, of the mastery of the senses and the submission of the individual to the demands of the society. In Freudian terms he is a living example of the triumph of the superego over the id and as such has become the standard of righteous conduct for countless generations, the radical opposite of his demonic counterpart, the grotesque caricature of unbridled self-indulgence and contempt for legitimate authority, the ten-headed *rākṣasa* tyrant, Rāvaṇa.

It is this characterization, surely, and not his status for Vālmīki and the Hindu tradition as an *avatāra* of Viṣṇu, that has led Buddhist, Jain and Muslim authors, dancers, sculptors, painets and singers of tales to adapt the Rāmakathā to their own purposes and their own cultures. Thus he becomes an exemplar of the Buddhist virtues of self-control in the *Dasaratha Jātaka* and the Thai *Ramakien,* an ideal practitioner of *ahiṃsā* in the Jain *Rāmāyaṇas,* a paragon of the clever and resourceful Islamic prince in the *wayang* dramas of the Malay-Indonesian world and the exemplar of sagacity, restraint, and self control in the Chinese and Japanese popular versions of the

Jātaka tales. Moreover, in addition to the towering antagonists Rāma and his radical antithesis the unrestrained demon king Rāvaṇa, Vālmīki has peopled his poem with a cast of characters designed to be exemplars of various kinds of both normative and sociopathic behavior in traditional Asian society. In this way Vālmīki's Sītā is crafted as the very archetype of the ideal Indian wife, held up as a shining example to this day while Lakṣmaṇa has become the archetype of the perfectly deferential and devoted younger brother similarly held up for emulation right down to the present. On the other hand Kaikeyī has become proverbial as the insubordinate wife, the dreaded figure who, as the modern idiom has it, "eats her husband." Rāvaṇa, the terrible but fascinating ten-headed monster is a grotesque paragon of unrestrained desire, the negative ego-ideal and quintessential "other" to Rāma. Hanumān, the powerful, wise and resourceful yet comical and endearing *vānara* hero becomes, in the *Rāmāyaṇa* tradition, the great model for the loyal, self-restrained and devoted servant subordinating everything to his master's interests while, on the other hand the gargantuan *rākṣasa* Kumbhakarṇa is a grotesque parody of insatiable appetites. Similarly, the characterization and fate of such figures as Śūrpaṇakhā present unforgettable cautionary tales of what happens to women who stray beyond the bounds of sanctioned behavior set by the patriarchy for which the *Rāmāyaṇa* has served as a powerful instrument.

These paradigmatic figures, particularly the positive ego ideals like Rāma, Sītā, Bharata, Lakṣmaṇa, the righteous *rākṣasa* Vibhīṣaṇa and Hanumān are, with culture-syntonic modifications to suit the local customs and conceptions of the many nations which hold the *Rāmāyaṇa* dear, clearly in harmony with the normative and desirable personalities as they are constructed by the great mainstream cultures of Asia whether Hindu, Buddhist, Islamic, Taoist or Confucian. By the same token, Vālmīki's negative or ambivalent characters such as the manipulative junior wife and step-mother Kaikeyī, the vacillating sensualist Daśaratha, and above all the monstrous enemy of all social, moral, and religious constraints such as Rāvaṇa and his voracious brother Kumbhakarṇa provide counter examples that serve to entertain, titillate and scandalize audiences while more clearly defining the virtuous and exemplary characters through the stark contrasts they present.

Heroes and heroines and their opposites, paragons of filial

piety, fraternal loyalty, ascetic self-control, wifely devotion, etc. and exemplars of everything the cultures of region abhor abound in its religious and literary texts. Heroes who are strong but compassionate, masterful but self-restrained, desirable but ascetic and who, in short, combine the ideal virtues of the warrior and the sage are heavily fore-grounded in many Asian written and oral texts. Rāma in particular, whom Vālmīki has crafted to all but uniquely combine the virility of the *kṣatriya* or warrior with the mildness, compassion and selflessness of the brahmanical sage, is surely the most fully developed exemplar of the type. In some ways the tradition's alternative exemplar may well be the historical Buddha himself, the prince turned world renouncer and compassionate spiritual warrior. But the narrative of the life of the Buddha remained very closely tied to the systems of thought and religious praxis that he and his many followers developed. Thus he became an exemplar of the idealized personality only in those lands in which, through a variety of historical circumstances, one or more schools of Buddhism became established. For non-Buddhists, if regarded at all, he could at best be seen, as in the tradition of the Vaiṣṇava *Purāṇas*, as merely a minor figure, an apostle of a false and delusive doctrine. Moreover, the life of the Buddha, exemplary though it may be, is that of a religious renunciant and a monk. It only partially serves the needs for entertainment, emotional engagement and moral guidance of large and diverse populations that include *bhikṣus*, mandarins, princes and *paṇḍits* as well as merchants, villagers and peasants. In this realm, the Rāma story with its tales of love, war, abducted princesses, ten-headed villains, monkey armies and flying palaces is unsurpassed. For it has provided audiences of dozens of countries belonging to all social classes and religions with an endlessly fascinating array of literary, artistic and performance media combining the spiritual and the moral with the excitement and romance of a complex epic narrative of love, intrigue and war.

Along with Rāma's principal mission, the destruction of the dreaded *rākṣasa* king and his hosts, his most quintessential and defining moment is his stoic and unwavering obedience to his father's promise to deprive him, on the eve of his consecration as king, of his rightful inheritance and banish him as a pauper to the wilderness for fourteen years. The fact that this promise was deceitfully extorted from the unwilling monarch by a cunning wife only serves to make the heroism of Rāma in his unvarying adherence to the truth of his father's word the greater and the contrast between his self-control with the sensual infatuation of father more stark.

What we see in this analysis, in effect, is that the *Rāmāyaṇa,* in whole and in parts, has had an unusually broad appeal throughout much of Asia because Rāma himself, with all the variations and shifts that his character is subject to in the vast array of cultures in which his story has found currency remains a recognizable and attractive model for an idealized heroic personality. Critical, in most cases to this characterization is a particular pattern of behavior in which the hero subordinates his own interests to those of his father, sacrifices the personal in favor of the family or the larger society, and chooses renunciation over indulgence. This is one of the most powerfully normative constructions of the ideal personality in traditional India and it clearly has considerable resonance in other Asian settings. Rāma is by far the most popular of the various figures who exemplify these virtues, figures such as the *Mahābhārata's* Bhīṣma, Pūru, and Rāma Jāmadagnya and the Bodhisattva in many of the popular *Jātaka* tales.

This type of hero is a particularly favored ego ideal in Southern Asia from the Vedic Age times until the present day.[19] It differs strongly from some other major heroic types in the salient texts of the region such as the equally fascinating, figure of Kṛṣṇa. Moreover, it contrasts very profoundly with a particularly favored western heroic type of hero. Figures of this kind from such characters as Achilles, Oedipus, Hamlet, and the heroes of innumerable western novels, plays and Hollywood films are generally rebellious against authority. They contest, challenge, and even overcome and supplant their fathers or father figures often putting their own interests and emotions ahead of those of their family or social group.

By way of contrast Rāma cheerfully and unquestioningly accepts being wrongfully deprived of his rightful inheritance and goes quietly into exile without a word of blame for his father or even his scheming stepmother who has brought about his ruin. Bhīṣma unhesitatingly and voluntarily renounces both his right of succession to another imperial throne and the imperatives of marriage and progeny to gratify his father's infatuation for a fisher girl. Pūru willingly exchanges his youth and virility for his father's senescence and impotence. Rāma Jāmadagnya beheads his own mother to please his jealous father.

In compensation for these heroic acts of deference and renunciation these figures are, in the end, rewarded and have been held up for centuries as culturally central models for behavior. By contrast Achilles sulks in his tent in a fit of pique over his king's appropriation of a prize of war, letting his friends and allies die rather than swallow the insult. Hamlet broods and agonizes and plots to do away with his wicked uncle. All self-respecting Hollywood action heroes thumb their noses at authority figures to pursue their own plots of intrigue and revenge.

Thus, if we examine the most normative, popular and influential mythical and literary texts of Europe, from the Homeric epics onwards, we see a general favoring and reflection of cultural norms that are quite different from those fore-grounded in the *Rāmāyaṇa* and other foundational texts of the elite and popular literatures of many Asian nations. Figures of this latter type are exceptional in European literature and it is therefore hardly surprising that characters like Rāma should resonate faintly if at all with western authors and audiences. Homer's creations, the *Iliad* and the *Odyssey* and Vālmīki's *Ādikāvya* are Indo-European epic poems of approximately the same antiquity and with rather similar themes of quests and battles to recover or avenge abused heroines. But the delineation of their heroes and other central figures is as different as can be imagined. The *Rāmāyaṇa*, which in one form or another has spread so widely through a variety of scholarly, commercial and religious exchanges into the folk, and elite texts of most if not all of Asia appears to have made virtually no impression on the lands to the west of Iran just as the western epics, before the era of colonialism at any rate appear to have had little if any impact in Asia. Thus although we can find Persian, Philippine, Japanese and Mongolian versions of the *Rāmāyaṇa* or at any rate of *Rāmāyaṇa* stories, and although the more picaresque tale and fable cycles of early India such as the *Pañcatantra* had enormous success in Europe and the Middle East we do not find Greek, Latin, Arabic, Celtic, Germanic or Slavic *Rāmāyaṇas*.

If this broad and very preliminary sketch of the distribution patterns of *Rāmāyaṇa* related texts should hold up upon what I would hope would be further detailed studies by scholars specializing in the various languages and cultures of Asia, then it would, I think, give us some cause to resist Cotter's totalizing deconstruction of Asia as a cultural region. For it would appear that there are some areal social and cultural values other than his "bright thread of Buddhism" that, to one degree or another, mark Asia as something more than a random "patchwork of people, climates and languages." Of all the important cultural mechanisms through which these core Indian values were spread, first from the ancient *janapada* of Kosala throughout the Indian subcontinent and from there across the length and breadth of Southern Asia, none, I would argue, has been of greater significance from antiquity to the present day than the *Rāmāyaṇa*.

Notes and References

1. Quoted in Bose, Sugata. "20th Century Rediscovery of Asian Universalism: Rabindranath Tagore's Interpretation of the Epics" in *Ramayana in Focus: Visual and Performing Arts of Asia.* Singapore: Asian Civilizations Museum. 2010. pp. 167-173.
2. Letter to Nirmalkumari Mahalanobis dated 15 July 1927. Op cit. p. 167.
3. For a book length exposition of this important concept, see Nye, Joseph S., Jr. *Soft Power: The Means to Success in World Politics*. New York, Public Affairs. 2004.
4. For a broad general account of the history of the many Middle Eastern and European translations and re-workings of the Pañcatantra cycle of tales, see Keith-Falconer, I.G. N. Kalãlah and Dimnah of the Fables of Bidpai: being an account of their literary history, with an English translation of the later Syriac version of the same and notes. Cambridge, Cambridge University Press. 1885.
5. These well-known verses are recited, along with several others, at the commencement of the Ramayanaparayana, or recitation of the poem as practiced in various Smarta and Vaisnava traditions. See, for example, Srimadvalmikiramayana Amukham Ramayanamahatmyadisahitam. Kalpathi-Palghat. R.S. Vadhyar & Sons. No Date.
6. Cotter, Holland "Dizzying Realm of Asian Art." *The New York Times.* Friday, March 26, 1999 Section B, p. 33.
7. For a general survey of Asian *Rāmāyaṇas,* see Lokesh Chandra, "*Rāmāyaṇa*, the Epic of Asia" in *The Rāmāyaṇa Tradition in Asia.* V. Raghavan, ed. Sahitya Akademi Delhi 1980. pp. 651-2.
8. Compare the recent press coverage of the Allahabad High Court's decision in the much-discussed case of the disposition of the contested site in Ayodhya.
9. *Bhagavad Gītā* 4.7-8. Shastri Gajanana Shambhu Sadhale, ed. *Śrīmadbhagavadgītā Śaṁkarādyekādaśaṭīkopetā.* Bombay. Gujarati Printing Press. 1935.

10. Cf. *Bhāgavata Purāṇa* 1.3.13 and 24. *Śrīmadbhāgavatapurāṇam: Śrīdharasvāmiviracitayā Bhāvārthabodhinīnamnyā Saṁskṛtaṭīkayā samupetam.* Acharya Jagadishalal Shastri, ed. New Delhi. Motilal Banarsidas. 1988.
11. Aśvaghoṣa, *Buddhacarita* 1.43: *vālmīkir adau ca sasarja padyam.* Johnston, E. H. ed. and trans. *The Buddhacarita or Acts of the Buddha* (1936). Delhi. Motilal Banarsidass (Reprint 1972).
12. Kulkarni, V.M. "Jain Ramayanas ansd their Sources." In *The Ramayana Tradition in Asia.* V. Raghavan, ed. Delhi. Sahitya Akademi. 1980. pp. 226-241.
13. For a general survey of Asian *Rāmāyaṇa s,* see *The Ramayana Tradition in Asia.* V. Raghavan, ed. Delhi. Sahitya Akademi. 1980.
14. Sahai, Sachchidanand. *The Ramayana in Laos: A Study in the Khvāy Thuarāphī.* Delhi. B. R. Publishing Corporation. 1976.
15. See Sweeney, P.L. Amin. *The Ramayana and the Malay Shadow-Play.* Kuala Lumpur. The National University of Malaysia Press. 1972 and Saran, Malini and Khanna, Vinod C. *The Ramayana in Indonesia.* Delhi. Ravi Dayal. No Date.
16. U. Thein Han and U. Khin Zaw. In *The Ramayana Tradition in Asia.* V. Raghavan, ed. Delhi. Sahitya Akademi. 1980. Pp. 301-314.
17. Francisco, Juan. "The Ramayana in the Philippines." In *The Ramayana Tradition in Asia.* V. Raghavan, ed. Delhi. Sahitya Akademi. 1980 pp. 15-177.
18. On the political resonance of the *Rāmāyaṇa,* see Pollock, Sheldon. "Ramayana and Political Imagination in India." *Journal of Asian Studies* 52.2: 261-297.
19. Goldman, R. P. "Fathers, Sons, and Gurus Oedipal Conflict in the Sanskrit Epics." *Journal of Indian Philosophy.* Vol.6, 1978, pp. 325-92. See also Ramanujan A.K. "Is There an Indian Oedipus?" in *Vishnu on Freud's Desk: A Reader in Psychoanalysis and Hinduism.* T. G. Vaidyanathan and J. Kripal, eds. New Delhi Oxford University Press. 1998.

6
Rethinking India's Past

Johannes Bronkhorst

The Brahmanical tradition has exerted a profound influence on India, from an early time onward. This tradition, like all traditions, had a certain vision of the past, and its enormous success has given it ample opportunity to impose that vision. The task of the historian, here as elsewhere, is to verify the prevailing vision of the past, and correct it where necessary.

One of the features of Brahmanism is that it has always presented itself as old and unchanging. Indeed, the claim was made, at least since the Grammarian Patañjali in the second century BCE, that Sanskrit, the language of Brahmanism, was not just old but beginningless. The same view came to be held with regard the Veda, the literary corpus connected with Brahmanism: the Veda was not just old but beginningless.

It follows that Brahmanical civilization, too, was thought of as tremendously old, and as the background of other cultural and religious movements in India. This view came to prevail, and survived until today. Buddhism, in particular, was thought of as a reaction against Brahmanism; it was taken for granted that when Buddhism arose, Brahmanism had been around for a very long time, also in the region where the Buddha preached.

My researches over the years have convinced me that this vision of the past is not correct. It is true that Brahmanism had been around for a long time when Buddhism arose, but not in the region where the Buddha preached, nor in many other regions of India. Brahmanism is an ideology that spread all over India, and over much of Southeast Asia, to be sure, but this spread had hardly begun at the time of the Buddha. At that time Brahmanism was largely centred in one part of the subcontinent, the part which the grammarian Patañjali and others called Āryāvarta. These authors give a rather precise description of the extent of Āryāvarta, which shows that only a part of the Ganges plain was included. This was in the second century BCE, two and a half centuries after the death of the Buddha.

Brahmanism, then, was a *regional* ideology, still during the last centuries preceding the Common Era. All this changed in subsequent centuries, but we do not know in detail just how, when, why and where. We only know that the spread of Brahmanism owed nothing to conquering armies, as was the case with Islam. Nor was it imposed by an existing empire, as happened to Christianity during the days of the Roman empire. It was not spread by religious missionaries either. Indeed, the spread of Brahmanism had very little to do with religious conversion. No one converted to Brahmanism in the ordinary religious sense of the term. In fact, it is not very useful to think of Brahmanism as a religion at all. Brahmanism was primarily an ideology, a socio-political ideology, with clear ideas as to the correct order of society and the correct way of running a state. In this ideology the role of Brahmins was central.

It is true that some of the activities Brahmins engaged in, especially ritual activities, but not only those, can rightly be considered religious. But accepting the elevated position of Brahmins in society and making use of their ritual and other services did not require a change in belief. Numerous inscriptions testify to the fact that many Indian kings made use of these services without for that matter rejecting movements such as Buddhism and Jainism. On the religious level, Brahmanism was not, or barely, in competition with these alternative movements. We have a number of names of scholars who were Buddhists and Brahmins at the same time, without the slightest awareness of a contradiction: socially these scholars were Brahmins, philosophically they were Buddhists. Note that the reverse situation is impossible, and therefore never recorded in our sources: one cannot be socially a Buddhist while at the same time a Brahmin by conviction. This, incidentally, is an asymmetry that historians of Indian philosophy rarely take into consideration: in the debates between Brahmins and Buddhists, Brahmins could be convinced by Buddhist arguments and yet remain Brahmins; but Buddhists who were convinced by

Brahmanical philosophical arguments did not become Brahmins, nor could they remain Buddhists.

The spread of Brahmanism, then, is a historical phenomenon that is, as yet, only little known and poorly understood. At the same time, it is a phenomenon of a vast scale that has no parallel in world history. In as little as ten centuries, a regional ideology had spread virtually over the whole of the Indian subcontinent and into Southeast Asia right up to Vietnam and the farther reaches of Indonesia. That is to say, an area as large as, if not larger than the Roman empire and with presumably more inhabitants underwent, for a varying but substantial number of centuries, the determining imprint of an ideology that had succeeded in imposing itself without the help of armies, an empire, or religious conversion. Future research, I hope, will tell us more about how this could happen. In this lecture I can do no more than draw your attention to some specific developments.

Consider first the use of Sanskrit. Sanskrit was the language of Brahmanism. Others did not use it. The oldest texts of Buddhism and of Jainism used different forms of Middle Indic, languages different from Sanskrit. The oldest inscriptions in India are not in Sanskrit either: for some four hundred years inscriptions were made, but none of them in Sanskrit. The reason is obvious: Sanskrit was the language of a regional ideology, i.e. Brahmanism, that exerted little influence.

All this changed around the second century CE, in north-western India. All of a sudden political inscriptions in Sanskrit make their appearance. What is more, the Buddhists of that part of the subcontinent changed to Sanskrit. They possessed already an extensive literature in languages different from Sanskrit, but they decided there and then to translate much of that into Sanskrit. What had happened? It appears that Brahmanical ideology had succeeded in gaining the upper hand in the political centres of north-western India. Accepting the Brahmanical socio-political ideology implied using the language of Brahmanism, Sanskrit. The Buddhists of north-western India may initially not have accepted this ideology, but they did need the support of the royal court and this, it appears, obliged them to start using Sanskrit.

The adoption of Sanskrit, both in political inscriptions and by the Buddhists, implied far more than a mere change of language. It implied the adoption, at least in part, of the Brahmanical vision of society. Most of the early political inscriptions, which are not in Sanskrit, show no sign of being aware of the most fundamental Brahmanical social doctrine: that society is divided into Brahmins, Kshatriyas, Vaishyas and Shudras. Ashoka's famous edicts, for example, mention Brahmins on a number of occasions, most often together with Shramanas, but never ever use the terms Kshatriya, Vaishya and Shudra. It is safe to conclude that society in his time was not divided into these four so-called varnas. These four classes are a Brahmanical invention, part of their social ideology. Brahmanism imposed this division of society wherever it could, not because society was really divided in this manner, but because Brahmanism maintained it should. As a result, we find these four classes only mentioned in Brahmanical inscriptions.

I started this lecture pointing out that Brahmanism, even where it innovated, maintained that nothing had changed, that the world had always been like that. Brahmanism had always been there, and was the background for all other developments that had taken place. Brahmanism, seen this way, was the background from which Buddhism arose. We now know that this is not correct, historically speaking. Buddhism arose in a part of the Ganges plain that had not been brahmanized, and would remain outside the core area of Brahmanism for at least three further centuries. However, when Buddhism started using Sanskrit, around the second century CE, it adopted along with this language other Brahmanical notions. It came to think of itself as having arisen in Brahmanical surroundings. We see this most clearly if we contrast the accounts of the Buddha's life composed in Sanskrit with those composed in other languages. Ashvaghosha may have been one of the first Buddhists to write in Sanskrit. His life of the Buddha depicts his father as a truly Brahmanical ruler, who has Brahmanical priests and advisors, performs sacrifices (though no violent ones), and much else. None if this occurs in the lives of the Buddha composed in Middle Indic.

Our reflections so far show that the process of brahmanization was both subtle and profound. Buddhism did not disappear in the early centuries CE. Quite on the contrary, it would still flourish in India for many centuries to come. And yet, it had changed the way it perceived itself. Perhaps this is a general feature of brahmanization. It does not necessarily replace other movements and world views, but it affects them from within.

How did Brahmanism succeed in exerting such a profound effect on other world views and ideologies? I pointed out already that Brahmanism did not spread through armies, imperial imposition, or religious conversion. The question of Brahmanism's success requires much more study, but some observations can already be made, as it seems to me.

It appears that Brahmins often came to be asked by local rulers to settle in their kingdoms. In such cases they were most typically provided with the usufruct of a village and land, which allowed them to concentrate on other matters. These "other matters" would normally involve performing rituals, reciting their holy texts, i.e., the Veda, teaching their shastras, and other such things. The underlying supposition was clearly that the presence of a ritually active community of Brahmins would be advantageous for the kingdom. Some Brahmins would play a role at the royal court, as advisors in both ritual and political matters.

Why would local rulers believe that the presence of Brahmins at the court and in the kingdom would be good for both ruler and kingdom? Clearly this conviction preceded the invitation to specific Brahmins to come and settle in the kingdom. In other words, Brahmanical ideology sometimes travelled faster than the Brahmins themselves. How this happened in specific situations is a question that needs further study. However, it seems plausible that Brahmanical ideology responded to a need felt by local rulers both in South Asia and in Southeast Asia.

We know that the political history of South and Southeast Asia during the first millennium CE saw the rise and decline of numerous regional kingdoms. Inscriptions report ad nauseam the military feats of rulers, who conquered and destroyed each other's territories almost without restraint. Assuming that these inscriptions are to at least some extent reliable, the military competence of many of these rulers left little to be desired. But for acquiring and maintaining a kingdom more is required than mere military competence. What these rulers needed, once they had won their battles, was practical advise as to how to run their kingdom, and how to protect it against unforeseen dangers. Brahmins were specialized in these two realms. Their undisturbed ritual occupations provided the best supernatural protection imaginable, and they combined that with theoretical competence in matters of polity.

It is interesting to compare these Brahmanical skills with what

Buddhists had to offer to rulers. Buddhism had begun as a religion of people who had left society, and who had therefore very little to say about how society should be run. It is true that Buddhism did not remain for long a movement exclusively of renouncers. It may still have been like that during the realm of Ashoka, but there are clear indications from northern India that this changed during the last centuries BCE. Buddhism at that time came into the possession of monasteries and much else, and this is no doubt a reason why it came to depend ever more on the active support of political rulers. We have seen already one of the consequences of this new dependence: Buddhism adopted the language of the Brahmins, Sanskrit, because like the Brahmins it sought access to the centres of political power.

Buddhism, then, needed the support of political rulers. What could it offer in return? We have seen that the Brahmins could offer a lot in return, enough to convince most Indian rulers that they could not risk *not* to support Brahmins. How about the Buddhists?

It appears that the Buddhists had a hard time competing with the Brahmins at the royal courts, and that this became, in the long run, one of the main reasons why Buddhism did not survive in India. Brahmanism offered, apart from supernatural protection, lots of practical advice to rulers: how to organize society, how to run their kingdom, etc. etc. Buddhism, still during the early centuries of the Common Era, offered nothing of the kind. As stated earlier, Buddhism had no vision of society and of how it should be run. True, there are a number of Buddhist texts that proffer advice to rulers, but a closer inspection only shows how useless this advice is. Kings should give money to the poor and avoid violence. This is hardly the advice that will secure that a king will stay in charge for long in the ruthless environment of incessantly competing kingdoms characteristic of India during those centuries. Some of these Buddhist authors admit, though implicitly, that their advice is totally unrealistic by recommending kings to give up on being a king and become a monk instead. With regard to the ritual protection offered by Buddhism to rulers we can be brief: during the early centuries of the Common Era they offered next to nothing of the kind.

A close inspection of the sources has led me to conclude that for a long time, say during the first five centuries of the Common Era, Buddhism left many of the skills that might be useful for rulers to Brahmins. We saw that Buddhism came to adopt a semi-

Brahmanical vision of society. This implied that certain activities were left to Brahmins. These included, of course, ritual activities, political counselling, but lots of other activities as well, among these: predicting the future on the basis of various indications and astrology. One of the surprising consequences of this is that there are practically no surviving names of Buddhists who engaged in astronomy and mathematics, this in spite of the fact that Buddhists were active in other sciences, such as medicine and, of course, philosophy. Astronomy and mathematics, in the Indian context, were inseparable from astrology, and astrology was the domain of Brahmins. In short, for a number of centuries Buddhism in India did not intrude into the realms of activity that the Brahmins considered their own. By the time they tried to change this, with the advent of tantrism, it was too late. Buddhism had not been able to compete credibly with Brahmanism, and its decline may be looked upon as its inevitable consequence.

Contrary to Buddhism, Brahmanism offered advantages that rulers could scarcely do without. This was not the result of historical coincidence. It can be argued that to at least some extent Brahmanism during the last centuries preceding the Common Era had prepared the ground, that it had developed the tools and methods which in due time turned out to be very efficacious. It is possible to look upon the Brahmanical literature composed during the centuries around the beginning of the Common Era as playing a role in the project Brahmanism was entering upon. This literature shows that the Brahmins of that period had two major concerns. On the one hand, they were concerned to create a separate identity for Brahmins: Brahmins are expected to follow a life-style that is different from all others. Purity plays a central role and finds expression through the observance of numerous rituals and sacraments, through the Brahmins' purity of descent both on the paternal and maternal side, and through the distance maintained from persons and things that are considered polluting. This concern finds expression in those texts that were primarily meant for internal consumption, among them various texts on dharma and ritual. Beside this, there are Brahmanical texts from this period that concentrate rather on the image that Brahmins were concerned to project onto society at large. A text like the Mahabharata projects an image of Brahmins as sometimes wise, sometimes unpredictable, but always powerful and scary; Brahmins like to live in peace in their hermitages, and may seem in this way inoffensive, but numerous stories remind us that they can be deadly if crossed. Political advice is given much attention, as are indications how to fit into the social hierarchy that is the hallmark of Brahmanism.

It would be worth a detailed study to analyse the model of Brahmanism that arose during the crucial centuries around the beginning of the Common Era. This model referred back, at least in part, to the Vedic tradition, but other aspects were quite new. Even new notions—such as the idea of the Brahmanical ashrama, an idea that is absent from Vedic literature—were presented as old, as having been in existence from time immemorial. This model was to become surprisingly successful in subsequent centuries.

Such a detailed analysis has not yet been undertaken. I hope to be able to contribute to it in years to come, but obviously the task is far too great for a single individual to accomplish. I do hope that others, too, will take up the challenge, and join me in rethinking India's past along the lines here suggested.

7
The Changing India: Dynamism of Ancient Indian Culture

Patrick Olivelle

Thomas Szasz in his *The Second Sin* remarks: "In the animal kingdom, the rule is, eat or be eaten; in the human kingdom, define or be defined."[1] The critique of orientalism and post-colonial discourse have alerted us to the dangers of thinking with other people's categories; yet the heat of this kind of rhetoric has not been matched with the light that comes from the careful study of our own intellectual histories. A close examination of the Indian nationalist discourse of the past few decades shows how in the very act of rejecting Western dominance and definitions the nationalists have completely surrendered to what they reject by adopting in even more extreme forms the very categories of orientalist discourse of the 19th and early 20th centuries. For both activist and scholar alike, these are the categories they/we think with; they are so much part of us that we fail to see them as different, as alien.

Speaking now for scholars, we have failed to look carefully enough at the intellectual lenses, provided mostly by previous scholarship, through which we perceive the past. One such lens is the view of an unchanging India, most famously expressed by one of the luminaries of 19th century Indology, Max Müller (1859, 18): "The Hindu enters this world a stranger; all his thoughts are directed to another world; he takes no part even where he is driven to act; and when he sacrifices his life, it is but to be delivered from it." Albert Schweitzer's (1960 [1936], 19) statement about world renunciation and asceticism echoes Max Müller's words and is not very different from comments one hears even today. He says: "When Hellenistic thought turns towards world and life negation, it is because in the end it begins to have misgivings about the world and life affirmation which for centuries had seemed a matter of course. . . . In the thought of India, on the other hand, world and life negation does not originate in a similar experience. It is there from the very beginning, self-originated, born as it were in a cloudless sky." Although exposed repeatedly for the fraud that it is, the spectre of the "changeless India" raises its head repeatedly and in most unexpected of places.

I was, for example, recently asked to participate in a book project on "Hindu Economics and Business" edited by a prominent Indian economist. Its first part covered the period before 500 BCE; its second part covered the period 500 BCE until 1947 CE—evidently nothing much changed during these two and a half millennia that would prevent this period being studied as a unified whole. A well-known anthropologist of Indian origin talks about the Hindu ideology of food, bringing examples from the Upani˘ads and from a Delhi taxi driver. Nothing much changes in India. So here we have contemporary scholars in various ways buying into the 19th century colonial depiction of an "unchanging India" where time stands still and villages continue to exist today as they did three thousad years ago. It is instructive to see how India and Hinduism are essentialized into static realities immune to the dynamics of social and economic changes even by scholars in such disciplines as Economics and Anthropology, which should be at the forefront of debunking changelessness in any society.

An awakening in the academy occurred with the publication, with all its shortcomings, of Edward Said's *Orientalism* in 1978. Long before that, however, as Trautmann (1997, 18) has shown, the work of Bernard Cohn had dealt with the "construction of the colonial sociology of India". Cohn showed that "the knowledge of India that is current today is the product of the colonial situation" (Trautmann 1997, 18). This kind of colonial knowledge, once the engine behind colonial power, is today not merely confined to impotent ivory-tower intellectuals. That it does exercise influence in the corridors of power is shown by the memoirs of Henry Kissinger in his analysis of the India-Pakistan crisis of 1971. Kissinger's assessment reeks of colonial views of an unchanging India when he says that "the Indian subcontinent has existed through the millennia as a world apart" and that invading armies and empires came and left "leaving multitudes oblivious of either the coming or the going."[2]

Unfortunately, not just scholars but even public intellectuals within India itself, including those espousing nationalist causes, continue to see India's past through the eyes of the colonial and even missionary lenses given to them over a century ago. The shedding of colonial rule occurred with the stroke of a pen at midnight on August 14, 1947, but the shedding of colonial categories of thought and scholarship is an enduring battle. Today I want to look at two central categories that scholars and even the general public continue to use to understand ancient Indian social divisions. And they are the concepts of *dharma* and the twice-born or *dvija.* Take any introductory textbook to Indian culture or religion written in India or the west, and you will see a central place given to these concepts as defining categories of Indian civilization and of Hinduism. They are presented, at least implicitly, as present from the very beginning as unchanging categories that were formative of Indian culture. I want to subject these two categories to historical analysis in order to show that even these so-called central and immutable concepts and categories of Indian civilization are very much the products of a dynamic social, religious, and political history. They are not the fossilized remains of an unchanging India but the historical products of a dynamic and changing India.

The Emperor and the Ascetic: Political History of *dharma*[3]

Because I have written several articles on the history of the term *dharma* (Olivelle 2004b, 2006a, 2006b), and edited a volume containing studies by 18 scholars on the semantic history of this term (Olivelle 2004a), I will only present here a synopsis of those findings. Briefly, then, the term emerges as a neologism (it is not found in cognate Indo-European languages, including Avestan) in the *Ṛgveda,* where it is used 68 times with a somewhat wide semantic range: foundation, institute, moral order.[4]

One would have expected that this term, which made such a promising start in the *Ṛgveda*, would grow in significance and centrality in the vocabulary of the middle and late Vedic periods to become the central concept that it became in later Indian history. This, however, was not to be the case. Except for changing its gender from the neuter *dharman* to the masculine *dharmaḥ*, it became a marginal term in the later Vedic lexicon. Indeed, its use within the other Vedic Saṃhitās, the Brāhmaṇas, and even the

Upaniṣads, which together form an enormous corpus of literature, is infrequent. Parallel to its relative infrequency, we can detect also a semantic restriction of the term. It is used most frequently with reference to Varuṇa, the heavenly king par excellence, and to his earthly counterpart. If we exclude verses cited from the *Ṛgveda* and repetitions, all the *Yajurvedic Saṃhitās* combined use it 28 times; in the enormous corpus of the Brāhmaṇas, it occurs just 13 times; and in the four ancient prose *Upaniṣads*, it is found in only 9 passages.

Independent Uses in Later Vedic Texts

YAJUR VEDA SAṂHITĀS

dharman	MS = 9	KS = 3	TS = 2	VS = 4	Total = 19
dharmaḥ	MS = 6	KS = 1	TS = 1	VS = 2	Total = 9

** In all but MS repeated phrases are omitted from the count.

BRĀHMAṆAS

dharma	TB 1				
dharmaḥ	AB = 1	TB = 4	ŚB = 7	GoB = 1	Total = 13

UPANIṢADS

Dharmaḥ does not occur

dharmaḥ	BṛU = 4	ChU = 3	TaitU = 2	AitU = 0	Total = 9

A startling statistical fact emerges from this: the term *dharma* occurs 68 times within the relatively short Ṛgveda, whereas it is used in just 51 independent passages in the literature of the middle and late Vedic periods. The semantic range of *dharma* is by and large restricted to the sphere of the king, occurring most frequently within the context of the consecration of the king (*rājasūya*). The term is clearly not central to the theology and ritual exegesis of these Vedic texts. The term is also conspicuous by its marginality in the post-Vedic ritual literature of the *Śrauta* and the *Gṛhya Sūtras*. I think we need to rethink our assumptions regarding the centrality of *dharma* within the cultural history of India.

By contrast we see that *dharma* is employed by Aśoka as the pivotal concept in a new imperial ideology articulated in his many edicts. The term is used over 100 separate times (excluding copies of the same edict given in different locations). Aśoka used *dharma* as the central concept to construct an imperial ideology—one may even call it an imperial theology—that gave legitimacy to his rule and a religious/moral foundation to his empire.

Unlike the Vedic texts, however, Aśoka gives us quite a clear picture of what he meant by *dharma*. In Rock Edict 3 he instructs his ministers to teach the *dharma* in the following words: "Obedience to mother and father is good (*sādhu*). Giving (*dāna*) to friends, acquaintances, and relatives, and to Brāhmaṇas and Śramaṇas is good. Not killing is good. Spending little and possessing little is good." Other lists add the proper treatment of slaves. Similar sentiments are expressed frequently in the edicts, which he frequently refers to as "*dharmalipi*" — "inscriptions relating to *dharma*", or perhaps "dharmic inscriptions". In the long Pillar Edict 7, where he uses *dharma* 30 times, he defines the practice of *dharma* as consisting of compassion, liberality, truthfulness, purity, gentleness, and goodness. For Aśoka, then, *dharma* was an essentially moral concept; and teaching *dharma*, which Aśoka looked upon as one of his major imperial obligations, meant teaching his subjects how to lead a good and moral life. For the first time we even have the translation of this term into Greek and Aramaic in the tri-lingual Minor Rock Edict IV of Kandahar, where the Greek *eusebeia,* meaning something like piety, and the Aramaic *qsyt,* with a meaning related to truth, are used as equivalents of *dharma*.

The semantic development of *dharma* within the middle and late Vedic period that saw it closely associated with kingship made it a likely candidate for adoption by an ancient Indian emperor. But how did a term that had a restricted semantic compass, referring to social order and laws, become an ethical concept divorced from law in the Aśokan inscriptions. I think for this we must look at the ascetic communities, especially Buddhism, that predated Aśoka.

This semantic transformation and the central position accorded to *dharma*, I believe, suggest that Aśoka's use of *dharma* was mediated by its appropriation sometime before Aśoka by the emerging ascetic communities. This appropriation was probably part of the broader adoption of royal symbols and vocabulary by ascetic leaders and communities; remember that *dharma* had become part of the royal vocabulary especially in the context of the royal consecration.

Within the historical religion of Buddhism, *dharma* stands at the very heart of its theology, defining the very essence of what the Buddha, the Universal Emperor (*cakravartin*) of a new moral universe, is thought to have discovered. here *dharma* defined the truth discovered by the Buddha, the truth that conferred authority on him. It forms part of the Triple Gem (*triratna*) that defined the core of Buddhism: Buddha, *dharma*, and Sagha. In this transfer from king to ascetic, however, *dharma* came to be redefined in terms of doctrine, especially moral doctrine, and it was given a centrality within religious discourse that it lacked in the Vedic lexicon. Especially in its use with regard to the non-monastic life of Buddhist laity, one can see how *dharma* came to acquire an essentially moral meaning, as in the five *śīlas,* or moral precepts, that they were expected to follow.

The term and the concept *dharma* acquired such a prominence and centrality through both Buddhism and the Aśokan imperial ideology that it was impossible even for the Brahmanical tradition to ignore it. My hypothesis is that the emergence of the Dharmaśāstric literature, a genre of expert texts devoted to the concept of *dharma*, first in the form of prose *sūtras* and then in metrical treatises beginning with Manu, was a direct consequence of Buddhist and Aśokan reforms. That a *śāstra*, an expert tradition of knowledge, be devoted to *dharma* would seem improbable from its marginal use within the theologies expressed in the middle and late Vedic texts. *dharma*, however, came to define the very essence of the Brahmanical religion, and the term *varnāśramadharma,* the *dharma* of social classes and orders of life, became a synonym for this tradition.

We have come a full circle. A brand new term invented by ancient Brahmanical poets of the Ṛgveda has become the central and defining term for the Brahmanical religion and way of life with considerable help from their rivals for religious authority and influence, the ascetic communities, and from an emperor with dreams of conquering the world through and for *dharma*.

How Brahmins Became Twice-Born: Semantic History of *dvija*[5]

General introductions to Indian culture and religion present the concept of "twice-born" as a fundamental aspect of Indian or Vedic society. The widely used and excellent introduction to India's cultural past, A. L. Basham's *The Wonder that was India,* comments on the class division of ancient Indian society: "A sharp distinction was made between the three higher classes and the śūdra. The former were twice-born (*dvija*), once at their natural birth and again at their initiation, when they are invested with the sacred thread and received into Āryan society" (Basham 1967, 139). Similar comments are found in most textbooks and even in scholarly tomes. Clearly, modern scholarship takes the concept of *dvija* associated with the rite of Vedic initiation to be a fundamental aspect of ancient Indian reflection on society. Does this consensus stand up to scrutiny? I think not.

The earliest descriptions of the rite for becoming a Vedic student (*brahmacārin*) is found in two hyperbolic eulogies, the one in the *Atharva Veda* (11.5) and the other in the *Śatapatha Brāhmaṇa* (11.5.4). In both places the initiation of the pupil is compared to the birthing process: the teacher becomes pregnant with the pupil, and the pupil becomes a fetus (*garbha*), and in the third night the pupil is born as a Brāhmaṇa. This analogy parallels the more common conception that the consecration for a sacrifice (*dīkṣā*) constitutes a new birth of the sacrificer (*dīkṣita*) (*Aitareya Brāhmaṇa* 1.3.1; *Śatapatha Brāhmaıa* 3.2.1.11; Gonda 1965, 337).[6] Even though, as in other initiation rites, the birth metaphor is used here, the term *dvija* is absent, as is any clear emphasis on the newly born status of the student. No connection is also made between this initiatory birth and the ideology of *varṇa.* Further, the initiate was probably an adult or a young man, with the mention of his long beard.

The most extensive descriptions of the rite of initiation are given in the *Gṛhyasūtras*, a class of texts devoted to domestic rites. The dating of these texts is problematic, but many of the early ones were probably composed prior to the rise of Dharmaśāstric literature. None of the *Gṛhyasūtras* present the rite of Vedic initiation as the second birth of the boy. The teacher who initiates him is not referred to as his father, or the Sāvitrī verse that is taught to him regarded as his mother. Neither do these texts use the term *dvija* with reference to the initiated boy.

Indeed, the term *dvija* and the parallel *dvijāti* are absent in the entire Vedic corpus, including the *Upaniṣads.*[7] They do not occur even in the subsequent ritual literature; the terms are absent in the *Śrautasūtras* and in most of the *Gṛhyasūtras.*[8] They are also missing in the texts of the grammatical tradition, which are generally good sources of terms in normal circulation. Yāska's *Nirukta*, Pāṇini's *Aṣṭādhyāyī* and Kātyāyana's *Vārttikas* on Pāṇini do not mention these words not mention these words. Quite surprisingly, even the voluminous *Mahābhāṣya* of the great 2nd century BCE grammarian Patañjali also does not use this term.

Although in itself it does not provide conclusive proof, this chart of the occurrences of the terms *dvija* or *dvijāti* in the ancient literature is instructive:[9]

Chart of *Dvija/Dvijāti* in Early Literature

Vedic Texts	= 0 (with the exceptions given in note 10)
Śrautasūtras	= 0
Gṛhyasūtras	= 0 (see fottnote 8)
Pāṇini	= 0
Kātyāyana	= 0
Patañjali	= 0
Āpastamba Dh	=0
Gautama Dh	=4
Baudhāyana Dh	=13
Vasiṣṭha Dh	= 13
Mānava Dh	= 166
Rāmāyaṇa	= 214
Mahābhārata	= 1535
Yājñavalkya Dh	= 40

The absence of *dvija* or cognate terms with the technical meaning of a twice-born human being in the theological vocabulary of the Brāhmaṇas, the early Upaniṣds, and most of the ritual *sūtras* indicates that something new was being signified by this term when it makes its appearance in the Dharmasūtras. Curiously, then, a term that became central in the later theological and sociological discourse within the Brahmanical tradition, a term that is ubiquitous in modern scholarly descriptions of ancient Indian society, is missing in almost all texts prior to about the second century BCE. Even if we grant that its absence in Pāṇini and Kātyāyana can be explained because of their brevity and subject matter, it becomes much harder to explain its absence in Patañjali's *Mahābhāṣya,* a long text that is within the mainstream of Brahmanical theology and contains references to many aspects of the *varṇa* system.

It appears, then, that the highlighting of Vedic initiation as a second birth of the initiated boy and his designation as a *dvija* along with its close relationship to the *varṇa* system were theological innovations within the expert tradition dealing with *dharma,* a tradition that was itself probably something of a novelty and produced a rich literature from about the 3rd century BCE. The oldest extant text of this tradition, the *Dharmasūtra* of *Āpastamba* (1.1.15-18), states: "He should never offend the teacher, for he gives birth to him by means of vedic knowledge. That is his most excellent birth; his parents give birth only to his body." This statement simply reiterates the discussions in the *Atharva Veda* and the *Śatapatha Brāhmaṇa* referred to above. We detect, however, that at a very early stage in the history of the Dharmaśātric tradition a theology that highlighted the rebirth aspect of Vedic initiation was brought to the foreground. *Āpastamba*, nevertheless, never uses the terms *dvija* or *dvijāti* either with regard to the initiated boy or with reference to the three upper classes (*Varṇa*) of society, a practice common in later texts; these terms are absent in his vocabulary. So, we have another piece of evidence for the newness and novelty of this concept. Even one of the most ancient texts of the Dharmaśāstric tradition does not use the term. We shall not be far wrong in thinking that this innovation took place toward the end of the second century BCE or perhaps in the first century BCE.

The Dharmasūtra of Gautama is the earliest extant text to use the term *dvijāti,* using it four times; he does not use *dvija.*[10] Gautama also states that "initiation is a second birth" (1.8), but it is unclear whether his use of *dvijāti* is connected to the conception of initiation as a second birth. At least he does not make that connection explicit. The term *dvijāti* for Gautama is not limited to Brahmins; he uses it as a term that comprehends the three upper *varṇas.* For example, at 10.1 he says: "Study, sacrifice, and giving gifts pertain to *dvijātis*" (*dvijātīnām adhyayanam ijyā dānam*). In the very next sūtra he goes on to state that teaching, officiating at sacrifices, and receiving gifts are additional activities of Brahmins. It is probable that in the other three places also Gautama uses the term to comprehend the three upper *varṇas.*

A pattern in the use of the two terms *dvijāti* and *dvija* begins to emerge in the *Baudhāyaṇa Dharmasūtra*. As is well know, only the first two *Praśnas* belong to the original sūtra; the last two *Praśnas* are later additions with large sections composed entirely in verse

(Olivelle 1993, 86-87; Olivelle 2000, 191). In the first two *Praśnas* *dvijāti* is used six times,[11] while *dvija* is used only once (1.1.13), while it occurs six time in book four (5.3, 20, 21, 24; 7.9; 8.8). It is clear that Baudhāyana uses *dvijāti* generally to refer to the three upper *varṇas,* once actually using the expressing *trayo varṇā dvijātayaḥ* ("the three twice-born *varṇas:*" 2.5.4). Only once does he use the term with specific reference to Brahmins, and here he uses the compound *dvijātipravara* (2.3.29). A noteworthy point in the use of *dvija* in Baudhāyana's work is that it always occurs in verses, probably indicating that this term entered the vocabulary late and with specific, if not exclusive, reference to Brahmins. The older term appears to have been *dvijāti,* and it was used more generally with reference to the upper three *varṇas.*

There is an explosion in the use of *dvija/dvijāti* in literature close to or after the beginning of the common era, as we can see from the above chart. In all the Dharmaśāstric texts that follow Gautama and Baudhāyana the twice-born is a central concept in their theology and the sociology based on the *varṇa* system. We see the extensive use of the *dvija/dvijāti* also in the two Epics where the term in used in every book of the two epics, although its distribution is uneven.

It is significant that there is no cognate term in Pāli with reference to Brahmins, and in Buddhist hybrid Edgerton give only one example - Dvijātirāja as name of Buddha in a former life. Clearly, this concept was confined to later Brahmanical theology and did not have an impact on the Buddhist vocabulary. The earliest inscriptional evidence I have traced is the Nasik Cave Inscription of Vāsiṣṭhīputra Pulumāvi, circa 149 CE.

The *Arthaśāstra* uses the term only once in probably a late passage (1.3.8), and the *Kāmasūtra* does not use at all. In the *Arthaśāstra* passage (*dvijātiśuśrūṣā,* obedience to *dvijātis*) the reference is clearly to Brahmins within the context of the *varṇa* system. The absence of the term in these two texts, the final redactions of which were carried out probably in the early centuries of the common era, indicates that the term was still restricted to theological discourse. That the term had become somewhat common by first or second century CE is indicated by its use by Aśvaghoṣa in both his poems.[12] He was, however, a man who was deeply versed in Brahmanical theology, and was himself probably a Brahmin before becoming a Buddhist monk.

Conclusion

Taken together, then, the theological and institutional innovations represented by the concept of *dharma* and the notion of the wice-born indicate a dynamic socio-religious situation in India between roughly the 4th century BCE and the 2nd century CE. As historians our task is to study this period to find out the religious, social, political, and economic reasons for these innovations within religious thought and practice. But first we must shed the lenses provided by earlier scholarship and begin to regard ancient India as a dynamic and fast changing society. We must begin to read familiar texts with unfamiliar eyes and with new questions.

The main question that historians must ask is why these innovations happened during this particular time in history, especially the innovations that occurred around the beginning of the common era. It is, of course, a very difficult question to answer, but I think these are the kinds of questions historians need to ask of the existing body of data from this period, including texts, inscriptions, and archeological and art historical remains. Often in historical work it is more important to ask the right questions than to get the right answers. But one thing is abundantly clear: the couple of centuries before and after the beginning of the common era were an exceedingly dynamic period when new theologies were beginning to be constructed within both the Brahmanical and the Buddhist traditions to confront, challenge, and cope with the social, political, and economic changes happening all around them. This was the time when the Indian heartland was exposed to foreign incursions and the establishment of rulers of central Asian extraction—Śakas, Kushana, and the like. This was also the time, as Sheldon Pollock (2006) has shown, when Sanskrit emerges as the language of the court, of inscriptions, and of court poetry. This is the kind of historical dynamism that falsifies the essentialized conception of Indian history and culture as static and unchanging. Henry Kissinger would have learned a significant lesson if he has lived during these vibrant times.

Bibliography

Basham, A. L. 1967. *The Wonder that Was India*. 3rd ed. (1st ed. 1954); London: Sidgwick and Jackson.

Brereton, Joel. 2009. "*Dharman* in the Ṛgveda." In Olivelle 2009a, pp. 27-67.
Edgeron, Franklin. 1953. *Buddhist Hybrid Sanskrit Grammar and Dictionary*. 2 vols. New Haven: Yale University Press.
Gonda, Jan. 1965. *Change and Continuity in Indian Religon*. The Hague: Mouton.
Horsch, Paul. 2009. "From Creation Myth to World Law: The Early History of dharma." In Olivelle 2009a, pp. 1-26. (original German 1967).
Kane, P. V. 1962–75. *History of Dharmaśāstra*. 5 vols. Poona: Bhandarkar Oriental Research Institute.
Lariviere, R. W. 2004. "*Dharmaśāstra*, Custon, 'Real Law' and 'Aprocryphal' Smṛtis." In Olivelle 2004a, pp. 611-627.
Lingat, R. 1973. *The Classical Law of India*. Berkeley: University of California Press.
Müller, F. Max. 1859. *A History of Ancient Sanskrit Literature*. London: Williams and Norgate.
Olivelle, P. 1993. *The Āśrama System: History and Hermeneutics of a Religious Institution*. New York: Oxford University Press.
____. 2000. Dharmasūtras: The Law Codes of Āpastamba, Gautama, *Baudhāyana*, and *Vasiṣṭha*. Delhi: Motilal Banarsidass.
____. 2004a. (Edited volume) *Dharma: Studies in Its Semantic, Cultural, and Religious History*. Special double issue of Journal of Indian Philosophy. Vol. 32, pp. 421-873.
____. 2004b. "The Semantic History of *Dharma*: The Middle and Late Vedic Periods." In Olivelle 2004a.
____. 2005. *Manu's Code of Law: A Critical Edition and Translation of the Mānava-Dharmaśāstra*. New York: Oxford University Press.
____. 2006a. "Power of Words: The Ascetic Appropriation and the Semantic Evolution of dharma." In Patrick Olivelle, *Language, Texts, and Society: Explorations in Ancient Indian Culture and Religion* (Florence: Firenze University Press), pp. 121-135.
____. 2006b. "Explorations in the Early History of Dharmaśāstra." In Patrick Olivelle, *Language, Texts, and Society: Explorations in Ancient Indian Culture and Religion* (Florence: Firenze University Press), pp. 155-177.
____. 2008. *Life of the Buddha: Buddhacarita by Aśvaghoṣa*. The Clay Sanskrit Library. New York: New York Univeristy Press.
____. (ed.) 2009a. *Dharma: Studies in its Semantic, Cultural and Religious History*. Delhi: Motilal Banarsidass.
____. 2010 "*Dharmaśāstra*: A Literary History." In *Hinduism and Law: An Introduction*. Ed. T. Lubin, D. Davis, and J. K. Krishnan, pp. 28-57. Cambridge: Cambridge University Press.
____. Forthcoming-a. "Kings, Ascetics, and Brahmins: The Socio-Political Context of Ancient Indian Religions." In *Dynamiken der Religionsgeschichte zwischen Asien und Europa*. Ed. Volkhard Krech and Marion Steinicke. Leiden: Brill.
____. Forthcoming-b. "Patañjali and the Beginnings of Dharmaśāstra: An Alternate Social History of Early Dharmaśūstra Production." *Aux abords*

de la clairière: Colloque en l'honneur de Ch. Malamoud. Bibliothèque de l'Ecole des Hautes Etudes - Sciences religieuses. Paris: Brepolis.

Pollock, Sheldon. 2006. *The Language of the God in the World of Men: Sanskrit, Culture, and Power in Premodern India.* Berkeley: University of California Press.

Said, Edward. 1978. Orientalism. New York: Pantheon.

Smith, Brian K. 1994. *Classifying the Universe: The Ancient Indian Varṇa System and the Origins of Caste.* New York: Oxford University Press.

Trautmann, Thomas. 1997. *Aryans and British India.* Berkeley: University of California Press.

Wezler, A. 2004. "Dharma in the Veda and the Dharmaśāstras." In Olivelle 2004a, pp. 629-654.

References

1. Cited in B. K. Smith 1994, 2.
2. Cited and discussed in Trautmann 1997, 20.
3. A version of this section on *dharma* was published in Olivelle, forthcoming-a.
4. For a discussion of the semantics of *dharma* in the *Ṛgveda,* see Horsch 2009 and Brereton 2009.
5. A version of this section on *dvija* was published in Olivelle, forthcoming-b.
6. Gonda (1965, 233) notes: "The complex ceremonies and ritual acts, of tuition and observances was considered the preparation for a new birth; hence the name *dvija* – applied to the members of the first three classes (especially the brahmans) who had passed through the initiation into the Veda." However, this appellation was never used in the early period, and the connection of *dvija* to the new birth within initiation was made only through a new theological interpretation and at a much later date.
7. We do find the term *dvijanman* in the *ṚgVeda* 1.60.1; 1.140.2; 1.149.4, 5; 6.50.2. But none of these usages pertain to a person who has undergone Vedic initiation. The two births there probably refer to the birth of fire in heaven and on earth. The *ṚgVeda Khilas* (4.2.6) use *dvijāti* with reference to humans, but the date of the Khilas is uncertain and they are probably quite late. The only place where the term occurs in the *Atharva Veda* (*Śaunaka*) is 19.71.1 (*dvijānām*). This has no parallel in the Paippalāda recension, and the parallel in *Taittirīya Āraṇyaka* (Pariśiṣṭa) 10.36 has the term *dvijātā,* which even Sāyaṇa thinks may refer to the two births in the sun and *Brahmaloka*. So the reading, authenticity, and meaning of this term in *Atharva Veda* (*Śaunaka*) is quite uncertain.
8. The exceptions are the *Āgniveśya Gṛhyasūtra* (2.3.3, 14, 16, 19) and the *Vaikhānasa Gṛhyasūtra* (5.8, 10; 4.12), both of which can be dated to the first half of the first millennium CE. It is also found in the *Baudhāyana Gṛhyasūtra* 2.9.14, but given that it occurs there within a series of verses

one may have reservations regarding its authenticity. The term also occurs in later sections (*paribhāṣā śeṣa*) of some *Gṛhyasūtras*: See Lubin 2005, 87, n. 23.

9. In looking at these raw numbers, one must make allowance for both the length of each text and the subject matter of some texts that may not have called for the use of this term.
10. See *Gautama Dharmasūtra,* 10.1; 12.1; 17.1; 21.4.
11. 1.7.1; 2.3.29; 2.5.4; 2.7.3; 2.18.14 (twice).
12. *Buddhacarita,* 1.44, 45, 47, 48, 84; 2.36; 7.13; 9.80; 11.71 (but here with reference to fire); *Saundarananda,* 2.35, 51; 8.19; 18.1.

Part III
Art and Culture

8
Indian Culture in a Globalized World

Muzaffar Ali

Sarv o saman bhi mauj e naseem e sahar bhi hai
Aye gul tere chaman mein koi chashm e tar bhi hai

— Jazbi

The poet asks of the flower

'The cypress tree, the fragrant jasmine and the gentle morning breeze are there in your garden, but is there someone whose eyes are moist at this sight?'

Culture can be best equated to a garden; garden of various scales and hues. If not designed and laid out imaginatively, looks ugly and if not tended it dies. It is created by sensitive humans for human pleasure and habitation. In every civilization the concept of a garden to share natures beauty with fellow humans, is a highly evolved form of expression. It helps the flight of imagination in which many creative disciplines flourish.

It is the source of music and poetry, symbolism and realism. It evokes a deep sensitivity and thoughtfulness. It is both hidden and the revealed.

And finally in every faith all ones good deeds are rewarded in the form of an abode in a perennial garden, the Garden of Paradise.

In its decline powerful cultures have thrown up a voice of anguish in various art forms. Human helplessness is the single biggest symptom of cultural decay. It is an expression of the soul which feels that a particular culture can be the true reflection of that state and the only ray for a renaissance in that milieu.

When I made my first film, 'Gaman', on the village migrant leaving his 'garden' and with him the ethos that made him. I was expressing that anguish of the soul, the successive loss of a culture in Awadh, since 1856. 'Gaman' was an ode to the break up of a rural culture and its values and I was elated at what Faiz wrote when he saw it.

'Muzaffar Ali's Gaman is a poem in visuals. Its tragic lyricism, its muted eloquence, is deeply perceptive; its sensitively conceived and truthfully captured slice of reality around us, the heart break of the human situation in town and country, makes it sheer delight, a veritable tour de force.'

26-8-78 Faiz Ahmad Faiz

The thumri of Gaman '*Aaja sawariya tohe garwa laga loon, ras ke bhare tore nain'* wrenched the heart in a similar way the poem of Wajid Ali Shah, the last Nawab of Awadh, did, which he penned as he left Lucknow after being deposed.

Dar o deewar pe hasrat se nazar karte hain
Khush raho ahle watan ham to safar karte hain.

It was nothing but the anguish of the ripping apart of a carefully crafted composite culture. He was like Ram leaving Ayodhya. Or the separation of Radha from Krishna.

Indian culture has been soaked in separation - song, music and dance. Human existence is all about Adam leaving the Garden of Eden, and all lifelong he lives with the dream of the lost paradise and the final return to it.

Culture as a dynamic dimension of a nation in a material world has been seen as a commodity. In this sense it has to be seen as a relevant function which ensures the aesthetic and human equilibrium of society and keep it fragrant and meaningful for its people and for those outside of it. It is a reflection of what we are going through in time with a backdrop of the refinement of the past, and as a commodity, with an eye to the future. While culture is shaped by the distillation of the past in modern societies, it is an all important way to present identities and a dignified way to hold your held up in the world without affectation and arrogance. This in today's context has enormous economic and political spin offs. Mostly intangible, but with both immediate and long term effects. Nations rise and fall, but their powerful extension into culture, makes them bounce back from their bad times and keeps them alive.

Culture in its truest sense is an extremely egalitarian function of society, free from domination and exploitation. It is a deeply human instinct which sifts the good from the bad on a long term basis. Its appeal may be specific in its attributes, but attractive in a wider sense. People want to share their culture and are also equally attracted to other cultures. This characteristic makes this phenomenon sustainable. It is this fragrance that is the backbone of all art and the quest to know and the urge to share.

The evolution of a free thinking socially relevant art is the evolution of a healthy democracy. Evolved democracies have a vision of an art form, which expresses their inner dialectics in a way which is relevant for shaping the minds and at the same time shaping their outward manifestation. Cinema though, intelligently crafted on the lowest common denominator principle, is entirely escapist and negatively affects the vulnerable rural and hybrid urban culture. Cultures are shaped by art. Art creates a sensitive perception of a dynamic reality. Today the most powerful medium that is forming mindsets and giving birth to perceptions that is shaping a cultural reality is the language of moving images. And films are being produced oblivious of the delicate human objective of how we need ourselves to be structured within and presented to the world. It is a medium of mass hysteria instead of an artistic tool of shaping an aware, reflective, concerned and caring democratic mind.

Culture is an individual, collective, communal, regional or a secular way of experiencing a happening. The scale, colour, decorum of these happenings were either feudal, folk or tribal. They became larger than life in scale, or unimaginable and in amazing feats of artistic expression. The tradition of the theatre and stage, carnivals and processions, weddings, birth and funerals, congregations and festivals all became part of the continium of presenting a milieu and its beliefs. With the abrupt end of feudalism, the society was bereft of scale, fanfare and decorum of doing things. Finer values were lost at both the collective and individual level. Spaces created for large public happenings became meaningless. Even folklore lost its lustre. This had begun to happen in small measures from the advent of colonialism. In most cultural centres western way of life had made inroads with specially designed policies. Although the British ushered in a sea change in intellectual development, but along with it, they deliberately decimated the valuable traditions that were a legacy of a centuries old composite culture.

Lord Macaulay said the following about India in 1835 in British Parliament.

"I have traveled across the length and breadth of India and I have not seen one person who is a beggar, who is a thief. Such wealth I have seen in this country, such high moral values, people of such calibre, that I do not think we would ever conquer this country, unless we break the very backbone of this nation, which is her spiritual and cultural heritage, and, therefore, I propose that we replace her old and ancient education system, her culture, for if the Indians think that all that is foreign and English is good and greater than their own, they will lose their self-esteem, their native self-culture and they will become what we want them, a truly dominated nation."

This created a communal rift which suited their divisive designs to dominate the subcontinent till partition became the only way to transferring power. Today English has become a language of Indian culture and it is being used to revive all the values of the past; the history, much of the poetry through translation. This growing interest, is also, in some small measure, driving people to learn the lost languages.

The advent of post Independence culture was controlled by those who had the means but not necessarily the regard for the past. The experience of culture moved into the hands of the world of sound and moving images. It did give a fillip to language but the quality and content suffered. In a newly found independence it was difficult to set high world norms in production design. Story, song and star were king and business went skyrocketing. To deal with a population already bereft of their cultural moorings finer details were unimportant. It was dangerous to be real and it was not possible to be artistically unreal. Politics was grappling with issues of basic development which were entirely alien to the make belief world of Indian cinema. However some issues kept being expressed but without a large political will and vision to impose a global agenda to make it viable and artistic. Neither history could be recreated with credibility and authenticity to present our composite culture and nor could we sustain presenting our contemporary realism, to either ourselves, or the world at large. The followers of Satyajit Ray had lost their path!

Today perpetuating culture is a politically driven commercial phenomenon.

Powerful nations invest in dominating the world through globalizing their culture and policies. And it is through this they maintain their supremacy. Economics has become the bottom line, whether it is peace or warfare, whether it is tourism or armaments. The major 20th century miracle of man's mind which has seen the two 'World Wars' is Advertising. The art of 'Subliminal Seduction' by the 'Hidden Persuaders' in an age where 'Medium is the Message'. This is born out of a nation which designs its global policy and follows it through to the last detail. It becomes part of mindless comedy as much as it is part of their carefully worked out serious artistic expression. And these dimensions of a global culture are evident outside their domain with a larger than life visibility and almost a part of our own psyche! It is therefore important to understand this before we tread into a realm called 'global'.

The two key factors here are Indianess and Globalization. We have to understand these independent of each other and then together as a dynamic phenomenon taking into account the interdependence of social, cultural, economic and political dimensions. Factors that are organic - that are born out of a free will and acceptance of beauty, and the others that are through subjugation of colonial and economic compulsion. We live in a multilayered cultural milieu with a universal life style deeply impacted by air travel and modern marketing. The cultured third world has been at the receiving end of products that are considered good for them. Today it is increasingly difficult to turn the tide around and stand up to decide what is good for ourselves on a massive scale. Such large scale acceptability is not possible until we can start with a movement to place our style in the best possible milieu for the world to follow. To understand what we were, how we evolved from one form of culture to another, to organically evolve to a culture of co-existence.

We need to look back to take the much needed leap forward empowered by the beauty of the past. We need to impart soul to the movement in a larger than life and holistic way to make the difference. We need to combat with our own people who are creating a mindless sameness in society for purely commercial gains. They are turning the rural landscape into a synthetic sheet of fabric reflecting the bright Indian sun in unnatural ways. All you need is to see with the inner eye.

There is no doubt that today we live in a 'One World' concept, with one part deeply interdependent on the other. But who is setting the agenda and who is calling the shots? We want to uphold this interdependence, but just turn the table around for a change, a welcome one for all. Like we have done partially with eastern thought - such a Yoga, Vedanta, Tao and Sufism; with history and culture and craft. We need to put it all this in a context and make it into sustainable movement. We therefore need to sharpen our design and marketing skills and set the clock right.

Let's take how the skills evolved, where they reached their pinnacle and how they were distorted and what is their source of renaissance today. All art forms are interrelated and a renaissance for one is a renaissance for all. It does not take place when painters paint for the drawing rooms of the elite or filmmakers do run of the mill movies. We need to see the hidden.

We need to reflect how light is used to create sympathy for an artistic effort, to bring out the gossamer sensuality of a fabric draping a human form or embellishing space. We need to learn and reflect with a poetic sensibility to direct the effort of a million hands. We need to feel for ourselves not as a production centers or consumers but as creators of a drama the world is waiting to see unfold from the east.

Coming from the west it is relevant to read what D.W. Griffith, the father of American Cinema, wrote in 1924.

"100 years from now, the most important single thing which the cinema will have helped in a large way to accomplish will be that of eliminating from the face of the civilized world all armed conflict. Pictures will be the most powerful factor in bringing about this condition. With the use of the universal language of moving pictures, the true meaning of the brotherhood of man will have been established throughout the earth."

In an ideal globalized East- West equilibrium is the free and fair exposure of the best of both to the other, or rather each other. Our first exercise is to use communication arts to understand the best of ourselves. There is so much romance and pathos in this vast land that has to be discovered.

Indian society was always stratified and unfortunately it is being more stratified today for different reasons. While politically it is being casteized it is also being regionalized and any national unification that is taking place is through English and sadly through a mindless form of Bollywood through Hindi. The finer aspect of language, culture and sensitive thought needs to be expressed through the language of moving images to explain ourselves to ourselves. We need to understand the philosophy of a nation to be able to present an integrated cohesive vision of what we broadly define and dream of being Indian. Thus even before we move into syncretic domains in large regional diversities we need to understand basic human emotions and values that have given culture its dynamic and evolutionary form.

We can either take a purist outlook of an extremist trying to purge our selves of external influences or a human evolutionary vision which will position ourselves strongly in an increasing globalized society.

Syncretism is the essence of globalization and there is no nation that can boast of centuries of co-existence and an evolution of a Hindu- Muslim culture which later ushered the integration of Christianity and Western culture into its fold. Though the west came more through colonialism we had the mechanism to absorb the best and repel the unwanted.

So therefore we need to understand emotions as they exist in various sub-cultural pockets and put them in a historical context of the evolution of a vast syncretic culture.

We need to understand the beauty and essence of rituals and customs and protect them for what they represent. A simple act of entering a home barefoot. Something which is common to us from Kerala to Kashmir. It is common to Mosques and Mandirs, Dargahs and Khanaqahs - any place which enriches you spiritually, intellectually and emotionally. There is a vibration in the soul that connects the mind and body and one human being to another.

Meaningful Tourism is a powerful way of evolving the meeting of mind and souls. Superficial tourism, like superficial films can play havoc and create an image imbalance that is irreversible. A qualitative approach is needed along with modern ways to connect and reach out.

Today we are straddling two horses. War and Peace. For us it is a happier scenario if it is travel and tourism. The more tourism grows the more we can keep war at bay. Promoting tourism is another function of globalizing culture and perpetuating world peace. Today we would like to believe in equality of nations. In a free and fair world we need to negate all symptoms and signs of an exploitive relationship be it economic or cultural, or a mix of both. We to need give and receive. Learn and teach. Impart to the world what it needs and import from it what is necessary to improve what we give. This bridge, this equation is the fountainhead of a universal renaissance. India has to express to the world what it takes to be India. We need not be chauvinistic. We can express the fine intangible things that we are trained to see and recognize.

Culture like a garden appeals to every sensibilities and every sensibility is universal. The sensibility of surrender where you put your voice down and just listen. To things that we take for granted - the wind through the trees, the song of birds. Where we don't see ourselves but behold the beauty of nature, their colour and fragrance, and sight of trees and flowers. We see how different flowers and trees grow on the same soil. We see and enjoy the wonder of coexistence. In each breath we feel every element of nature in a milieu in which pure souls thrive. Culture is the most unique blend of aesthetics and human sensibility.

Only those cultures survive that strive to reach this balance or whatever reaches this balance survives as culture. What is the deliberate human effort in procreating culture remains an open secret. It is the quest for universal truth that each one of are born with. The quest for beauty, the quest for oneness of man. culture is therefore in a Sufi way, the same flower growing in different soils. All we can do is celebrate it. As Marx said, 'nothing human is alien to me.' We can celebrate Leonardo da Vinci as much as we can celebrate Rabindranath Tagore, we can celebrate Rumi as much as we can celebrate Valmiki or Tulsidas or Khusrau..., we can translate the Upanishads in Persian as we can translate the Quran in English. Today culture is a house without doors, a garden without boundaries. And there is no external thief.

The biggest responsibility in a fast changing advertising and market driven world is discover the essence of this truth and provide a continuity of this search to the youth. The youth must not get subsumed in indulgent escapist consumerism. They should feel free to dream and follow their heart. They should see the chemistry of culture and understand their own role in the light of the past. There is a role for every occupation in the making of cultures. Such free and pure minds are the first to recognize when culture or a belief system is being used to exploit man and subjugate societies. This is the need for peace and harmony in a globalized world.

9

Notes from Afar[1]: Sanskrit Literature and the Western Operatic Canon

Sally Sutherland Goldman

From its introduction to the West by Sir William Jones, the place of Kālidāsa's *Abhijñānaśākuntalam* (*The Recognition of Śākuntalā*)[2] in the European imagination, especially that of the Germans, cannot be underestimated.[3] Despite the fact that the play was known, admired, and appreciated, its adaptation into the operatic canon, one of the more popular entertainment forms of the 19th century, although attempted a number of times—as evidenced by such works as Schubert's *Sakontala* (1820), Perfall's *Sakuntala* (1853), Reyer's (ballet) *Sacountala* (1858)—was never really successful.

Thus, as early as 1820, the famous Austrian composer Franz Schubert (1779–1828) began work on a two act opera called Sakontala. The libretto for this opera was written by an Austrian professor of physics and a friend of Schubert, Johann P. Neumann (1774–1849). Neumann based his libretto on Jones' translation of Kālidāsa's *Abhijñānaśākuntalam*, which, in turn, had been translated into German by Georg Forster in 1791 and into French in 1803 by A. Bruguière. The opera was never completed nor, obviously, performed, in Schubert's time. In fact, the work was not actually produced until modern times.[4] The narrative basically follows Kālidāsa's story, but simplifies the resolution, creating a tighter plot for the demands of the western audience and stage. In Act I of Neumann's libretto, King Duschmanta (Duḥṣanta/ Duṣyanta) falls in love with the young maid and daughter of the sage Kanna (Kaṇva), Sakontala (Śakuntalā), and gives her a ring as a token of his love and of his promise to marry her. Sakontala, distracted by her love for the king, fails to pay appropriate homage to the sage Durwasas (Durvāsas), who takes offense and curses her: The king thus becomes unable to recognize Sakontala. Sakontala begs for forgiveness and Durwasas modifies his curse: The king will recognize her if she shows him the ring. Demons are introduced who cause her to lose the ring. When she finally comes to the royal court with her father Kanna (Kaṇva), the king rejects her. In Act II, the king's signet ring is discovered by a fisherman. The fisherman attempts to sell it, but is arrested for attempting to sell the king's property and is brought before Duschmanta. The fisherman tells the court that he has found the ring inside of a fish. Upon seeing the ring, the king's memory is restored and finally the two lovers reunite in a final scene with a chorus, while Kanna prononces that it is always best to trust the wisdom of the gods.

In the middle of the opera, Schubert abruptly stopped work on it. We do not know why he ceased this project. There has been speculation that he might have been uncomfortable with Neumann's third act of the libretto, in which he had added new elements to the original.[5]

The narrative, at least for the first two acts, while not completely true to the original, does little violence to it, and translates well into operatic style. What is particularly interesting is that the narrative does not fall into line with those of others of its period. Here, the focus is on love, memory, recognition, and truth. The ever-popular classic "love" triangle, in any configuration whatsoever, is entirely missing.[6] The love between Sakontala and Duschmanta is thwarted, not by another male [unheard of in the Indian context], but by a religious/social transgression against an elder authority figure. While such transgressions lie at the heart of many Indian narratives, they are not normally the "stuff" of western opera. Additionally, the dramatically early (in Western works, the marriage is normally at the culmination of the work, not at the beginning) and somewhat unusual *gāndharva* marriage[7] of Sakontala and Duschmanta might have been a source of discomfort for both the composer and librettist. It seems that Schubert at least, was interested in recreating Kālidāsa's drama as opera, with some intention of adhering to the original plot and its developments. Thus, it is to Schubert, that one must attribute the first, if unfinished, opera based on an Indian narrative, rather than a western narrative about India. Nevertheless, while a number of the operatic versions of Śakuntalā were popular in their time, no version of the opera has ever gained the long-term popularity that so many other operatic works have.

While numerous libretti locate themselves in India and even tell tales that purport to be of India, up until the middle of the 19th century they, in fact, are, with the exception of the Śakuntalā story, in no real way "of India." Toward the end of the 19th century, however, there arose a marked increase in the number of operas whose libretti could claim to be based definitively on narratives derived from directly from South Asian textual traditions. Many of these came directly from Sanskrit literature. This can, in part, be tied to the increased accessibility of texts and translations of the Sanskrit originals to the European audience.

This is evidenced, for example, by the 1871 dramatic cantata *Nala und Damayanti* (*Nala and Damayantī*)" written by the German composer Ferdinand Hiller. The work was very popular in its time.[8] The narrative of the *Nalopākhyāna*, whose earliest extant version is found in the *Mahābhārata*, was known at least by 1844 in Europe from the text of the *Nalodaya*, which scholars originally attributed to Kālidāsa and which was edited and translated into English by William Yates.[9]

1884 saw the first appearance of a new opera based on an old favorite. Paul Felix von Weingartner (1863–1942), an Austrian composer, conductor, and pianist premièred and new version of the Śakuntalā story (*Sakuntala*—[Opus 9]; [Opus 94, 1941]). The choice, in all likelihood, was a result of his fascination with the occult, astrology, and eastern mysticism. This interest came to influence both his world-view and his music. *Sakuntala* was his first opera and the well-known composer and pianist Franz Liszt, who mentored the young Weingartner, helped him produce it. The opening performance suffered from technical difficulties and was not exactly successful.[10] Weingartner revised the opera as Opus 94, and it was performed again, a year before his death, in 1941. Weingartner's interest in India did not stop there. His second opera was based on yet another of Kālidāsa's plays, the *Mālavikāgnimitram*, and entitled *Malawika* (*und Agnimitra*) (Opus 10, Komische Oper in 3 Aufzügen). Composed in 1885, it was first performed on June 3, 1866 in Munich. Clearly, outside of the Śakuntalā narrative, this opera is the first evidence of an Indian narrative being adapted to the Western operatic tradition. Following the *Śākuntalā*, the *Mālavikāgnimitra* was one of the earlier works, along with the *Raghuvaṃśa*[11] and the *Kumārasaṃbhava*,[12] translated into a European language. In 1840 Otto F. Tullberg had translated the work into German, and in 1881 Ludwig Fritze offered a second translation.[13] We do not know if either of these was the inspiration for Weingartner's opera, and I have not yet be able to obtain a copy of the libretto, if it even exists, but we do know that the opera was not widely performed, if ever, after its debut. It has completely disappeared from the modern operatic canon.

This period saw a number of other such productions. Thus, in 1884, Ludwig Philipp Scharwenka (1847–1917), a German composer, wrote a choral work based on Śakuntalā (*Sakuntala*), which was extremely popular at the time.[14] It is one of his most famous works, and yet virtually unknown in modern times. In 1887, Antonia Smareglia, an Italian composer, wrote *Re Nala* ("*King Nala*"), which, unfortunately, has been lost. In 1894, Natale Canti composed his opera, *Savitri: iddilio drammatico indiano in tre atti* (*Savitri: A Dramatic Indian Idyll in 3 Acts*), with a libretto composed by Luigi Alberto Villanis. Unfortunately information on these operas is scant, and we can assume that they were not popular enough to warrant more that a few performances.

At about the same period, an English composer by the name of Isidore De Lara, upon being urged to convert an early cantata, "The Light of Asia," into an Italian opera, reworked the piece into a full opera entitled, *La luce dell'Asia.* This opera, first performed at Covent Garden in London in1892, was based on the life of the Buddha. Although no longer part of the regularly performed canon, this opera appears to have had a bit more success than the ones mentioned above. In 1904 the opera was re-titled, *Le reveil de Bouddha* (*The Dream of Buddha*).

In the early 1900s, the popularity of operas taken directly from Indian stories continued to grow. Thus, in 1902, Erazm Dluski, a Polish composer, wrote an opera *Urwasi.* This was followed in 1905, by an opera composed by Zimmerman based on the Śakuntalā story. In 1904 Ferdinand B. Hummel composed and premièred a work based yet again on Śakuntalā, while in 1899 Anton (Stepanovich) Arensky, the first Russian to write an opera based on an Indian narrative premièred his *Nal' i Damayanti* in Moscow. It was described as "a grand opera,"[15] and recordings of it in full or in part are available.[16] Thus we can see that "India" and Indian narratives, particularly those based on famous works from the

Sanskrit literary canon had truly come of age. The sheer number of these operas is telling of the popularity of the subject matter,[17] while their lack of longevity speaks to other concerns.

Most remarkable among the composers of this period is the English composer Gustav Holst. As a young man, Holst became interested in Hindu philosophy and Sanskrit literature, and would remain fascinated with the East for some two decades of his life,[18] while his interest can be seen as early as 1895, when he began to think about setting some of the hymns of the *Ṛgveda* to music, it was not until somewhat later that he began his quest in earnest. According to Raymond Head, in his, "Holst in India (i): 'Maya' to 'Sita,'" in the late 1890s, the composer was influenced by R. W. Frazer's *Silent Gods and Sun Steeped Lands*, which was the source of his first exposure to the concept of *māyā*, and Kālidāsa's *Meghadūta*, which at that time some thought to be the finest poem ever composed. This introduction led the young Holst to look for more translations from the Sanskrit.

A prolific translator of Sanskrit during this period was Ralph Griffiths, who had spent a large part of his life in India.[19] Griffiths, although a serious scholar, sought to popularize and make accessible the Sanskritic corpus. *Specimens of Old Indian Poetry*, one of his earliest endeavors, was first published in 1852. It contains a version of the Savitri story. Griffiths's *Idylls from the Sanskrit* (1866), which contains a second version of the Savitri story, the story of Rama and Sita and a couple of verses of Kālidāsa's *Ṛtusaṃhāra*), was his second attempt. These were then, in short order, followed by his *The Ramayana* (1868), *The Ramayana of Valmiki* (1870–1875), and *The Hymns of the Rig Veda* (1889–92).[20] Holst was clearly familiar with these works and some were in his personal library and it is generally agreed that Griffith's works substantially influenced Holst's choices and lyrics.[21]

Although Holst's daughter, Imogen, believes it was in the 1890s that her father began his study of Sanskrit, Head convincingly disputes this, as Dr. Mable Bode, who would eventually become Holst's Sanskrit teacher, was not only not teaching at SOAS (School of Oriental and African Studies) in London—where the two would eventually work together—during this period, but she was finishing her doctorate and, following that, studying with Sylvain Lèvi in Paris.[22] In 1899, Holst began working on his opera *Sita*. It was to be revised by Holst numerous times before he actually finished it [or put it aside for good] in 1907–1908. The three act opera, although it has never been performed officially and is not widely known, has been the subject of interest to scholars of Sanskrit and of music.[23]

Holst's is the first such opera to be based on the Rama story. While, in all likelihood Holst's libretto was inspired by and, perhaps, in part based on Griffiths' translation, the story strays a fair distance from the original of Vālmīki. As evidenced from opera's title the focus of the story is not on Rama, but rather on his wife, Sita.[24] The first act begins as the goddess Mother Earth, enthroned, beseeches Vishnu:

> "Save us from one who knoweth no mercy,
> Who knoweth no law.
> Chief of the Rakshas!
> Great Lord of Lanka
> Ravana, surnamed the Dread one.
> When he rides through the world
> Birds cease their song.
> Beasts crouch down trembling.
> E'ven the wind dies in angst and dread.
> Fire cannot burn him,
> Water o'er-whelm him.
> "No god overcome him
> He has e'ven fought with Death.
> No spell hath he weaved.
> To save him from man.
> Man he deemed feeble,
> Unworthy of thought.[25]

One might note that this passage, is reminiscent of Vālmīki's *Bālakāṇda* 1.14.10, where the sun and other natural phenomena are represented as diminished by fear of Ravana.[26]

In the first act, we are already in the Dandaka forest. Lakshman enters fighting two Rakshas. More Rakshas appear and Lakshman calls out to his brother Rama, who enters and attacks the Rakshas. Lakshman is struck down and falls to the ground. Rama searches for him, discovers him lying on the ground and he thinks him dead. Lamenting his lost brother he cries to the gods:

> "Ye Gods on high, is this your will?

Send me a comrade, send me a helper.[27]

He then calls upon Mother Earth to help him:

Lonely am I.
My brother is dead.
None (save) the foe near me.
Indra, great heaven's lord
From thou foster Sweet mother Earth
Smiling around me
Ha! Now within my breast,
Hope burneth fiercely.
Hear me ye gods.
Your servant am I.
Send me a comrade.
Show forth thy power![28]

At this Sita, slowly rises up from the earth. Clearly Holst has taken considerable liberty with the *Ramayana* narrative.

Mother Earth has sent Sita to be Rama's companion. But Sita warns him:

My home is with thee and all earth's creatures.
With thee to protect me, what more can I ask?
Yet hark to me further.
Earth and her daughter only may dwell where there is trust.
Where there is faithfulness.
Ne'er must thou doubt me!
Lest back to her bosom my mother recall![29]

Sita swears her love for Rama and thanks her mother, the Earth for sending him her daughter as his bride. The two profess their love for one another, falling into each other's arms. Rama spies something moving, and they discover Lakshman, who is severely wounded, but still alive. Rama begs Sita, through the agency of her mother, to mend his brother's wounds, which she does. Lakshman once more healed, swears loyalty to Sita. The trio moves into the Pancavati forest, and encounter Surpanakha, who announces that she is the sister of Ravana, and a bride worthy of Rama.

Rama rejects Surpanakha, telling her:

> Did I wish for one who would bow to me,
> Crawl to me,
> Tremble and fear me?
> Not a wife would I choose but a dog![30]

Insulted, Surpanakha rushes toward Sita but Lakshman comes between them, threatening to kill her. The threesome moves on into the forest, leaving Surpanakha, trembling and cowering in the path. Ravana comes and Surpanakha tells him what has happened and convinces him to take vengeance.

Act II begins in the Pancavati, where the demon Marica is surrounded by other rakshas. They demand to hear of Ravana's might, and Marica tells them of it. Ravana and Surpanakha enter. Ravana demands that they win Sita as a bride for him. But Marica warns that "No Rakshas chief can conquer Rama" (p. 70). Ravana threatens, and tells his plan: a rakshas, in the form of a fawn will draw Rama away, so that he can abduct the beautiful Sita. Lakshman enters, having hunted to no avail, the entire night. Sita sees the fawn, and demands it, Rama follows it, leaving Lakshman to guard Sita. Lakshman is drawn off by the feigned cries of Rama, and Sita is abducted by Ravana. Sita refuses to submit to him and calls to her mother the Earth. Ravana, with Sita in tow, arrives in Lanka to the victorious cries of the rakshas.

In Act III, Rama returns and bemoans the loss of his beloved. Surpanakha enters and tells Rama that Lakshman is in the forest, being helped by a troop of men. She also tells Rama that Sita no longer loves him, and is now in Lanka as the queen of the Rakshas. She tells Rama where Lanka is, just across the "torrent." Lakshman returns with a group of men. They build a bridge across the waters.

In Lanka, Surpanakha approaches Sita, who has sworn to kill herself that night and wishes only to sleep. But, hearing that Surpanakha has brought news of Rama, she gets up. Surpanakha convinces Sita that Rama is on his way to claim her, and, that, she must dress appropriately for her reunion with Rama—she must look like a queen. As they make their way Ravana stops them, demanding that Sita hear his last warning:

> "Bow to my will, ere the sunset or
> beware the doom that awaits thee.[31]

Once more, Sita resists, vowing her undying devotion to Rama. As the sun rises, Rama, his men working through the night to build the bridge, arrives. Ravana, calls upon the darkness to encompass the earth, Sita prays to her mother the earth for the sun to rise. Darkness does not heed Ravana's command. As the sun ascends into the sky, Rama and his men arrive in Lanka. Engaging Ravana in a duel, Rama kills him. Rama has Sita brought, but seeing her dressed as a queen, rejects her:

> I am blind.
> But 'tis not the darkness,
> The Queen of the Rakshas.
> The bride of the Dread one is dazzling mine eyes,
> Is scorching my heart.[32]

Sita reminds Rama of her words:

> Beware.
> Did I not warn thee never to doubt.
>
> Faith then is dead.
> Dead too is home.
> Love is dead.
> I am alone.
>
> The voice of my Mother.[33]

The goddess earth rises up, her gaze killing Surpanakha, and returns to the earth with Sita. But, as she leaves, she tells Rama who he really is: None other than incarnation of Vishnu. The opera ends with Mother Earth proclaiming:

> Bow not to me Rama . . .
>
> Rama thy deed proclaims thee a mortal,
> Yet in thy bosom dwellest the spirit upholding creation.
> Thou art He by whom the Earth is.
> Vishnu, Preserver of all.[34]

The opera, although not adhering to the original and containing modifications that might cause an audience steeped in the lore of the *Ramayana* considerable unease—for example, Lakṣmaṇa's nearly demise and revivification or Hanumān and Rama's other monkey allies replacement by a band of woodsmen—does contain much of the essence of the *Ramayana.* Following in line with much of the scholarly interpretive ideas of the period, Holst reads the *Ramayana* as a nature myth, wherein Sita, daughter of the earth goddess, is her earthly representation. It is to her mother that Sita repeatedly calls upon in her times of need,[35] Ravana is Darkness personified, and uses his powers to cast the earth in darkness; Rama, is Vishnu's incarnation on earth and is also closely aligned with the powers of light, i.e., the sun. The battle between Rama and Ravana is enacted as a struggle between the rising sun and the darkness of night.[36]

The opera highlights the power of faith and trust. Rama, failing to trust Sita, seeing her in royal garments rejects her. As soon as she realizes that Rama has failed to keep his word, she calls upon her mother to take her back. Given the demands of the operatic conventions and the expectations of the western audience, Holst has, to my mind, cleverly combined the *agniparīkṣā* of the original and Sita's final appearance in the epic, where she swears her fidelity to her husband, and in so doing returns to the earth with her mother. Of particular note here, is that unlike earlier operas, such as Richard Stevens's *Widow of Malabar* (circa 1780), where *satī* [suttee] and similar practices were marked as the representative of the most heathen or pagan of practices and was given as a rationale for colonial rule, Holst erases the Sita's purification trial entirely, making the rejection of Sita an outcome of Rama's failure to trust and Sita responsible for her own fate. This erasure is not unique, for as Head notes, "Holst cleverly de-Indianizes the story. Throughout the entire opera, in fact, he [Holst] was careful to strike out direct references to Hindu culture."[37] Moreover, we can't ignore the somewhat cruel irony in the fact that the opera, using one of the most fundamental narratives of the sub-continent becomes tool to defend the colonial establishment, wherein the representation of the colonial power, the power of light and good, must control the land mapped onto the body of the feminine, which has fallen into the hands of darkness and ignorance.

It is a shame that the opera has never been performed, but Holst felt that the music he composed for it was too influenced by that of

Wagner. Moreover, he likely lost faith in it, as the opera, which had been submitted as an entry in the Recordi composition, did not win. He thus associated the opera with failure. In any case he refused to allow the opera to be performed. One assumes that his daughter was obliged to continue her father's wishes after his death. Perhaps one day Holst's *Sita* will see the light of day. Head sums it up most eloquently, "*Sita* also sums up a whole Western feeling about India: by investing Hindu mythology with European expression, Holst created a work which is a unique expression of the need which Europe had for an Indo-Aryan Orient."[38]

Holst eventually did go on to study Sanskrit. It is clear that he had worked his way through the first part of Edward Perry's A Sanskrit Primer (Boston: Luzac & Co. 1885, 34d ed. 1901) and eventually studied under the tutorship of Dr. Mable Bode, a Pāli scholar. How much Sanskrit he eventually learned is unclear, but it is certain that Dr. Bode, who became a lifelong friend and supporter of Holst, helped in particular with his study of the *Rig Veda*. We know that he was familiar with R. Griffith's *The Hymns of the Rig Veda*, a copy of which he owned. But it is also clear that he had access to A. A. Macdonell's article "Mythological Studies in the *Rigveda*" (*JRAS* Jan. [1895], pp. 65-189]) and his *A History of Sanskrit Literature* (London: 1900, 2nd ed. 1905). It appears that Holst also knew J. Muir's *On the Interpretation of the Veda* as well as F. Max-Müller's edition of the *Rigveda*. Holst would go on to write his *Choral Hymns from the Rigveda* (1907–12) a truly remarkable set of works. (Fourteen pieces were from the *Rig Veda* for voice and piano [nine were published as Opus 24] 1907–1908; fourteen pieces were for chorus and orchestra, and published as Opus 26 in four groups, 1908–1909).[39] In 1908, during this Indian Period, Holst would also compose a cantata based on Kālidāsa's *Meghadūta*, "The Cloud Messenger (1909-10) and "Two Eastern Pictures," based on the poet's *Ṛtusaṃhāra*.

One of the most popular of Holst's works from this period is his one act opera "*Sāvitri*."[40] Holst knew of the Sāvitrī episode from Griffith's *Specimens of Old Indian Poetry* and *Idylls from the Sanskrit*, mentioned above. The opera focuses only on the most crucial moment of the episode, that moment when Sāvitri encounters Yama, "Death." Holst modifies the story in one significant way, he incorporates *māyā*, "illusion," into the story. Holst was a lifelong devotee of the *Upaniṣads*, and it is one of the few books that he always kept with him and was fascinated with the concept of *māyā*.[41] The importance of *māyā* to Holst's *Sāvitri* is evidenced in Satyavan's words:

> It is Maya!
> Dost thou not know her?
> Illusion—dreams—phantoms.
> But to the wise,
> Maya is more.
> Look around:
> All that thou see'st,
> Trees and shrubs,
> The grass at thy feet,
> All that walks or creeps,
> All that flies from tree to tree,
> All is unreal:
> All is Maya.
> Our bodies, our limbs, our very thoughts.
> We ourselves are slaves to Maya.
>
> These, wandering thro' the world of Maya,
> Are perchance shadows of that which is.[42]

And then at the end Satyavan, says:

> Then this was but a dream!
> Yea, so, too, was my weariness.
> Maya had seized me,
> I was her slave;
> Now hath she fled.
> Naught remains but thou and thy love.

Thou alone art free from Maya:

> Thou alone art real.[43]

Death, sums up the force of *māyā*:

> Unto his kingdom
> Death wendeth alone.
> One hath conquered him,

One knowing Life,
One free from Maya;
Maya who reigns where men dream they
are living;
Whose power extends to that other world
Where men dream that they are dead.
For even Death is Maya.[44]

As Head has pointed out, in the opera one can see the influence of both William Morris' socialist ideas and Walt Whitman's transcendental philosophy at work. Moreover, Head continues, the piece is remarkable both musically, as the binary of the text is reflected in the music, and for its synthesis of Holst's attraction to the narratives of Sanskrit and his contemplation of *māyā*, "illusion."[45] The remainder of the libretto, though limited, more or less replicates the encounter between Sāvitri and Yama. However, much in the fashion of *Sita*, Holst is careful to distance the narrative from India. Satyavan and Sāvitri are a simple woodsman and his wife. Satyavan is no longer the son of a disposed king, nor is she a princess. Her devotion and love to her husband remain, and in a very similar vein to the original, Holst's Sāvitri begs of Death:

"Ah! Death, the just One,
Whose word ruleth all,
Grants me a boon;
He giveth me Life,
The life of a woman, of wife, of mother.
So hath he granted that which alone
Fulfils his word.
If Satyavan die, my voice is mute;
My feet may never travel the path.
Then I were but a dream,
An image, floating
On the waters of memory.
Satyavan only can teach me the song,
Can open the gate to my path of flow'rs,
The path of a woman's life.
Away, Death!
Back to thy kingdom,
Alone must thou travel,
True to thy word.[46]

For Holst's *Sāvitri*, as for Vyāsa's, a woman is mute, her voice silenced without her husband.[47] For only with her husband can a woman be a wife or a mother. Holst has no difficulty in envisioning a woman as fully dependent on and only completed by a man, her husband.

Thus, by the late 1800s and early 1900s, operatic libretti draw extensively on Indian narratives, although in many cases significantly modifying the original to meet the needs of the operatic tradition and the western audience. Not unexpectedly, the most popular among these is the Śakuntalā story. This is not an unlikely choice as the story was one of the earliest to be introduced into Europe, and it soon became one of the chosen works of the European cultural and intellectual elite. What often goes unnoticed, though is the popularity of other narratives, such as that of Nala. The culmination of this trend is seen in the work of Holst, who more so than any other composer, used Indian narrative as the basis for his works. Of particular note is that despite the ongoing popularity of these narratives in the operatic imagination of the West during the 1800s and early 1900s, there is virtually no memory of them in the modern canon.[48] Nevertheless the immense influence that the Sanskrit literary tradition has had on the operatic tradition of the west, is an important and often overlooked indicator of the extent to which Indian culture has permeated western culture to its very core.

Notes

1. The following is an excerpt of a much longer, original paper, which is under currently under revision, discusses numerous additional operas beginning from approximately 1650 up through contemporary works, and aditionally focuses on operas in which the narratives for the libretti are more variously derived.
2. Jones' translation of *Abhijñānaśākuntam* was published in 1787.
3. See Dorothy M. Figueria, *Translating the Orient* (Albany: State University of New York Press, 1991).
4. http://schubertusa.weebly.com/schubert-opera-sakontala.html.
   In 2002, Schubert's opera was reconstructed by Karl Aage Rasmussen, a Danish composer. The basis of this reconstruction was a complete handwritten libretto of the play, which had been discovered by Dr. Thomas Aigner in an antiquarian bookshop in Vienna, and various sketches that had been made on by Schubert.
5. Karl Rasmussen suggests this. See note 4 above.

6. See, for example, Scott L. Balthazar, "Aspects of Form in the Ottocento Libretto" (*Cambridge Opera Journal* vol. 7, No. 1, March 1995, pp. 23–35), p. 24.
7. Early Brahmanical/Hindu tradition recognized eight types of marriage. Of these, the *gandharva* marriage, commonly understood as a "love" marriage, took place when a man and a woman, in love, married secretly and without the consent of their respective families. The marriage between Duṣyanta and Śakuntalā is considered the classical example of such a type of marriage. See Robert Goldman, "Carried Away: Abduction, Abjection and Anxiety in the Indian Epic Image" (in *A Pantheon Rediscovered*, Edited by Phyllis Granoff. New Delhi: Oxford University Press. In Press) and Srikanta Mishra, *Ancient Hindu Marriage Law and Practice* (New Delhi: Deep & Deep, 1994), pp. 65–103.
8. Ferdinand Hiller (1811–1885) composed a great number of works. His "Nala and Damayanti" was considered one of his most important pieces and is described as "a dramatic cantata, founded on the ancient Hindoo poem." The work, Op. 150, is for solo voices, chorus and orchestra; the English translation by Natalia Macfarren, publisher: London Novello; Ewer.
9. *The Nalodaya, or, History of King Nala, a Sanscrit poem by Kālidāsa.* Translated by William Yates. Calcutta: Printed at the Baptist Mission Press, 1844.
10. According to Adam Walker, the Weimar orchestra of the 1880s was far from its peak of a few decades earlier—and the opening performance of *Sakuntala* in 1885 "ended in shambles with the singers going one way with orchestra another" (*Franz Liszt: The Weimer Years 1848–186,* New York: Knopf and Cornell University Press,1989, p. 271).
11. *Raghuvansa, Kálidása carmen sanskrite e latine by Kālidāsa.* Translated by Adolf Friedrich Stenzler. London: John Murray [etc.], 1832.
12. *Kumára sambhava: Kálidásœ carmen Sanskrite et Latine by Kālidāsa*; Adolphus Fridericus Stenzler. London: sold by A.J. Valpy, 1838; *The Birth of the War-God, (Kumára Sambhava,) a Poem by Kálidása.* Translated from the Sanskrit into English Verse by R. T. H. Griffith, London, 1853 and translated into German as *Kālidāsa's Wolkenbote*, C Schütz; H H Wilson. Bielefeld: Velhagen & Klasing, 1859.
13. *Malavika et Agnimitra: drama indicum: Kalidasae adscriptum* by Kālidāsa.; Otto Fredrik Tullberg Bonnae ad Rhenum: H.B. Koenig, 1840; *Malavika und Agnimitra ein indisches Schauspiel,* by Kālidāsa; Ludwig Fritze. Leipzig, P. Reclam [1881?]. The play was also translated into French (*Agnimitra et Mālavikā; comédie en cinq actes* by Kālidāsa; Victor Henry. Paris, Maisonneuve et C. Leclerc) in 1889 and into English (*Malavikagnimitra*, translated into English by F.

Hall [JASBe. 28) Malavikagnimitra of Kalidasa) in 1859 and by C. II. *Tawney*. First edition. Calcutta) in 1875.

14. *The Athenaeum, Journal of Literature, Science, the Fine Arts, Music, and the Drama*, January to June 1885, no. 2997, April 4, 1885, p. 450.
15. *Who's Who in Music: A Biographical Record of Contemporary Musicians*, compiled and edited by H. Saxe Wyndham. Boston: Small, Maynard and Company, 1913, p. 6.
16. http://goliath.ecnext.com/coms2/gi_0199-157590/Arensky-Symphony-2-Suite-3.html.
17. The subject matter itself speaks to availability of certain works from the Sanskrit, which in turn is a reflection on cultural prejudices and attitudes, needs, and concerns of the European and English intellectuals, religious leaders, politicians, and the like.
18. Holst's fascination with India has been a subject of scholarly interest. Raymond Head has written three articles that focus on the topic ("Holst and India (I): 'Maya' to 'Sita' " [*Tempo, New Series*, No. 158, 1986, pp. 2–7]; "Holst and India (II)" [*Tempo, New Series*, no. 160, 1987, pp. 27–36]; "Holst and India (III)" [*Tempo, New Series*, no. 166, 1988, pp. 35–40]), while Gabriella Olivero Ferero and Daniela Roeslla have recently produced an excellent and detailed monograph, on Holst's opera *Sita* (*Sita: Un'opera indedita di Gustav Holst: Passioni Dall'India All'Occidente* (Parma: Loca dle Cairo [2007]). In addition, Del Bontá's article, "Songs of India" (*Opera Quarterly*, 1984, pp. 5–15), notes Holst's study of Sanskrit as well.

    See Head 1986, p. 2. Head in his article brings up a number of incidents and influences that helped to propel Holst's fascination with India. He also notes how this fascination for India was part of a larger cultural mood. Among one of the most influential figures in Holst passion for India was Walt Whitman, who himself had a lifelong passion for India (as seen in his poems such as "A Passage to India" ([183, Leaves of Grass. Philadelphia: David McKay. 1900 [http://www.bartleby.com/142/183.html]). Holst, in tribute to the poet philosopher wrote a work entitled "The Walt Whitman Overture" (1898), which was first performed in 1980s (Head 1986, p. 3).
19. "Ralph Griffiths (1826-1905) [was] a retired Indian Civil Servant, who, in addition, had been Boden Sanskrit Scholar at Oxford University in the 1840s. Griffiths went to Benares College in 1854, becoming its Principal in 1863. He stayed there until 1878 when he was appointed Director of Public Instruction in the North Western Provinces and Oudh. After he retired in 1885 Griffiths stayed on in India." Head (1986), p. 4.
20. Ralph T.H. Griffith, *Idylls from the Sanskrit* (London: Smith, Elder, and Co, 1866); *Scenes from the Ramayana* (Metrically Translated by Ralph T. H. Griffith) (London, 1870); *The Ramayan of Vālmīki translated into English Verse by Ralph T. H. Griffith* (London: Luzac

and co, 1895); *Hymns of the Rig Veda, 4 vols* (London: 1889; Benares; E.J. Lazarus and Co. 1889–1892).

21. See Ferrero and Rossella 2007.
22. Head 1986, pp. 4–5.
23. See Ferrero and Rossella 2007.
24. Diacritics, in general, have been omitted in keeping with the spelling conventions used by Holst in his works.
25. Ferrero and Rossella 2007, pp. 58–59.
26. See 1.14.10 (*The Rāmāyaṇa of Vālmīki: An Epic of Ancient India. Volume I, Bālakāṇḍa: Boyhood* [Introduction and Translation by R. P. Goldman, Annotation by Robert Goldman and Sally Sutherland. Princeton: Princeton University Press, 1984]). See, too, 6.78.45 and notes (*The Rāmāyaṇa of Vālmīki: An Epic of Ancient India. Volume VI, Yuddhakāṇḍa:* Translation and Annotation Robert P. Goldman, Sally J. Sutherland Goldman, and Barend van Nooten [Introduction by Sally J. Sutherland Goldman and R. P. (with Robert P. Goldman). Princeton: Princeton University Press. 2009]).
27. Ferrero and Rossella 2007, p. 60.
28. Ferrero and Rossella 2007, pp. 60–61.
29. Ferrero and Rossella 2007, p. 61.
30. Ferrero and Rossella 2007, p. 65.
31. Ferrero and Rossella 2007, p. 88.
32. Ferrero and Rossella 2007, p. 93.
33. Ferrero and Rossella 2007, pp. 93–94.
34. Ferrero and Rossella 2007, p. 95.
35. In Vālmīki's epic, Sītā only calls upon her mother during her last appearance in the epic story in the epic's final book, *Uttarakāṇḍa.* See Sally J. Sutherand (Goldman), "Draupadī and Sītā: Aggressive Behavior and Female Role-Models" (*JAOS*, vol. 109, no.1, pp. 63–79, 1989) and Sally J. Sutherland Goldman, "Gendered Narratives: Gender, Space, and Narrative Structures in *Vālmīki's Bālakāṇḍa*" (in The Ramayana Revisited. Edited by Mandakranta Bose. New York: Oxford University Press, 2004, pp. 47–85).
36. The opera focus on the oppression of Mother Earth, clearly portrayed a nature divinity, being oppressed by evil powers, a theme certainly that would have appeal in the ecologically minded world of today.
37. See Head 1986, p. 7.
38. See Head 1986, p. 7.
39. See Head (1987, pp. 28–36) for a detailed appraisal of the surviving works.
40. *Sāvitri.* (1976) Edition Eulenburg, No. 1097. London: Ernst Eulenburg Ltd. With a forward by Imogen Holst. This is the spelling that Holst uses in his work. In order to maintain consistency, diacritics have been omitted in general be omitted.
41. See J.B. Trend, "Savitri: An Opera from the Sanskrit" (*Music & Letters*, vol. 2, no. v. 1921, pp. 345–350), pp. 346–347.

42. Sāvitri 1976, pp. 7–8, 9.
43. Sāvitri 1976, pp. 739–40.
44. Sāvitri 1976, pp. 42–43.
45. Raymond Head 1987, p. 30.
46. Sāvitri 1976, pp. 31–37.
47. For a discussion on the use of voice and the Sanskrit heroine, see Sally J. Sutherland Goldman, "Sītā Speaks: The Voice of the Heroine in *Sundarakāṇḍa* of the *Vālmīki Rāmāyaṇa,*" (in *Questioning Ramayanas: A South Asia Tradition,* edited by Paula Richman, Berkeley: University of California Press, 2001, pp. 223–238; Delhi: OUP, 2001, pp. 223–238).
48. The reasons for this are beyond the scope of this paper, but one might well look to the changing political dynamic of post-World War II and the redefinition of India as a "third world nation."

10
The Sufi Shaikhs and the Formation of the Early Mughal Regime

Muzaffar Alam

> "After you experience the unbounded Divine Beauty you see His Grace present both in a *kafir* and a Muslim".
>
> Mir Abd al-Wahid Bilgrami (d.1608) in *Sab'a Sanabil*

> "In my father's realm there was room for practitioners of various sects and beliefs, just as the followers of all religions have a place within the spacious circle of God's mercy".
>
> Jahangir in his Memoir, *Tuzak-i Jahangiri*

In the sixteenth century with the ascendancy of the Mughals, an important step in the development of political culture and ideology occurred in India. The changed social milieu enabled the emergence of a new set of reflections on social and political questions that had been debated in India since at least time of the founding of the Sultanate of Delhi. How could the existing ideas that derived from Arabo-Persian and Central Asian traditions be adapted to a situation where power in a large part of the countryside was in the hands of non-Muslim family and kin groups? How was one to resolve the demands of an imperial center with powerful local and regional traditions? This problem was by no means unique to the Mughals, but they proclaimed in unequivocal terms the need of a new political vocabulary and syntax to legitimate the coordination between the diverse cultural groups. Indeed, so successfully did the Mughals wed existing political discourse with pragmatic innovations that many of the local Hindu elites began to identify themselves, to a certain degree, not simply with the Mughal state system but also with the Mughal Persian culture. I have discussed elsewhere some of the idioms in which the Mughals articulated and reinforce their political management. This paper is an attempt to understand one such idiom, namely Sufi ideology and Sufi practice. We will see if the Sufi Shaikhs and their orders had a role in the formation of this politics. Did they all share the same position, or did they differ with one another? How do we explain the difference in their approaches, if any? Was it because of some immediate pragmatic consideration or was rooted in their diverse views of religious truth?

The Sufi Reception of 'Hindu' Traditions

The Sufi shaikhs encouraged and promoted many things held in common by Hindus and Muslims. They shunned ritualism and ceremonialism, spoke the language of the commoners and gave an impetus to linguistic and cultural assimilation. All types of people are reported to have visited the early Chishti sufis, who believed and preached that the highest form of prayer was the removal of misery of those in distress.[1] Several Sufi practices were borrowed from the rituals of the local Hindus.[2] The famous Siddha treatise, *Amrita-Kunda*, on *Hatha-Yoga* principles, was translated into Arabic and then into Persian as early as the thirteenth century.[3] The *masnawis* and *dohas* written by the Sufis excited the imagination of the people of all classes and contributed a good deal to bring Sufism to a popular level. Badauni reports that verses from Mulla Daud's *Chandayan*, among the celebrated early Hindvi *masnawis*, occupied the distinction of having been recited even from the mosque pulpit in Delhi.[4] Similarly Mulla Qutban of Jaunpur, the author of *Mrigavati*, Manjhan, the author of *Madhumalati* and Malik Muhammad of Jayas, the author of *Padmavat*, the best-known of the Muslim Hindi *masnawis*, also show familiarity with and appreciation for Hindu mythology, Hindu manners, yogic rituals and Nath cults.[5] At a more popular level, Sufism developed several offshoots, even absorbing some evidently anti-Islamic features, without much regard for the regular Islamic rituals and prayers.[6]

The Sufi shaikhs also intervened in politics, at times supporting and at other times opposing the authorities. In the thirteenth century, when the rulers found themselves in difficulty in the face of the theologians' demand for the implementation of *sharī'a* as they projected it, requiring compulsory conversion or annihilation (*imma al-Islām, imma al-qatl*) of non-Muslim subjects, it was the Sufis and the Chishti Sufis in particular who had provided an ideological rationale for a pragmatic, more tolerant politics. In the assessment of the Sultan and his nobles, the theologians' demand was clearly impossible to carry out. It was, however, also difficult to simply set it aside.

There was little help in the manner in which the early Muslim political theorists carried the *siyasa-shari'a* discourse from the Islamic lands. The Sultan thus tried to establish his links with the Sufis in a rather exaggerated way, as is illustrated by the several anecdotes connected with his early life. Of many incidents from his past, he remembered and mentioned in public only those that included one or the other Sufi's prediction of his kingship while he was still a slave in Bukhara and Baghdad.[7] He mentions that the wealth and power that he was endowed with was all due to the blessing of the dervishes,[8] that long ago they saw gleams of royal power (*saltanat*) shining in the face of this person, that they also foresaw that due to his grace, in his worldly kingdom, religion too would be secure.[9] Nizam al-Din mentions that in his struggle against his rival Nasir al-Din Qabacha, Iltutmish had the full support of the eminent Suhrawardi Shaikh of Multan, Baha al-Din Zakariya.[10]

These incidents, almost all reported in Sufi texts, indicated the response Iltutmish received from the Sufis in his search for legitimacy. In Sufi circles and Sufi memory, he was projected as a pious and devout Muslim.[11] Hasan Sijzi, the compiler of Shaikh Nizam al-Din Aulia's conversations, records that while the Sultan attended to the business of governance all day long, in the night he kept awake bending his knees before God.[12] Nizam al-Din Auliya is reported to have said that "The lamp of his (Iltutmish) power was illumined with the light of Divine Support".

The Sufi attitude here is to be seen here in light of the conditions that prevailed around the time of the establishment of the Delhi Sultanate, both in India and Central Asia, from where the early Muslim conquerors came. The new comers, on the one hand, were surrounded by a rather hostile populace in India; on the other hand, the Mongols had torn apart the fabric of Muslim power in Central Asia. Many members of ruined ruling dynasties, noblemen, saints and scholars looked to North India as a place where they could settle in peace. The rulers of the newly-gained lands in India could not thus have afforded any policy or action which would reinforce the position of their foes. Even a temporary strategic retreat to the land beyond the Indus in the Islamic East was unthinkable. In a bid to minimize local Hindu hostility, it was pragmatic to emphasize that their conflict was only with those who challenged their paramount authority. With the rest of the local population, they had no quarrel. Delhi thus emerged as a sanctuary of Islam and Muslim migrants. A liberal and tolerant attitude to the religious and social practices of the local Hindus was adopted almost out of compulsion.

The Doctrine of *Wahdat al-Wujud*

There was also however a ground to legitimate all these political developments in the Sufi belief in unity in multiplicity, known as *wahdat-al wujud* (Unity of Being). The doctrine had interesting parallels in India and had no difficulty in accommodating numerous versions and interpretations of non-dualism given by Indian philosophers and saints.[13] The atmosphere thus appeared to be conducive for greater interaction between different sects and appreciation of their apparently divergent thoughts and practices, as all were believed to be one in the ultimate analysis. This was also expressed in the Nirguna Bhakti assertion of the fundamental unity of Hindus and Turks. The alignment of Ram with Rahim, Hari with Hazrat, Krishna with Karama, Muhammad with Mahadeva perhaps represented more than a mere verbal equation.[14]

In the sixteenth century, the influence of the ideology of *wahdat al-wujud* was very strong in northern India. Muhammad Ashraf Simnani, the ancestor of the famous saintly family of Kachhauchha (in the modern district of Faizabad) was an eloquent defender of the doctrine. Besides writing a number of treatises to explain it, Simnani popularized the use of the expression *Hama Ust* (All is He), thus emphasizing the belief that anything other than God did not exist. Rudauli (in the modern district of Barabanki) was another major Sufi centre where the doctrine received unusual nourishment. The *khanqah* of Shaikh Ahmad 'Abd al-Haqq (d. 1434) there has been mentioned as the 'clearing house' of the Hindu *yogis* and *sanyasis*. Shaikh 'Abd al-Quddus (1456-1537) was amongst the eminent sufis associated with this *khanqah*. His *Rushd Nama*—a treatise on *tauhid* (monotheism) which consists of his own Hindavi verses and those of his preceptor (*pir-i dastagir*), received inspiration from the 'syncretistic' religious milieu of Rudauli. Some of these verses with slight variations appear significantly in Nath poetry as well as in the *dohas* of Kabir.

This set of sentiments and philosophical approach found a fascinating expression in the mid-sixteenth century in the *Haqaiq-i Hindi* of 'Abd al-Wahid Bilgrami (1510-1608), in which Bilgrami sought to reconcile Vaishnava symbols and the terms and ideas used in Hindu devotional songs, with orthodox Muslim beliefs. According to Bilgrami, Krishna and other names used in such verses symbolized the Prophet Muhammad, or 'Man', or even sometimes the reality of human being (*haqiqat-i insan*) in relation to the abstract notion of the oneness (*ahadiyat)* of the Divine Essence. *Gopis* sometimes stood for angels, sometimes the human race, and sometimes its reality in relation to the relative unity (*wahidiyat*) of the Divine attributes. Braj and Gokul signified the different Sufi notions of the world (*'alam*) in different contexts, while the Yamuna and the Ganga stood for the sea of unity (*wahdat*) and the ocean of gnosis (*ma'rifat*), or otherwise the river of *hads* (origination) and *imkan* (contingent or potential existence); the *Murali* (Krishna's flute) represented the appearance of entity out of non-entity and so on.[15] There are unmistakable imprints of these doctrines on the ideas of Abu'l Fazl, the noted ideologue of Akbar`s court.[16]

With the establishment of the Mughal regime in India in the sixteenth century, however, there also began a new and very powerful Sufi tradition, the doctrinal basis of which was radically different from even diametrically opposed to the one that had nourished the erstwhile religious and cultural synthesis. This was the doctrine of *Wahdat al-Shuhud*, propounded and promoted by the newly arrived Naqshbandi shaikhs, who had virtually served as the royal *pirs* of the Mughals in Central Asia. They challenged the validity of *Wahdat al-Wujud*. The trajectory to the non-sectarian politics that we generally associate with Akbar was thus not so smooth. Still under the Mughals, or at least under the early Mughals, non-sectarian politics scaled the highest pinnacle. The course of Sufi-Sultan relations as they evolved during the early decades of the Mughal rule thus assume special significance, and for a better appreciation of it, we may go back to Central Asia, whence the Mughals and the new Sufi shaikhs came.

The Mughals and the Naqshbandi Shaikhs in Central Asia

In the late fourteenth century, the Mughals' great ancestor Amir Timur himself is reported to have maintained close relations with Amir Kulal, the *pir* and preceptor of Shaikh Baha al-Din Naqshband, after whom the eponymous *silsila* came to be known.[17] In the fifteenth century, however, things changed with the emergence of Khwaja Ubaid-Allah Ahrar (d. 1490), the second great figure in the *silsila* after Baha al-Din, with whom the Naqshbandis expanded the frontiers of their influence far beyond Mawarannahr into Iran and Ottoman territory. Now, the relationship between a Naqshbandi master and his disciples, in particular the ones associated with power, also acquired a special social and political significance. Khwaja Ahrar was not only the spiritual preceptor (*pir*) but also a kind of paramount political patron of his disciples, amongst whom were a large number of the Timurid rulers and their nobles in Central Asia.[18] He saw himself as having been divinely ordained to protect the Muslims from the evil of oppressors (*Musalmanan ra az sharr-i zalama nigah darim*) and to help them achieve their purpose (*maqsud-i Muslimin bar-awurdan*).[19] This he thought he could achieve by "trafficking with kings and conquering their souls" (*ba padshahan bayast ikhtilat kardan wa nufus-i ishan ra musakhkhar kardan*). There was a clear awareness of a political role that he believed he had been assigned to play, and this was something *new* and *different* from a mere loyalty to the *shari'a* which the earlier Shaikh Baha al-Din had insisted upon.[20]

Ahrar's power and triumph is to be explained perhaps more in terms of his enormous and unprecedented wealth and organizing skill than his spiritual and Sufi qualities. He was probably the biggest single landowner of Central Asia of his time. He possessed thousands of acres of the best irrigated lands in Tashkent, Samarqand, Bukhara, Kashkadaria and other places.[21] These properties were critical for the system of protection and patronage that Ahrar developed. This included an economic network, in which a large number of people and officials, many of whom not even his spiritual disciples, were involved.[22]

Babur's own father 'Umar Shaikh Mirza was also a disciple of the Khwaja, who often visited the Mirza and treated him as his son.[23] A measure of the Khwaja's intimacy with the Mirza was the fact that at Babur's birth, he was " requested to choose a name for the child and he blessed him with the name of Zahir al-Din Muhammad. [But a]t that time the Chaghatai were very rude and uncultured (...), and not refined (...) as they are now; thus they found Zahir al-Din Muhammad difficult to pronounce, and for this reason gave him the name of Babur".[24] Although Khwaja Ahrar had died by the time Babur rose to power, the prince nevertheless attributed several of his achievements to the Khwaja's blessings. For example, shortly before he took Samarqand in 1501, Babur saw the Khwaja in a dream, and with the blessings of the Khwaja "[he] really took Samarkand a few days later."[25]

Between 1500 and his conquest of India, Babur came into contact with Shah Isma'il Safavi and with his help avenged himself upon the Uzbeks for the devastation they had wreaked on the Timurids and their associates in Central Asia. Because of his close relations with the Safavid Shah, Babur is also alleged to have temporarily developed Shi'a leanings. A Naqshbandi shaikh of the time, Ahmad ibn Jalal al-Din Khwajagi, reportedly, admonished him for his seeking help from the Shah of Iran and asked him instead to accept Shaibani Khan as a *khalifa*.[26] Be that as it may, Babur nevertheless remained a lifelong devotee of Khwaja Ahrar. Of interest here is an anecdote pertaining to Babur's victory over Ibrahim Lodi in the battle of Panipat in 1526. The anecdote is reported by a seventeenth-century historian, Muhammad Sadiq. Sadiq writes that as Babur's army was too small in opposition to a near-countless Afghan brigade, he felt overwhelmed and feared that he might lose the battle to the enemy. He then contemplated the image of Khwaja Ahrar as he had heard it described. All at once there appeared a horseman dressed in white, fighting against the Afghans, who were thereupon completely routed. Later, after the fight, one of his nobles told Babur—when he narrated the incident to them—that the horseman in white as he described was Maulana Ahmad Khwajagi. The same day, Babur sent one of his close courtiers to Khwajagi with several gifts together with a portrait drawn on a piece of paper.[27] The saint seems to be the same Ahmad Khwajagi who had earlier resented Babur's seeking help from the Safavid Shah. The letter sounds like a statement of repentance for Babur's earlier comportment and a reaffirmation of his devotion to Khwajagi Ahmad in particular, and to the Naqshbandi saints in general.

Though Babur himself does not mention this incident, his continuing faith in and loyalty to the Naqshbandi order is pretty clear. On November 6, 1528, when he fell ill in India, he decided to render into poetry a treatise of Khwaja Ahrar entitled *Risala-i Walidiya* with a belief that this was how he would be able to cure himself of the disease.[28] Babur also invited to Hindustan Khwaja Ahrar's grandsons and his great-grandson. At a feast that he gave in their honor in Agra in 1528, they were seated at his right and received rich presents.[29]

However, they did not choose to stay in India. In fact, one of them, Khwaja Khawand Mahmud set out for India only in the spring of 1530, and Babur had already died before his arrival. He was nevertheless received in Agra with great honour by the new ruler, Humayun.[30] Soon however, "for some [unspecified] reasons", he left for Kabul and died there.[31] In Dughlat's account, there is a clue to the reason why he did not stay at Humayun's court. Khwaja Khawand had apparently come with the intention of occupying the exclusive position of the royal spiritual master. But while Humayun welcomed and showed respect to him, he was also simultaneously devoted to a Shattari Sufi saint, Shaikh Phul, "for he, Dughlat writes, had a great passion for the occult sciences—for magic and conjuration".[32] The sorcery and magic that Dughlat mentions were the Sufi prayer and litanics known as *da'wat-o-asma-i hasana*, in vogue among the Shattaris in India. Humayun's fascination with the Shattari saints, we may guess, could have been because of his own interest in astronomical sciences.

Dughlat's account, which includes Humayun' brother Mirza Kamran's relations with the Khwaja too, shows the Timurids' continuing faith in and their devotion to the family of Khwaja Ahrar. Humayun, therefore, was perturbed over the Khwaja's decision to depart from his court, and begged him to stay, but the latter would not listen to his entreaties. Dughlat also notes that in those days, he often heard the Khwaja say: "I have seen in a vision, a great sea which overwhelmed all who remained behind us in Agra and Hindustan; while we only escaped after a hundred risks"; and Humayun's defeat at the hands of Sher Shah eventually came about three years later, just as the Khwaja had predicted.[33] The unfortunate Humayun thus missed the blessings of the Naqshbandi Khwaja of his ancestral homeland. However, his relations with the Khwaja appear to have been somewhat restored later.

The Mughals were connected with some of the great Naqshbandi lineages matrimonially too. A daughter of Babur was married to Nur al-Din Muhammad, a descendant of Khwaja 'Ala al-Din 'Attar, who was the first *khalifa* (or disciple) of Khwaja Baha al-Din Naqshband. Their daughter, Salima Begam, as we will see below, was later married to the powerful Mughal noble Bairam Khan. Humayun's younger son, Mirza Muhammad Hakim, the ruler of Kabul, gave his sister, Fakhr al-Nisa in marriage to Khwaja Hasan Naqshbandi, a descendant of Baha al-Din Naqshband, after the death of her first husband, Abu al-Ma'ali. Khwaja Hasan thus became very powerful in Kabul for a time in the later sixteenth century.[34]In the early phase of Mughal settlement in Hindustan, the presence of certain Naqshbandi saints as *pirs* (but not necessarily as the royal *pir*) and as important members of the Mughal elite, is thus unmistakable.

The second phase of Timurid contact with the subcontinent begins with Humayun's return from his exile in Iran. Humayun, as we know, died soon after his return and resumption of power in Delhi. The process of recovery of the lost territory, its consolidation and further expansion only took place in Akbar's time. We may now turn to how the Naqshbandi Khwajas figured at this critical juncture of the shaping of Mughal power.

Akbar encounters the Central Asian Shaikhs

At the beginning of Akbar's reign (1556-1605) Khwaja 'Abd al-Shahid, who had earlier visited Babur's court, arrived anew from Samarqand. Akbar received him "with respect and kindness" and granted him a *pargana* in Punjab, where he lived for about two decades, was widely respected, with people from all walks of life visiting him to acquire grace from his holy presence. The Khwaja, according to the chronicler Bada'uni, was a symbol based on the earlier model of Khwaja Ahrar. In 1574, however, the Khwaja left India. The reason and occasion for the Khwaja's departure seems to have been the rapid decline of the Naqshbandis from the favour of the Emperor. To gain a clearer sense of this decline, we may examine the career of another noted Naqshbandi, Sharaf al-Din Husain, who also visited Akbar's court early in his reign. Sharaf al-Din Husain too rose in eminence in the Mughal court through the influence of Maham Ananga and Adham Khan, important figures of the early years of Akbar's reign. He received the high rank of *amir*, and was given grants in Ajmer and Nagor. The emperor gave him his half-sister Bakhshi Banu Begam in marriage.[35] In the 8th year of Akbar's reign, his father Khwaja Mu'in "hearing of his son's exaltation and grandeur", also arrived from Kashghar, and received from the emperor respect and treatment, and favours such as "kings show to dervishes".[36]

The Naqshbandis at this stage were held "in great esteem", to the extent that Mulla Mubarak, whom Bada'uni portrays as a man opportunistically inclined doing what was most rewarding at a given moment, "adapted himself to their rule".[37] Soon after, however, the Naqshbandis' position seems to have declined, even though some of them held a couple of offices until about the end of the 1570s. A major factor behind the turn in the Emperor's attitude could have been the revolt of Sharaf al-Din Husain himself in 1560s. Akbar decided to tackle this with an uncompromising firmness. He refused to listen to any plea, even to Khwaja 'Abd al-Shahid's recommendation on the matter,[38] which must have disappointed the Khwaja and forced him in 1574 to leave for Samarqand. Bada'uni writes that the saint "felt much grief at the refusal [to accept his advice] and left much saddened, even though the emperor did not neglect any marks of due honour and respect".[39]

Towards a New Regime

The grief of the Khwaja, however, seems to be much more because of the new developments at Akbar's court, where, he realized, there would be little place left for the Mawarannahri Naqshbandis to live in their erstwhile style. In several modern writings on Mughal India, we have excellent accounts of the details of these developments.[40] Without repeating them here, a few choice details from those accounts will suffice here. In the first place were a series of Akbar's policies in consideration of the religious susceptibilities of his non-Muslim subjects. The most momentous of these was the emperor's marriage to a Rajput princess early in his reign, and a number of administrative measures such as the abolition of pilgrimage taxes and the hated *jizya*, and cessation of the forcible conversion of prisoners-of-war to Islam. Secondly, by the mid 1560s there had also evolved a new pattern of emperor-noble relationship which suited the needs of a new Mughal state, to be defended now by a nobility of diverse ethnic and religious groups, amongst whom the Hindus and the Shi'as now occupied a significant position. The Mughals were originally Hanafite Sunnis and Akbar too, until the 1570s at least remained faithful to this tradition. On the other hand, the new non-Muslim and non-Sunni recruits into Mughal state service were not asked to abandon their old customs and beliefs. On the contrary, several non-Muslim rituals began to be integrated into the emerging Mughal dispensation.

Further, the years between 1560 and 1575 also saw a rapid change in the position of the Chaghatai nobles, mainly intended by the emperor to buttress the power around his person. The revolts by the old guard—the Mirzas, the Qaqshals and the Atka Khail, for instance—, which followed and also precipitated measures aimed at weakening their strength, showed the intensity of their disapproval and resistance to this change. Their *jagirs*, hitherto concentrated in one region, were dispersed, while nearly all the civil and financial offices were now being staffed by the non-Chaghatai groups.[41] The fortunes of the Naqshbandis, who had an established affinity with the Chaghatais, according to one report, were previously ensured because of the high and unmatched strength of the latter in the early years of Akbar's reign.[42] Their preeminence then would very likely suffer a serious setback in the wake of the increasing corrosion of the power of the Chaghatai nobles.

Akbar thus moved away from the pattern of rulership of the erstwhile Timurids, in which power was shared in a measure with members of the nobility and the Naqshbandi Sufi lineage, to a kind of universal kingship, emphasizing the undisputed and all-encompassing power of the ruler. Akbar's new image of power clashed with Naqshbandi ideals. Akbar's new imperial capital, Fathpur Sikri was built in large measure in deference to the place's association with a saint, but it was he, the emperor, not the place or the saint, who was to be lauded as the centre of authority in the new Timurid polity in India.[43] The new regime that he envisaged was also incompatible with the Naqshbandi Khwajas' perception of a Muslim state. In their view, a major task of the ruler with whom they had contact, as is illustrated from Khwaja Ahrar's relations with the rulers of his time, was not simply to ensure the welfare (*rifahiyat*, *khair*) of the Muslims, but also to discourage and abolish the customs of strangers (*rusum-i biganagan*). Muslim society was to be totally free from the evil (*sharr*) of non-Muslim social practices, an ideal manifestly not upheld by Akbar's state.[44]

The Naqshbandi shaikhs were accustomed to great influence. We have discussed Khwaja Ahrar, but after him too, several other saints of the lineage combined wealth with their spiritual accomplishments to strengthen their intervention in the political domain. Khwaja Ju'ibari and Khwaja Mushtari, two members of the same family of Naqshbandi shaikhs in Uzbek-ruled Mawarannahr, were also celebrated for their legendary wealth. Their joint property is said to have surpassed even that of Khwaja Ahrar.[45] Makhdum-i A'zam (d.1543), a disciple of Maulana Muhammad Qazi (d. 1516), a noted *khalifa* of Khwaja Ahrar established an ascendancy over the ruler of Kashghar in the same way as had Khwaja Ahrar had over the earlier Timurid Sultans. The power in his family remained for decades, until in 1678 one of his descendants, Khwaja Afaq dislodged the ruler in Yarkand and became the ruler himself.[46] The Naqshbandi Ahrari shaikhs, who had a strong memory of a share in power, would then have found it difficult to adjust to a political environment under Akbar where the king not only asserted his sole authority, but could also ignore the recommendation of a Naqshbandi sheikh who was a direct descendent of the great Khwaja Ahrar.

Akbar thus weaned himself away from the Naqshbandis, in part because he had lately begun to see, in the activities of several supporters of the lineage at the court of his half-brother in Kabul, Mirza Hakim, and in their contact with the people of his court, the seeds of a formidable challenge to his ambition for exclusive state power. In early 1580s, when the emperor assigned the task of suppressing several serious rebellions in Gujarat and in the east to his nobles and deputies, he led and commanded in person the expedition to deal with Mirza Hakim in Punjab.[47] Kabul later served as the centre for re-launching the Naqshbandi order in India, even after the termination of Mirza Hakim's regime. However, in distancing himself from the Naqshbandis, Akbar did not turn indifferent to the Sufis in general. Like Iltutmish, he came to look for legitimacy from the non-Naqshbandi shaikhs, in particular the Chishtis. Considering that the Chishtis had earlier been close to the Afghan rulers, it is worth reviewing their response.

The Mughals and the Chishti Shaikhs

In 1526, when Babur established Mughal power in the subcontinent, Shaikh 'Abd al-Quddus Gangohi, a member of the Sabiri branch of Chishti order, was probably the most noted Sufi shaikh, with his deputies (*khalifas*), disciples (*murids*) and ordinary associates (*mutawassils*) spread over almost the entire upper northern Indian plain. They belonged to diverse groups, ranging from lowly weavers and peasants to the very high members of the political class, including the reigning monarch and many of his courtiers, nobles and commanders. Gangohi, like many Afghan nobles of the time, was unhappy with Ibrahim Lodi (r. 1517-26), though unlike them he did not welcome the Mughals who he saw as a scourge, set loose as divine retribution in the world of the sinful Afghans. But as he was nearly the sole royal *pir* of the Afghans, he was persuaded by his disciples to join with them in the Afghan camp, in order to bless them and pray for them in their fight against the Mughals. Gangohi anticipated the Afghan defeat, thought of fleeing, but eventually managed only to send his family away to Gangoh. He was constrained to stay back with Ibrahim Lodi's army along with his eldest son, Shaikh Hamid and his servitor (*khadim*), Sayyid Raja. With the Lodi Sultan's defeat and death, he fell into the hands of the Mughals, who first forced him to undo his turban, which they then threw around the necks of his son and *khadim*. The elderly *pir* of the Afghans was then forced to walk on foot from Panipat to Delhi, a distance of some forty miles, while his son and *khadim* were tied to the saddle of a horse by the long turban of the Shaikh.[48] Soon after, he was released, and he then spent the last eleven years of his life in Gangoh, where he died in 1537.

In 1530, when Babur died, the Afghan struggle against Babur's son Humayun continued unabated, and throughout these years, Gangohi remained opposed to the Mughals. He even allegedly had support and admiration for Sultan Bahadur Shah of Gujarat and the Sur chief Sher Khan, the arch-enemies of Humayun, while a disciple of his had a vision of driving Humayun away "in order that Islam may grow strong and there may be stability in the land".[49] It was believed that it was with Gangohi's blessings that Sher Shah could defeat Humayun and forced him to flee Hindustan.[50]

Gangohi, however, also seems to have tried periodically to develop good relations with the newly arrived Mughals. We have letters by him to Babur, Humayun and also to a Mughal noble, Tardi Beg. Besides the routine exhortations for pious acts and generous care for the learned and the saintly, Gangohi, in particular in his letter to Babur, also projects himself as an orthodox Sunni advocate of a rather narrow and bigoted juristic version of the *shari'a*.[51] Here, he somewhat contradicts his own position earlier elaborated in his *Rushd Nama*.[52]

Whether he succeeded in his effort or not is a moot point. There is not much evidence in the existing contemporary sources, political or Sufi, to show his, and for that matter of any other Chishti shaikh's, regular and sustained connection with the early Mughals. The position of *pir* to Babur and Humayun was still a preserve of the Naqshbandis of Mawarannahr.[53] Abu al-Fazl, however, mentions that Humayun with some of his companions at times used to visit Gangohi, and spend some time in his divinely inspired and animated assembly to experience truth and gnosis.[54] This mention was then copied with obvious additions and hyperbolic effects in almost all the later Chishti *tazkiras* and also in some Mughal chronicles. Among the principal Sufi *tazkira* writers who did so was the noted seventeenth-century scholar, 'Abd al-Rahman Chishti, the author of the *Mir'at al-Asrar*.[55] This embellished image of the long-standing nature of the Mughal-Chishti connection may be best understood in light of Akbar's endeavour to build his power in ways that differed markedly from earlier Timurid patterns.

I may mention here that Akbar's leanings to the Chishtis were not because their concerns were purely 'spiritual' and other-worldly or because they had no taste whatsoever for power and politics. Their past too had seen cases of conflict with rulers.[56] A significant feature of Chishti politics, as we briefly saw above, had, however, been their support to rulers in their endeavour to adjust the nature of Muslim power to the Indian environment.[57] In some Chishti treatises of Akbar's time, the Chishti doctrine of the *Wahdat al-Wujud* was expressed and elaborated in a much more forceful language. "The whole world is a manifestation of love (*'ishq*), and we see everything as perfect," writes a sixteenth century Chishti sheikh. He continues: "As you begin *iradat* (become a *murid* and join the order) you stop quarrelling over *kufr* and *iman*. There is no precedence of one religion over the other...After you experience the limitlessness of unbounded Beauty you can see His Grace present both in a *kafir* and a Muslim."[58] Nothing could have provided a stronger support to 'Akbar's dream'. Further, no Chishti shaikh ever amassed wealth comparable to that of Khwaja Ahrar and the Ju'ibaris. On the contrary, the Chishtis had generally pleaded for a kind of asceticism, and preferred to advise and bless the political authorities from a distance.

Akbar's visits to the shrine of Khwaja Mu'in al-Din, the founder of the Chishti *silsila* in India illustrate best his fascination with the order. According to Abu al-Fazl, one night, while on a hunting expedition in a village near Agra, Akbar heard people singing Hindi verses in praise of the Khwaja. The emperor was impressed by the saint's popularity, and thenceforthhe would often discuss the Khwaja's "perfections and miracles", and developed a "strong inclination" to visit to the shrine.[59] In the late 1560s, the emperor had invoked the *baraka* of Khwaja Mu'in al-Din Chishti for the survival of a child.[60] Later, Akbar undertook several journeys to Ajmer including one entirely on foot all the way from Fathpur to the holy city of the saint. Akbar's fascination with Chishti saints was not confined to Khwaja Mu'in Al-Din. He had also earlier visited the tomb of Nizam al-Din Auliya in Delhi, and in 1569 he began the construction of palaces in Fathpur Sikri, the abode of Shaikh Salim Chishti, through whose prayers Akbar believed he was blessed with a son who was named after the Shaikh.[61]

The new Akbar, as an exclusive devotee of the Chishti saints, both dead and alive, showed not simply concern for the religion of the others; he tried to facilitate conditions for the people *(jamhur anam)* to appreciate each other's religion and tradition as well. Here, one may note Abu'l Fazl's account of Akbar's motives in commissioning the translation of *Mahabharat.* In his introduction to the epic's Persian translation, he writes:

> The generous heart [of His Excellency] is naturally inclined toward the well-being of all the classes of the people *(islah-i ahwal-i jami' tabaqat-i baraya)*; friend and foe, relations and strangers are all equal in his far-sighted view.... He noticed the increasing conflict *(niza')* between the different sects of the Muslims *(farai'q-i millat-i Muhammadi)*, on the one hand, and the Jews and the Hindus *(Juhud-o-Hunud)*, on the other, and also the endless efforts to deny each other's [faith] among them. The sagacious mind [of His Excellency] then decided to arrange the translations of the sacred books of

> both the communities *(fariqain),* so that with the blessing of the most revered and perfect soul [the Emperor] of the age, they both refrain from indulging in hostility and disputes, seek truth, find out each other's virtues and vices and endeavour to correct themselves. Also in each community *(taifa)* a group of illiterates, fanatics and petty-minded people have gained prominence. Pretending to be leaders of religion, they have misguided the people with their frauds and fallacies *(tazwirat-o talbisat)* to treat as significant those matters which are far from the path of wisdom and prudence. These inauspicious impostors *(muzawwiran-i bi sa'adat),* because of their ignorance or dishonesty, hankering after their carnal desires, misinterpret the ancient scriptures, the wise sayings and doings of the sages of the past. When the books of both these communities are rendered into simple, clear and pleasant style, simple-hearted folks would appreciate the truth and be free from the [traps of] trivialities *(fuzuliyat)* of the fools who go around pretending to be learned and wise *(nadanan-i dana-numa).* It was therefore ordered that a translation in a plain style of *Mahabharat,* which consists of the most of the basic principles and rites of the Brahmans of India and is their most honoured, most sacred and most detailed book, be prepared in collaboration of the experts of [both the Persian and the Sanskrit] languages and under the judicious scrutiny of the learned and the wise of both the communities'.

It is difficult to measure the exact impact of the translations of such books on the manner in which the two communities viewed each other. It is noteworthy, however, that in seventeenth-century Mughal India, a number of Muslim scholars included the pre-Muslim Indian past in the histories they wrote and thus gave a message to their readers to appreciate and appropriate Indian tradition as part of human history.

Further, in a proclamation of the code of conduct and a working manual (*manshur al-adab-i Ilahi wa dastur al-amal-i agahi*) issued to the managers (*muntaziman*) and officials (*karpardazan*), including the princes, the high nobles, the *mansabdars*, the '*amils* and the *kotwals* in charge of the towns and the villages throughout the empire, the passage pertaining to religion, runs as follows:

> And they (officials) should not interfere *(muta'arriz)* in any person's religion *(din-o-mazhab)*.For, wise people in this worldly matter, which is transient, do not choose a thing that harms. How can they then choose to inflict losses on themselves in matters of faith which pertain to the world of eternity? If he is right, they [the state officials] would oppose the truth [in case they interfere]; and if they have the truth with them and he is unwittingly on the wrong side, he is a victim of ignorance *(bimar-i nadani)* and deserves compassion and help, not interference and indignation *(mahall-i tarahhum-o-i'anat ast na jai ta'aruz-o-inkar)*. They should be fair, well-disposed and friendly to all (*neko-kar, khair-andish wa dostdar-i har guroh*).[62]

Noteworthy here are also two contemporary observations on the existing atmosphere of the high Mughal period. They help us have an idea of the extent to which the Mughal state either followed or disregarded the demands of narrow religious considerations. One of these is a remark of 'Abd al-Qadir Badauni, the noted historian of Akbar's time, about the reception accorded in India to Mir Muhammad Sharif Amuli, the Iranian scholar and leader of the deviant Nuqtawi sect, who had to flee Iran for fear of persecution. Badauni, as we know, was a narrow-minded and bigoted Sunni. He detested the non-orthodox ideas of Amuli and disapproved of the prevailing situation in which deviants like Amuli were welcome. He writes: 'Hindustan is a wide place, where there is an open field for all licentiousness, and no one interferes in another's business, so that every one can do just as he pleases'. The other observation of the French traveller, François Bernier who visited India in Aurangzeb's time, is of even greater significance, because the politics that I have discussed above received a setback during Aurangzeb's reign. After commenting disapprovingly on 'strange' Hindu beliefs and rituals regarding the eclipse, Bernier remarks: 'The Great Mogol, though a Mahometan, permits these ancient and superstitious practices; not wishing, or not daring, to disturb the Gentiles in the free exercise of their religion.'[63] Even in matters like *sati* (the immolation of widows), the Mughals intervened only indirectly; Bernier writes that 'They [the Mughals] do not, indeed, forbid it (*sati*) by a positive law, because it is a part of their policy to leave the idolatrous population, which is so much numerous than their own, in the free exercise of its religion; but the practice is checked by indirect means'.[64]

The doctrine of *Wahdat al-Wujud* was thus resurgent in supporting the non-sectarian politics of the new regime. Jahangir also followed the example of his father, calling himself "*mazhar-i atamm*" (the perfect manifestation of the Perfect). Like God whose grace is for all, irrespective of his/her creed, the king too belongs to every member of his subjects[65]. He had close contacts with Hindu scholars and *yogis*[66]. One Sri Kant Kashmiri, who was a scholar of high repute, and had a profound knowledge of Hindu philosophy and religion, was appointed by him as the *qazi* of Hindus.[67] He held several discussions around spiritual and religious matters with Jadrup, the noted Vaishnavite divine at Ujjain and Mathura, and saw similarity between the Vedantic philosophy of the Hindus and Sufi thoughts among the Muslims.[68]

The Mughal nobles and others from amongst the elites too were not slow in following the examples of their masters. Hakim Kamran Shirazi reportedly met Jadrup when the latter was staying at Benaras, and it was in his presence that one of the Muslim nobles came to Jadrup and sought his views regarding the Prophet Muhammad.[69] 'Abd al-Rahim Khan-i Khanan patronized an illustrated Persian translation of Ramayana. Later, the tradition expressed itself more powerfully in Dara Shukoh's effort to explore the depths of Hindu religion and in his patronage of several Sanskrit works' translations into Persian.[70] These works include *Bhagavadgita, Yoga Vasistha*, and *Probodhacandrodaya.* Dara himself, completed a translation of the Upanishads named *Sirr-i Akbar*. After a critical examination of Hindu religions, he found that all religions are identical, leading to the same goal. His work *Majma' al-Bahrain* is devoted to highlighting the similarity between the beliefs and practices prescribed in Islamic *tasawwuf* and Hindu *Yoga*. The celebrated seventeenth-century savant Chander Bhan 'Brahman' compiled a treatise known as *Mukalma-i Dara Shukoh wa Baba Lal*, around the discussion the Prince had with the saint of that name.

All this created the conditions in which many Hindu Vedantists began to feel that there were several points in the *masnawis* of Maulana Rum and Islamic *tasawwuf* which they could call their own. Some Muslims likewise began to cherish the idea that among the Hindus, there were not only idol-worshippers, but also others who had a deep belief in the monotheistic doctrine.

Among the best interpreters and defenders of the doctrine of *Wahdat al-Wujud* during this century were Shaikh Muhibb-Allah (d. 1648) and Shaikh 'Abd al-Rahman Chishti (d. ca. 1683). The reputation of some of the treatises Shaikh Muhibb-Allah wrote to expose and elaborate on his doctrines brought him into close contact with Dara Shukoh. His *Risala-i Taswiya* (Treatise on Equality) evoked a storm of opposition in orthodox circles, and later under Aurangzeb—who is reported to have taken strong exception to its contents—it was ordered to be burnt in public. Shaikh Muhibb-Allah also laid emphasis on the acquisition of mystic knowledge from Hindu *yogis*. One of his eminent disciples, Shaikh Muhammadi undertook the study of and training in *yoga* from Brahmans after he had perfected his grounding in Islamic Sufism under Shaikh Muhibb-Allah.[71]

In another case, Shaikh 'Abd al-Rahman Chishti, a descendant of Shaikh 'Abd al-Haqq of Rudauli prepared a recension in Persian of the *Gita* entitled *Mirat al-Haqa'iq* (Mirror of Realities) presenting it as an ideal exposition of the doctrine of *Hama Ust*.[72]

The Mughals appreciated what they endeavoured to do and what they had achieved. In his memoirs, Jahangir contrasts boastfully the conditions that obtained in the territory under his rule with those that obtained then in the territories in control of the Uzbeks and the Safavids in Central Asia and Iran.[73] We find echoes of Jahangir's boast outside of the court as well. In the assessment of Shaikh 'Abd al-Rahman, the Mughals ensured the supremacy of *din* by their concern for social harmony (*mashrab-i i'tidal*). In Mughal India, he noted, unlike in Uzbek Central Asia and Safavid Iran, the followers of all religions (*adyan-o-mazahib*) lived in peace and performed their rites and social practices freely. And yet the Mughals, according to him, acted in complete accord with the injunctions of their Faith (*nusus*).[74]

The desire to build an empire where both Shaikh and Brahman could live with the least possible degree of conflict, also necessitated the generation of adequate information about the diverse traditions of the land. Akbar's historian, Abu' Fazl is not content in his *Akbar-nama* with a mere description of the heroic achievements of his master; he concludes his account in what he calls as the *A'in* (institutes) of Akbar, in which he describes the revenues, the peoples or the castes in control thereof, and, above all, the social conditions and literary activity especially in philosophy and law, of the Hindus, "who form the bulk of the population, and in whose political advancement the emperor saw the guarantee of the stability of his realm".[75]

The Sufi shaikhs thus promoted conditions in which the Mughals could build a class of allies out of heterogenous social and religious groups. While this class cherished universalistic human values and visions, the emperor was seen, in the words of Keshav Das, the noted Braj poet, as *duhu din ko sahib* (the master of both religions), possessing the attributes of Vishnu, the Hindu god.[76] *Din* in this atmosphere assumed a new meaning; the king could blend 'Hindu' social practices and Rajput court rituals with his Islam at the Mughal court. These practices included a wide range like applying *tika* (the vermilion mark) on the foreheads of his political subordinates, *tuladan* (the weighing ceremony), and *jharoka darshan* (the early morning appearance of the emperor on the palace balcony), for instance.[77] The influence of the illuminationist philosophy of Shihab al-Din Suhrawardi Maqtul apart,[78] it was perhaps to highlight the affinity with the Rajputs—in whose legends fire and light occupied special position—that Abu'l Fazl emphasized the legendary origins of the Mughals themselves from light.[79] The Mughals allowed the Rajput princesses to observe their rituals ceremoniously in their palaces. On the other hand, the alliance also received nourishment from the local Hindu culture in Rajputana and developments within the Rajput society. The Rajput saw the Mughals as a sub-category of their own *jati.* The Mughal emperor in their tradition held a high rank and esteem, called *Jagat Gosain* and was often equated with Ram,[80] the Kshatriya cultural hero and ideal and exemplary king of Hindu tradition. The Rajputs began to identify themselves with the Mughal house, to be defended in the same way as their own families and houses.[81]

Before we conclude, it is relevant to ask if all this represented merely the Mughals' endeavour to use a Sufi tradition and doctrine to promote their politics without any support or appreciation for it from the Sufi quarters. An answer to this question can be found in certain seventeenth century Chishti *tazkiras.* In 1581, on his way to Punjab, Akbar visited the *khanqah* of Shaikh Jalal al-Din, in Thanesar, a noted *khalifa* of Shaikh 'Abd al-Quddus Gangohi. Akbar was accompanied by the brothers Abu al-Fazl and Faizi. They had a long conversation with the shaikh, discussed with him the secrets of Divine Realities and mystical sensibilities (*haqa'iq wa ma'arif*). The emperor, as the recorded memory in later Chishti *tazkiras* goes, was so impressed with the shaikh's response that he even expressed a desire to give up kingship. The shaikh, however, dissuaded him from doing so, saying,

> "First you find a person who can match you and sit [on the throne] in your place, and then come for this work (...). Your justice for an hour is better than the prayers of a thousand of saints. Piety and sainthood for you lies in your being just to God's people (*khalq-i Khuda*) and in conferring benefits upon them. Remember God. Kingship does not prevent you from remembering Him".[82]

The Shaikh's response showed his appreciation or legimization of Akbar's authority much the same way as we saw earlier in Nizam al-Din Aulia's remarks about Iltutmish. The Chishti Sufis went even further in legitimating Mughal authority in attributing its source to their own ranks: Abd al-Rahman Chishti explains Akbar's power nearly solely in terms of Khwaja Mu'in al-Din Chishti's grace/*baraka*. He writes that when the fourteen year-old Akbar ascended the throne upon the death of Humayun in 1556, he became the sole ruler of the entire country with the spiritual blessing of the great Khwaja Mu'in al-Din Chishti. The Khwaja bestowed upon him and his descendents the rule of the country. Akbar returned his debt through sincere devotion to the Khwaja, visiting his shrine in Ajmer several times, building a grand mosque there, helping to settle the town, making arrangements for the safety and convenience of its residents.[83] Jahangir surpassed his father in his devotion and sincerity to the Khwaja, augmented the grants and visited the shrine in extreme humility and servitude, on occasion remaining in Ajmer for years together. After his death, Shah Jahan bestowed incalculable munificence upon the descendents of the caretakers of the shrine, and other people, associated with it, and enhanced the grant for it and built a magnificent mosque of marble in its precincts.[84] For both Akbar and Jahangir, Chishti uses the epithet, *rahima-hu-Allāh*, routinely used for a saint and meaning "May God bless him." This is noteworthy in the case of Akbar in particular, known in other significant Sufi literature— notably that of the Naqshbandi Mujaddidi, which has percolated into the memory of South Asian Muslims— as the defiler of Islam.

With regard to Jahangir, Chishti also adduces some details to emphasize the emperor's intimacy with the contemporary saints, including his own self. Chishti mentions a certain Saiyid Muhammad with whom Jahangir once had a long meeting, affirming his commitment to seeking the Truth, even placing his rulership at the command of the saint. The emperor confessed to the saint that he was unable to give up drinking, since he had become addicted to it since his childhood; he also admitted that he was unable to perform the daily five time prayers regularly. With this frank statement, the emperor sought Saiyid Muhammad's guidance (*hisbatan lillah mara rah-i Khuda benumayed)*. The following was the saint's response:

> According to our saints, prayer is the principal part of religion and so is abstaining from drinking. Because of your good intention, however, you have entered already into the circle of the Friends of Truth (*dūstdārān-i haqq*). God has created everyone for a particular task. You have been given the *khilāfat* and the country to rule. Your job is to protect this God-given country and fulfill the needs of the people with justice. Do keep remembering God all the time and regard Him as ever present and watchful. This is your duty (*haqq shināsī*) and that is sufficient.[85]

Chishti recounts that when Shaikh Usman, a Qadiri shaikh who was then in Agra, heard about this incident, he was delighted and also blessed the emperor. (Here, it is worth noting that the circle gathered in Chishti's image of sufis around the figure of the emperor admitted Qadiri sufis, but not Naqshbandis.)

The connections Chishti draws between the emperor and the Sufi saints sometimes had a more practical bent, namely an association with the management of the state. This point is illustrated nicely when Chishti notes that, while the state was under the care of Shaikh Pir Shattari, the king's person was to be taken care of by his own *murshid*, Shaikh Hamid Chishti, who died in 1622.[86] Since nobody was appointed in his place, the king, who fell ill upon his return from Kashmir, took a turn for the worse, leading eventually to his death. The role of Sufis in this vital task is again highlighted in a more personal way when Chishti recounts the penultimate days of Shah Jahan's rule. He noted that after Shaikh

Firoz, who had the responsibility of taking care of the person of the emperor, died in the month of Ramadan, the condition of the emperor began to deteriorate. Chishti himself was then appointed to his care, but fell ill in 1655, just four days after the emperor was struck with illness. For a few years, Chishti and the emperor were bedridden and thus the task of protecting the country could not be performed properly, despite the fact that there were several other persons present and active. Chishti draws a direct connection between the unfortunate and unavoidable slackening of Chishti vigilance and the consequent chaos which led to the war of succession, resulting in the eventual ascension of Aurangzeb, who in the words of Chishti rose to power with "the consensus of the *'ulamā* of the time," implying that Aurangzeb did not command the support of at least a section of the Chishti shaikhs.[87] (The *sama'* and *muhtasib* anecdote from *Sawati' al-Anwar* could be recounted here).

As for Shah Jahan, since he was trained by a Sufi, he was not only a true follower of *ahl-i sunna wa jamā'a* as understood in general by the Sufis, but the emperor reached a very high level of *tasawwuf* in his own right. While in Akbarabad, Chishti reports seeing the Prince Shah Jahan visiting Shaikh Sufi every day to learn not only about Sufic texts but also to read the *Tabqāt-i Nāsirī*, a historical text by Minhaj al-Din al-Siraj.[88] Amongst the valuable sciences the Sufi taught him was also the sciences of the exegesis of the Qur'an, *Hadīs* and different Sufic texts.[89] Chishti thus believed that it was destined that the emperor spent his last years like an ascetic (*tarikīn*), interpreting Shah Jahan's incarceration as a God-gifted spiritual opportunity for him to perfect his soul. Thus, in the final seven years of his life, Shah Jahan spent his days worshipping Allah, reciting Qur'an, and studying the books of exegesis of the Quran and Hadith. For Shah Jahan too Chishti uses the epithet, *Rahima-hu-Āllah.* [90] Such was the Chishti Sufi Saikh's evaluation of the new Mughal politics, a radically different perspective from that of the followers of the contemporary Naqshbandi tradition.

It was in the world of this politics that the poets aspired to build a new ka'aba:

> Biya ki ru ba-mihrab gah-i nau benehim,
> Bina'i 'Ka'ba-i digar ze sang-i Tur nehim
> Come, let us turn our face toward a new altar,
> we take stones from the Sinai and build a new Ka'aba.
>
> Faizi

And claimed that

> 'Arif ham az Islam kharabast-o-ham az kufr
> Parwana chiragh-i-haram o dair nadanad
> (The mystic is in ruins, both due to Islam and due to infidelity
> The moth doesn't distinguish between the candle in a mosque and a lamp in a temple.)
>
> Urfi Shirazi

In the weave of the sentiment of these verses, one can discern both the weft of the Mughal's pragmatic political innovations and the warp of Sufi ideology as it was brilliantly articulated by the Chishtis. If the Mughals elaborated a new synthesis of power, adapting Central Asian traditions of rulership to the demands of imperial rule amidst a diverse, non-Muslim populace, the Chishtis equally adapted the Sufi ideology and practice of *Wahdat al-Wujud* to the new religious and political landscape of Hindustan. In the mutuality and intertwining of Mughal and Chishti discourses, one can find a unique paradigm of Muslim rule and religious practice in a peculiarly South Asian context.

Notes and References

1. Amir Hasan Sijzi, *Fawa'id al-Fu'ad*, Lucknow, Nawal Kishore, pp. 13-14, 68 and 147; Amir Khwurd, *Siyar al-Auliya*, Delhi 1302 AH/1884-1885, pp. 38-39 and 46.
2. *Faw'aid al-Fu'ad*, pp. 137, 158-159; K.A. Nizami, ed., *Khair al-Majalis*, Aligarh, 1959, pp. 65, 66 and 150; cf also K.A. Nizami, *Some Aspects of Religion and Politics in India during the Thirteenth Century*, reprint; Delhi, 1974, pp. 178-179 in particular for the significance and meanings of the circulation of *zanbil*, and the *chilla-ye makus* ('inverted' *chilla*).
3. S.A.A. Rizvi, *History of Sufism in India*, Vol. I, Delhi, 1978, pp. 335.
4. 'Abd al-Qadir Badauni, *Muntakhab al-Tawarikh,* Vol. I, p. 230; for an analysis of *Chandayan* cf. Savitri Chandra, *Social Life and Concepts in Medieval Hindi Bhakti Poetry*, Delhi 1983, pp. 21-32.
5. For some comments on these Sufi poets of Hindvi cf. A. Rashid, *Society and Culture in Medieval India 1206-1556,* Calcutta 1969.
6. Ja'far Sharif, *Qanun-i Islam*, English tr. by G.A. Herklots, reprint; London, 1972, pp. 195-196, 289-292, 295-296; Aziz Ahmad, *An Intellectual History of Islam in India*, Edinburgh, 1969, pp. 44-45.

7. For these stories, and others pertaining to Iltutmish, see K.A. Nizami, *Salatin-i Dehli ke Mazhabi Rujhanat*, Delhi, 1958; Idem, *Studies in Medieval Indian History and Culture*, Allabhad, 1966, pp. 15-18.
8. Minhaj al-Siraj, *Tabaqat-i Nasiri*, Calcutta, Bibliotheca Indica, 1863, p. 167.
9. Nizami, *Studies*, p. 17.
10. *Fawa'id al-Fu'ad*, p. 120.
11. *Khazinat al-Asfiya*, p. 275.
12. *Fawa'id al-Fu'ad*, p. 213.
13. Cf. Rizvi, *History of Sufism,* Vol. I, pp. 322-96 for an abundance of details in this respect. Rizvi discusses Sankara's *advaita*, Ramanuja's *visishtadvaita*, Nimbarkar's *dvaitadvaita* and Chaitanya's *achinta-bhedabheda* and shows similarities between these and the doctrine of *wahdat al-wujud.*
14. For a different view cf. Aziz Ahmad, *Studies in Islamic Culture in the Indian Environment*, reprint; Karachi, 1970, pp. 144-145.
15. Mir 'Abd al-Wahid Bilgrami, *Haqaiq-i Hindi*, Aligarh Muslim University, Maulana Azad Library, Ms., Hindi translation by S.A.A. Rizvi, Kashi, V.S. 2014/1957; See also Rizvi, *Muslim Revivalist Movements in Northern India in the Sixteenth and the Seventeenth Centuries*, Agra, 1966, pp. 60-62. For Bilgrami's biography, see Mir Ghulam 'Ali 'Azad Bilgrami, *Ma'asir-ul-Kiram*, III, pp. 65-66.
16. Cf. Rizvi, *Religious and Intellectual History of the Muslims in Akbar's Reign,* pp. 339-373; Azra Nizami, *Social and Religious Ideas of Abu'l Fazl;* see also Irfan Habib, 'A political Theory for the Mughal Empire: A Study of the Ideas of Abu'l Fazl', *Proceedings of the Indian History Congress,* 59th Session, Patiala, 1998.
17.. Hamid Algar, 'A Brief History of the Naqshbandi Order' and ' Political Aspects of Naqshbandi History', in Marc Gaborieau, Alexandre Popovic and Thierry Zarcone, eds. *Naqshbandis: Historical Developments and Present Situation of a Muslim Mystical Order* (Istanbul-Paris: Institut Français d'Etudes Anatoliennes d'Istanbul, 1990), pp. 3-44 and 123-152.
18. Fakhr al-Din 'Ali ibn Husain Wa'iz al-Kashifi, *Rashhat 'Ain al-Hayat*, ed. 'Ali Asghar Mu'iniyan (Tehran: Bunyad-i Nikukari-i Nuriyani, 1977), pp. 516-69 for stories about Ahrar's relations with Sultans 'Abd-Allah, Abu Sa'id, Mahmud and Babur, for instance.
19. Ibid., p. 295.
20. I intend to maintain a distance here from the scholars who think that all through their history the Naqshbadi Sufis have been involved in one or the other sort of political activity. I have therefore emphasized the words 'new' and 'different'. See also Algar, 'Aspects of Naqshbandi History', pp. 123-52, and Jo-Ann Gross, 'Multiple Roles of a Sufi Shaikh: Symbolic Statements of Political and Religious Authority', in Gaborieau, Popovic and Zarcone, eds., *Naqshbandis*, pp. 109-21.

21. Compare O.D. Chekhovich, *Samarqand Documents* (Moscow, 1974), pp. 67, 72, 125, 244 and 247; al-Kashifi, *Rashhat*, pp. 227, 228, 246 and 328. See also Jo-Ann Gross, 'Economic Status of a Timurid Sufi Shaikh: A Matter of Conflict or Perception', *Iranian Studies*, Vol. 21, 1988, pp. 84-104. For Ahrar's estates in Kabul see also, Stephen f. Dale and Alam Payind, 'The Ahrari Waqf in Kabul in the Year 1546 and the Mughul Naqshbandiyyah', *Journal of the American Oriental Society*, Vol.119, No.2 (1999), pp. 218-33.
22. Cf. Jürgen Paul, 'Forming a Faction: The Himayat System of Khwaja Ahrar', *International Journal of Middle Eastern Studies*, Vol. 23, 1991, pp. 533-548.
23. Ibid., Beveridge trans., p. 15; Thackston translation, p. 41. Abu al-Fazl Allami, *Akbarnama*, Vol. I, ed. Agha Ahmad 'Ali and 'Abdur Rahim (Calcutta: Bibliotheca Indica, 1873), p. 219. see also *Baburnama*, Beveridge trans., p. 15, Thackston's translation, p. 41.
24. *A History of the Moghuls of Central Asia Being the The Tarihk-i Rashidi of Mirza Haidar Dughlat*, English translation by E. Denison Ross (reprint, London: Curzon Press, New York: Barnes and Noble, 1972), p. 173. *Akbarnama*, Vol. I, p. 225
25. Ibid., Beveridge trans., p. 132; Thackston's translation, p. 120.
26. See Fazl-Allah ibn Ruzbihani Isfahani, *Suluk-ul-Muluk*, British Library, London Ms. Or. 253, Preface, fol. 3a. Isfahani writes that with Babur's help, heresy, which is to say Shi'ism, spread in Mawarannahr and that he like the Iranian Shi'ite leaders played a detestable role in bringing the mosques and other religious centres of the region beyond the river Jihun under the control of the heretic Shi'as. The region was thus afire with their mischief (*fitna*). All this happened because he invited the red-capped Safavid *qizilbash* to come to his help in his fight against the Uzbeks to recover Samarqand and Bukhara. But for Ubaid-Allah Khan's gallant struggle (*jihad*), the rites and symbols of the true faith would have been completely routed in the region. See also the printed edition of this text by Muhammad 'Ali Muvahhid (Tehran: 1362 Shamsi/1984. For an English translation of this work, see Muhammad Aslam, *Muslim Conduct of State* (Islamabad:University of Islamabad Press, 1974), pp. 31-33.
27. Muhammad Sadiq, *Tabaqat-i Shahjahani,* British Library, India Office Library Ms., Ethé 705, fols. 192b-193a. Khwajagi Ahmad, a disciple of Maulana Muhammad Qazi, who was a disciple of Khwaja Ahrar, died in 949 A.H. He is buried in Dehbid.
28. *Baburnama*, trans. Beveridge, pp. 619-20; Dale, *The Garden of the Eight Paradises*, pp. 176-77.
29. *Baburnama,* trans. Beveridge, pp. 632 and 641-42; Dale, Ibid., pp. 427-28. Dale also mentions one unidentified Khwaja Chishti?
30. *A History of the Moghuls of Central Asia*, p. 398; *Akbarnama*, Vol. II, p. 301.

31. *A History of the Moghuls of Central Asia*, p. 398; Samsam al-Daula Shahnawaz Khan, *Ma'asir al-Umara*, Vol. II (Calcutta: Bibliotheca Indica, 1891), p. 575.
32. *A History of the Moghuls of Central Asia*, pp. 398-399. See also Persian text edited by Wheeler M. Thackston (Cambridge, Mass.: Harvard University Press, 1996), pp. 345-47. See also 'Abd al-Qadir Bada'uni, *Muntakhab al-Tawarikh*, ed. by Kabiruddin Ahmad, Ahmad 'Ali and W.N.Lees, Vol. III (Calcutta: Bibliotheca Indica, 1869), p. 4; *Ma'asir al-Umara,* Vol. II, p. 575. Humayun remained close to Shaikh Muhammad Ghaus until he lost the empire to the Afghans and fled to Iran. The Shaikh then left for Gujarat. When Humayun regained power he returned to Delhi. The emperor, however, died soon afterwards and the saint was disappointed at his reception by Bairam Khan, the regent of the young emperor, Akbar. He then retired to Gwalior where he died in 970 AH. See also K. A. Nizami, 'Shattari Saints and their Attitude towards the State', *Medieval India Quarterly*, Vol. 1, No. 2, 1950, pp. 56-70.
33. *A History of the Moghuls of Central Asia*, pp. 399-400; *Ma'asir al-Umara,* II, 575. Ross's translation of the phrase "*wa sargardan raft*" here is confusing. He adds the name of Maulana Muhammad in square brackets and translates the phrase as "[Maulana Muhammad] returned stupefied".
34 *Muntakhab al-Tawarikh,* Vol. II, p. 72. Commenting on Khwaja Hasan's absolute power some of the wits of the period used to say:

   If our Master be Master Hasan
   We shall have neither sack nor rope left.

   For his and other Naqshbandis position at Mirza Hakim's court in Kabul, see Sanjay Subrahmanyam, 'A note on the Kabul kingdom under Muhammad Hakim Mirza (1554-1585)', in *La Transmission du savoir dans le monde musulman périphérique, Lettre d'information*, No. 14, 1994, pp. 89-101; Munis D. Faruqui, 'The Forgotten Prince: Mirza Hakim and the Formation of the Mughal Empire in India', *Journal of the Economic and Social History of the Orient,* Vol. 48, No. 4, 2005, pp. 487-523.
35. *Akbarnama*, Vol. II, pp. 197 and 303; *Ma'asir al-Umara*, Vol. II, p. 809.
36. *Akbarnama*, Vol. II, p. 303
37. Bada'uni writes that he followed "many and various rules of life. For some time during the reigns of the Afghan emperors he used to keep company with Shaikh 'Ala'i, and in the beginning of the Emperor's [Akbar's] reign, when the Naqshbandi order was held in a great esteem, he adapted himself to their rule, and for some time he was attached to the Hamadani Shaikhs, and at last when the Iraqis were in great favour at the Court he spoke as one of their religion"; *Muntakhab al-Tawarikh*, English trans. Vol. III, p. 119.
38. *Akbarnama*, Vol. II, p. 303 for Sharaf al-Din's revolt.

39. *Muntakhab al-Tawarikh*, Vol. II, p. 174. Badau'ni also reports that the Khwaja commanded immense respect among the rulers of Kabul and Central Asia. On his way to Samarqand when he arrived at Kabul "it happened that Mirza Shah Rukh had just taken the people of Kabul captive, and was returning with them to Badakhshan. By means of the intercession of the Khwaja nearly ten thousand persons obtained deliverance (...)". Compare *Muntakhab al-Tawarikh*, Vol. III, pp. 65-66.
40. Compare, for instance, John F. Richards, 'The Formulation of Imperial Authority under Akbar and Jahangir', in Muzaffar Alam and Sanjay Subrahmanyam, eds. *The Mughal State, 1526-1750* (Delhi: Oxford University Press, 1998), pp. 126-67; Iqtidar Alam Khan, 'The Nobility under Akbar and the Development of His Religious Policy, 1560-1580', *Journal of the Royal Asiatic Society,* 1968, Parts 1-2; I. A. Khan, *The Political Biography of a Mughal Noble: Mun'im Khan Khan-i-Khanan, 1497-1575* (Delhi: Orient Longman, 1973), Introduction, pp. ix-xx.
41. I.A. Khan, *The Political Biography*, Introduction.
42. *Ma'asir al-Umara*, Vol. I, pp. 513-514.
43. John F. Richards, 'The Formulation of Imperial Authority'.
44. Compare *The Letters of Khwaja 'Ubayd Allah Ahrar and His Associates,* Persian text ed. Asom Urunbaev, English translation with notes by Jo-Ann Gross, Introductory essays by Jo-Ann Gross and Asom Urunbaev (Leiden: Brill, 2002), pp. 114, 128, 143, 145, 146, 166 and 169, letters nos. 49 (50), 59 (62), 282 (286), 284 (288), 304 (308) and 306 (310). See also Jürgen Paul, 'Forming a Faction', pp. 540-41. *Biganagan* means strangers, foreigners, which in the context implied the customs and practices introduced and established by the Mongols.
45. Compare David W. Damrel, 'Forgotten Grace: Khwaja Khawand Mahmud Naqshbandi in Central Asia and Mughal India', Unpublished Ph.D. Dissertation, Department of Religon, Duke University, 1991, pp. 80-81. Damrel cites Mansura Haider, 'Agrarian System in Uzbek Khanates of Central Asia', *Turcica*, Vol. 7, 1974, pp. 157-178, and Haider, 'Urban Classes in the Uzbek Khanates, XVI-XVII Centuries', in Graciela de la Lama, ed. *Central Asia: Papers presented at the 30th International Congress of Human Sciences in Asia and North Africa* (Mexico City: El Colegio de Mexico, 1976).
46. Compare Robert Barkley Shaw, 'The History of Khwajas of Eastern Turkistan' (ed. N. Elias), *Journal of the Asiatic Society of Bengal,* Vol. 66, Part 1, 1899, and René Grousset, *Empire of the Steppe,* cited in Algar, 'Political Aspects of Naqshbandi History', p. 128.
47. Subrahmanyam, 'A Note on the Kabul Kingdom'; Faruqui, 'The Forgotten Prince'.
48. Shaikh Rukn al-Din, *Lata'if-i Quddusi* (Delhi: Matba' Mujtaba'i, 1311 AH/1894), p. 64.
49. *Lata'if-i Quddusi,* pp. 79-80. For an English translation, see Simon Digby, 'Dreams and Reminiscences of Dattu Sarvani, a Sixteenth Century Indo-

Afghan Soldier' (in 2 Parts), *The Indian Economic and Social History Review*, Vol. 2, 1965, pp. 71-72. My translation of some of the words and phrases is different.

50. *Lata'if-i Quddusi*,p. 83; Digby, 'Dreams and Reminiscences', pp. 180-81.
51. *Maktubat-i Quddusiya,* pp. 224-25 and 335-39.
52. Simon Digby, 'Abd al-Quddus Gangohi (1456-1537 A.D.): The Personality and Attitudes of a Medieval Indian Sufi', *Medieval India- A Miscellany,* Vol. 3, pp. 1-66, in particular pp. 34-66; S.A.A. Rizvi, *A History of Sufism in India*, Vol. I (reprint, Delhi: Munshiram Manoharlal, 2003), pp. 339-49. Not much however can really be made of this apparently changed position of his, considering the fluid and ambiguous political conditions in which these letters were written. Features of indigenous devotional religion in fact continued to be part of his *tasawwuf.* He also never gave up teaching the *Rushd Nama* to his disciples. As someone recovering from the trauma and humiliation of Mughal captivity, Gangohi's uncompromisingly bigoted position in his letter to Babur could also have been intended to reinstate himself as a pious *pir*, with an unstated assertion that his close affinity with the erstwhile rulers had been for a purely religious objective, unconcerned with anything profane and this-worldly.
53. Babur however paid homage to the tombs of Qutb al-din Bakhtiyar Kaki and Nizam al-Din Auliya in Delhi. Compare Zain Khan, *Tabaqat-i Baburi*, trans. Sayed Hasan Askari, (Delhi: Idarah-i Adabiyat-i Delli, 1982), p. 92; Stephen F. Dale, *The Garden of the Eight Paradises: Babur and the Culture of Empire in Central Asia, Afghanistan and India,1483-1530* (Leiden:Brill, 2004), pp. 199 and 331. Babur also visited the shrines of some other saints, like the one of Shaikh Sharfal-Din Yahya Maneri in Bihar(Dale p. 444). Yahya was a Firdausi Suhrawardi and not a Chishti saint, as Dale mentions. For him see, S.A.A. Rizvi, *A History of Sufism in India* (reprint,Delhi: Munshiram Manoharlal, 2003), Vol.1, pp. 228-240.
54. Abu al-Fazl Allami, *A'in-i Akabari,* ed. Sayyid Ahmad Khan (reprint, Aligarh: Sir Syed Academy, Aligarh Muslim University, 2003), p. 214.
55. Compare 'Abd al-Rahman Chishti, *Mir'at al-Asrar,* British Library, Ms. Or. 216, fol. 483b ; Muhammad Akram ibn Shaikh Muhammad Ali ibn Shaikh Ila Bakhsh, *Sawti' al-Anwar*, British Library, India Office Library Ms, Ethé 654, fol. 381a. For an analysis of *Mir'at al-Asrar*, see Bruce Lawrence, 'An Indo-Persian Perspective on the Significance of Early Sufi Masters', in Leonard Lewisohn, ed., *Classical Persian Sufism from its Origins to Rumi* (London: Khanqahi Nimatullahi Publications, 1993), pp. 19-32. For 'Abd al-Rahman Chishti see also Shahid Amin, 'On Retelling the Muslim Conquest of India', in Partha Chatterjee and Anjan Ghosh, eds., *History and the Present* (Delhi: Permanent Black, 2002).
56. Digby, 'The Sufi Shaykh and the Sultan: A Conflict of Claims to Authority', *Iran*, Vol. 27, 1990, pp. 71-81; Sunil Kumar, 'Assertions of Authority: A Study of the Discursive Statements of Two Sultans of Delhi',

in M. Alam, F. N. Delvoye and M. Gaborieau, eds., *The Making of Indo-Persian Culture: Indian and French Studies* (Delhi: Manohar, 2000), pp. 37-65.

57. For a discussion around this question, see Muzaffar Alam, *The Languages of Political Islam: India 1200-1800* (New Delhi: Permanent Black, 2004), pp. 81-114.
58. Compare Mir 'Abd al-Wahid Bilgrami, *Sab' Sanabil*, Urdu translation by Muhammad Khalil Barakati (Bheondi, Maharashtra: Rizwi Kitabghar, 1981), pp. 330-31. Bilgrami wrote the treatise in Persian, of which the original is still unpublished, in 969AH/1562. Later in 974/1567 he compiled the better known, *Haqa'iq-i Hindi*, in which he gave Islamic meanings to the words and expressions explicitly 'Hindu'.
59. *Akbarnama*, Vol. II, p. 154 (text), English translation, p. 237; P.M. Currie, *The Shrine and Cult of Mu'in al-Din of Ajmer* (Delhi: Oxford University Press, 1989). p. 100; K.A. Nizami, *Akbar and Religion* (Delhi: Idarah-i-Adabiyat-i-Dilli, 1989), p. 104.
60. *Tuzak-i Jahangiri*, Thackston's translation, p. 21.
61. Richards, 'Formulation of Imperial Authority'; Currie, *The Shrine and Cult of Mu'in al-Din,* pp. 99-102 and 152-154; Nizami, *Akbar and Religion,* pp. 104-105, 111 and 117.
62. Rizvi, *Religious and Intellectual History of Muslims in Akbar's Reign* pp. 197, 355-6 and 366-369.
63. François Bernier, *Travels in the Mogul empire, 1656-1668*, English translation by A. Constable, reprint, New Delhi: S. Chand & Co., 1972, p. 303.
64. Ibid., p. 306.
65. *Majalis-i Jahangiri*
66. *Dabistan-i Mazahib,* p. 194. English transl., Vol. II, pp. 164-165.
67. Ibid., p. 194; English transl. pp. 164-165. For a detailed account of the nature of discussions which Jahangir had with the Pandits, see, *Tuzak- i Jahangiri* (text), p. 14; Eng. transl., I, pp. 32-3.
68. *Tuzak-i Jahangiri* (text), pp. 250-51, 252-53, 279, 280, 281; Eng. transl., II, pp. 49, 52-3, 104, 105, 108. Mirza Muhammad Mu'tamad Khan; *Iqbal Nama-i Jahangiri*, pp. 543-44, 556-7; *Dabistan-i Mazahib*, pp. 184-6; English transl. vol. p. 159. Jadrup died in AD 1637.
69. Ibid., p. 186; English transl.Vol. II, p. 145.
70. Compare Bikrama Jit Hasrat, *Dara Shikuh: Life and Works*. Calcutta: Vishwabharati, 1953. pp. 174-292; Kalika Ranjan Qanungo, *Dara Shukoh: volume 1, biography.* Calcutta: S.C. Sarkar & Sons, Ltd, 1952. pp. 241-268.
71. Rizvi, *Muslim Revivalist Movements*, p. 340. For an interesting discussion on the theme see Shah Muhibbullah, *Maktub Banam Mulla Jaunpur*, Maulana Azad Library, Aligarh, *Zakhira-I Ahsan*, no. 297.7/37, *Farsi Tasawwuf.*

72. Charles Rieu, *Catalogue of the Persian Manuscripts in the British Museum*, Vol. III, London, 1885, p. 1034. For a discussion on the *Mirat ul-Makhluqat*'s translation see Roderic Vassie, 'Persian Interpretations of the *Bhagvadgita* in the Mughal Period,with Special Reference to the version of Abd al-Rahman Chishti', unpublished Ph.D. thesis, School of Oriental and African Studies, University of London, 1988. See also Vassie, 'Abd al-Rahman Chishti and the Bhagavadgita: "Unity of Religion" Theory in Practice' in Leonard Lewisohn, (ed.), *The Heritage of Sufism*, Volume Two, Oxford: Oneworld, 1999. p. 367-377.
73. Jahangir, *Tuzuk-i Jahangiri*, p. 16.
74. 'Abd al-Rahman Chishti, *Mir'at al-Asrar*, British Museum, Or. 216, fol. 507a.
75. H. Blochmann's Preface to his translation of the *Ain-i Akhari*, Vol. I, reprint, Delhi, 1965.
76. Keshavdas, *Jahangir-jaschandrika*
77. Sri Ram Sharma, *The Religious Policy of the Mughal Emperors,*
78. J.F. Richards, 'The Formulation of Imperial Authority under Akbar and Jahangir', in Muzaffar Alam and Sanjay Subrahmanyam (eds.), *The Mughal State, 1526-1750,* Delhi, 1998, pp. 126-167.
79. Compare *Akbar-nama*, Vol. I, p. 122.
80. Norman P. Zeigler, 'Some Notes on Rajput Loyalties during the Mughal Period', in Alam and Subrahmanyam (eds.), *The Mughal State*, pp. 168-210.
81. This is best illustrated in Raja Ram Singh Hara's reported response to the anxiety expressed by Prince Muhammad A'zam's wife (who was a Safavid princess), who asked as to what the Raja was planning to defend her against the Marathas who were threatening her party: '(…) *asmat-i rajputiya wa asmat-i mughliya*'.
82. Muhammad Akram ibn Shaikh Muhammad 'Ali ibn Shaikh Ilah Bakhsh, *Sawati' al-Anwar*, British Library, India Office Ms. Ethé 652(I.O. Islamic 2705), fols. 389b-390b; 'Abd al-Rahman Chishti, *Mir'at al-Asrar*, British Library, Ms. Or. 216.
83. *Mir'at*, f. 230b.
84. Ibid. f.507a
85. Ibid. f.507b.
86. Ibid. f. 508a. For a reference to him and his role in initiating Abd al-Rahman into the Chishti Sabiri order, see Rizvi, *History of Sufism*, Vl. 2, p. 289.
87. *Mir'at,*ff. 508a-510a. Before Shahjahan's time too Chishti says he was in contact/sevice of the Mughal emperor. He writes that with Jahangir's permission and at his command he used to visit the northern hills, where he met Acharya Muni Bhadra, the agent of the Hill Raja and an expert of Indian hisory, from whom, he claims, he got some details about his book on Salar Mas'ud. cf. *Mir'at-i Mas'udi,* f. 92a. He reports in *Mir'at al-*

Asrar (f.508a) that he left for his village though, to live in reclusion (*gusha-i inziwa*) in 1618, when Jahangir left for Kashmir; he returned to the court apparently after Shahjahan's coming to Power. See also Rizvi, *History of Sufism*, II, pp. 288-289 and 368-369, and pp. 369-370 for the Naqshbandi saints' appreciation for Aurangzeb, who according to the author of *Khazinat al-Asfiya* (vol.I, p. 640, citing *Tazkira-i Adamiya*) was a disciple(*murid*) of Sihindi's son, Khwaja Muhammad Ma'sum Sirhindi.

88. Shaikh Sufi was a disciple of Shaikh Nizam al-Din of Amethi, an eminent Chishti saint of Awadh in the sixteenth century. See Rizvi, *History of Sufism*, Vol. 2, pp. 288-289.
89. *Mir'at,* f.508a.
90. *Mir'at,* f.510a.

11
Epic Identity and Humanism in Ancient India: A Refined Idea in a Rough World?[1]

Heeraman Tiwari

A culture of a people in many ways connotes their identity; I will begin, therefore, with the notion of identity in Classical India. Although the problem of identity in Indian thought has been discussed in many contexts, but I shall try and deal with it here from a philosophical point of view. In his engagement with the views of Rabindranath Tagore, Mahatma Gandhi had said: 'I hope I am as great a believer in free air as the great poet. I do not want my house to be walled in on all sides and my window to be stuffed. I want the cultures of all the lands to be blown about my land as freely as possible. But I refuse to be blown off my feet by any.'[2]

Individualism *vs* Universalism: A Philosophical View

In Indian philosophy, like in Greek philosophy, the problem of identity was closely connected with the problem of universals. The debate over universals and universalisation is first discussed in relation to word and its meaning. In the introduction to his Great Commentary (*Mahābhāṣya*) on Pāṇini's grammar, Patañjali[3] begins the discussion of the meaning of a word (*śabda*), and says: 'Now, what *is* the word *gauḥ*?' (*gauḥ* means cow). Patañjali then offers four possible answers: that 1) 'the word (cow) a visible object possessing a dewlap, tail, hump, hooves, (and) horns?'; 2) 'the word (cow) is shaking, moving, (and) blinking?'; 3) 'the word (cow) is white, dark, black, brown, or grey.'; 4) 'the word is that commonality which is undifferentiated among different kinds, and intact when things are cut up.' However, Patañjali rejects all the four answers as 'substance (*dravya*)', 'action (*kriyā*)' 'quality (*guṇa*)', and 'form' (*ākṛti*) respectively, and suggest further, fifth and sixth, answers: that 'the word ("cow" here) is that through the utterance of which there arises an awareness of objects possessing a dewlap, tail, hump, hooves, (and) horns.' Or, rather, 'the word is *dhvani* 'sound' which has a well-known meaning in everyday speech. For instance, "make a sound"; "do not make a sound"; "this boy is noisy" – one is so called when one makes sounds. Therefore, word is sound.'[4]

There is another view in ancient Indian philosophy that suggests that even when a word refers to a universal it always does so in relation to an individual. In other words, the referent of a word is such a property which generates awareness of commonality in a class of individuals as well as awareness of distinction from individuals of other classes. So how does an individual relate himself/herself to a larger class, say, the world, while being firmly grounded in individual identity? The answer will come, perhaps, through universal human values, for it 'is eternal and inheres in many individuals of the same class.'[5]

Humanism *vs* Self: an Ancient Dilemma?

For the sake of the present paper, let me appropriate the term 'humanism' for 'universal identity' and begin our discussion with a passage from V.S. Naipaul's latest travel writing. Almost echoing the ancient Indian notion of humanity Naipaul tries to universalise it through his perception of the treatment of animals in the service of humanity.

> "The land is full of cruelty which is hard for the visitor to bear. From the desert countries to the north long-horned cattle are sent for slaughter here in big ramshackle trucks, cargoes of misery, that bump along the patched and at times defective autoroute to Abidjan, to the extensive abattoir area near the docks. And there in trampled and vile black earth these noble creatures, still with dignity, await their destiny in the smell of death, with sometimes a calf all alone without a mother, finding comfort of a sort in sleep, a little brown circle on the dirty ground, together with the beautiful goats and sheep assembled for killing. The ground

> around the abattoir goes on and on. When sights like this meets the eyes of simple people every day there can be no idea of humanity, no idea of grandeur." [6]

In this passage Naipual ruminates on the humanity with melancholy as if he were suggesting that from the sufferings and wretched conditions of animals emerges the idea of humanity; from cruelty is born kindness. What is necessary is to be able to arrest that humanity which floats freely everywhere: the 'cargoes of misery' point the path to humanism; the wretched 'noble creatures' epitomise 'dignity', an absolute surrender to the service of human whim or requirement. The suggestion indeed appears very cruel. But if one looks at it closely, it resembles the conclusions of the Buddha: 'everything is misery', and to look for a path to emerge from this misery leads to *nirvāṇa* a complete bliss or 'state of compassion'.

Humanism in the Face of Violence

The idea of humanism is very old and in ancient India, when the Vedic and Brahmanic systems were perceived to be stained from certain excessive dogmas, Mahāvīra and the Buddha appeared on the scene to correct the human values by exhorting people to practise compassion and mercy towards all beings. Mahatma Gandhi too has tried to look for humanity in the most despicable of human conditions, almost like animal conditions described by Naipaul in the passage above. Gandhi had learnt his wounding journeys in South Africa and later in India to discover the essence of humanity from the journeys of the two great ancient Indian reformers: Mahāvīra and the Buddha. Both Mahāvīra and the Buddha carried out painful journeys. It is just that we have a better and closer account of Gandhi's journeys, and for Mahāvīra and the Buddha we have to rely on legends and stories. All three embarked on their journeys to rid the world of violence. Naipaul has compared Gandhi's journey in South Africa to "a kind of Calvary" which "altered his life and set him on the path of his life's work", that was conquering through the absence of violence, *ahiṃsā*; and this journey, according to Naipaul, turned Mahatma Gandhi from a shy young man to "a leader of men."[7] Like Mahāvīra and the Buddha, Gandhi thought of universal humanity where people will teach themselves how to be human. 'We are not really human,' Radhakrishnan said, 'if we do not feel that we are related to something that transcends the finite and the conceivable. We want not a mere improvement of the world, but an ideal transfiguration of it.'[8] The teachings of the *Bhagavadgītā*, too, hint at such an idealism and universal value or property, and there it is called *dharma*, righteousness or proper conduct or behaviour. In the Indian epic *Rāmāyaṇa,* its protagonist, Rāma, tells the monkey king, Vālin, that appropriating individualism in violation of universal *dharma* violates the essence of *dharma*, for 'righteousness or *dharma* is subtle (*sūkṣmaḥ*) and extremely difficult to realise (*parama durjñeyaḥ*), and the self in the inner core (heart) of all beings knows what is good and what is evil': *sụkṣmaḥ paramadurjñeyaḥ satāṃ dharmaḥ plavaṅgama/ hṛdisthaḥ sarvabhūtānāṃ ātmā vetti śubhāśubham.*[9] Was it not this universal *dharma* (universality of humanism) which the German poet Goethe referred to when he spoke these beautiful words?:

> '"What was it that kept you from us so apart?"
> I always read Plutarch again and again.
> "And what was the lesson he did impart?"
> "They were all human beings – so much is plain."'[10]

So how does one balance this dualism: individualism and universality? We may look for an answer in the ancient Indian epic *Rāmāyaṇa* and its traditions. As we understand it, humanism aspires to attain universal good through actions which are commensurate with universal values; but such actions always define a Utopian goal. For example, when he returns to Ayodhyā as a king, at the end of the war in Laṅkā, Rāma aspires to bring about perfect harmony and universality in his kingdom;[11] and he wishes to do so by following certain universal values which are based on equality and humanism.

Universal Humanism *vs* Utopia: Is It Viable?

Search for a perfect and most ideal society, or Utopia, has always engaged and exercised human mind. The *Bhagavadgītā* offers a world full of happiness, idealism, almost similar to the world of Homeric dream – where Kṛṣṇa advises Arjuna, when the latter is confused and distressed, almost depressed, by the prospect of having to kill his own relatives and friends in the impending war with his cousins, and presently suffers a massive nervous breakdown the symptoms of which are explicit in the text itself: *gāṇḍīvaṃ sraṃsate hastāt tvak caiva paridahyate/ na ca śaknomy avasthātuṃ bhramtīva ca me manaḥ*—'The Gāṇḍīva bow is slipping of my hands; my body is burning with fever; I can no longer remain standing, my legs are giving away, and my head is very giddy; I am about to collapse."[12] Kṛṣṇa here takes the role of an accomplished, caring psychologist and administers to his beloved patient, Arjuna, a most effective therapy by reminding him of his true identity, which is his *dharma*, the most cryptic and elusive of personal realisations, and advises Arjuna not to shirk his duty, for in so doing, Kṛṣṇa promises, Arjuna will attain the world of perpetual happiness: 'Where shines not the sun, or moon, or fire; no one ever returns from there; that is the ultimate world of mine.'[13] Ironically, this description sounds so much similar to the 'Black Hole' of the Physical universe.

The struggle for a perfect society suggested by the *Bhagavadgītā* is no different from the dream of a perfect society of the Judeo-Christian tradition.[14] The Vedānta philosophy, as we know, tries to deal with the essence of identity by espousing the soul's relationship with the world, *saṃsāra*, as engulfed in illusion. Illusion or *māyā* causes a sort of amnesia to the soul, *jīvātmā*; as a result, the soul fails to recognise its link with *Brahman*, the ultimate reality. The therapy to cure this amnesia of illusion for the soul is rumination, *nididhyāsana,* on the nature of both the world and the Brahman. The scriptures and other texts of great learning explained by a guide or a teacher help in this process. Radhakrishnan was inspired by philosophy of Vedanta, which he believed embodies complete humanism, 'the grandeur of spiritual oneness', and combines the sublime trinity of human nature—viz. religion, metaphysics and ethics—and Śaṃkara realises its fullness in his system. Radhakrishnan believed that 'in this philosophy are to be found the elements of an ethical science though not a perfected system of ethics. It is rationalistic, a type of moderate rationalism,'[15] and that the ancient Indian law of *Karma* not only connects a human individual with their past (through the memory impressions, *saṃskāras*) but also 'is a self-conscious, efficient portion of universal nature with his own uniqueness.'[16]

Past *vs* Present: the Enigma of the Connection?

But all of this refers to the fabled past, the time gone by, things that would have happened. How could the knowledge of our past, one may ask, help us today? One could say, quoting the celebrated American Sanskritist, Daniel H. H. Ingalls, that 'all dogmatic statements concerning choice of approach and motive in the study of the past are foolish. They are worse than foolish; they are pernicious.'[17] Ingalls suggests that 'it should be approached scientifically, social-scientifically or humanistically.'[18] Others have even suggested, as we shall shortly see, that the study of the past should not even be attempted. Our distant past, the argument goes, can be of little use in dealing with the challenges, circumstances and problems of modern world. Ramchandra Guha, for example, argues in his latest book, *Makers of Modern India* (Delhi, 2010) that 'there was little in the history and the politics of the remote past that could have aided Indians in interpreting and confronting the profound challenges that came in the wake of colonial rule.'[19] Guha goes on to say that despite its past history of 'hierarchy and inegalitarianism,' modern 'India can give the world the idea of a state and constitution that protects far greater religious *and* linguistic diversity than is found in any other nation. …We have demonstrated that nationalism can be made consistent with internationalism;'[20] and all this is due not to the 'richness and relevance' of India's distant past but to its 'modern political tradition'. Contribution of modern Indian tradition, according to Guha, has not been fully appreciated even by 'well-educated Indians' because of 'the widespread nostalgia for the very distant past. There is one kind of Indian who thinks that it was when the Hindu scriptures were composed that his civilization was the most advanced in the world. This orients them towards the study of sages and rulers of ancient times, in the belief that it may help the Hindus once more rule, or at least dominate, the world.'[21]

I am not advocating here that study of 'the remote past' and its traditions could help us construct or reconstruct the history of our past—or represent an ideal textual source for understanding our past—much less, it could provide ideal answers to the predicaments of today.[22] What I can say, however, is that no journey into our past can be complete and final; but if we traverse into the ancient Indian texts and their traditions that have over the centuries, some would even say millennia, shaped India's historical consciousness, with "a new angle of vision", it could help us reconstruct our ways of thinking, looking at it; it could help us prepare a "fresh cartography" of the past.[23] For even the act of writing the past, or the history of it, also involves writing oneself into it; the past cannot be fully divorced from the present and will, in all probability, linger in the future, too. Despite these various pronouncements, one can safely say that the study of the past can help us in assessing the present and preparing for the future: it 'broadens one's knowledge of man,' 'enables one to guess at the future'.[24]

However, responding to the neglect of India's contribution to ethical and political ideas in modern world, Amartya Sen has argued that there existed in India's remote past distinct, rational and scientific traditions of enquiry and debates which were anticipated and encouraged by the ancient Indian rulers. These thinkers of our distant past may have had some influence on the 'makers of modern India'.[25] Ingalls had suggested once that much treasure lies neglected in the attic of classical India that can contribute in shaping the ideas for the present and the future of both India and the West. One such treasure, suggested Ingalls, is 'the traditional Indian evaluation of human life … that may again come to be popular in many lands.'[26] One example of such an engagement with India's past could be the economist Amartya Sen' work, *Development as Freedom*, which opens with a classical Indian debate on 'the power of wealth' in fulfilling human wishes. The debate in question takes place around eighth century B.C. between sage Yājñyavalkya and his wife Maitreyī in the *Bṛhadāraṇyaka Upaniṣad.* Quoting the rhetorical questions of Maitreyī, *'How far would wealth go to help me get what I want?'* and *'What should I do with that by which I do not become immortal, if that is what I want?'*, Amartya Sen says that such a debate in Indian philosophy illustrates 'both the nature of the human predicament and the limitations of the material world.'[27] Sen's other famous recent works advocating engagement with 'the remote past' of India to understanding the nature of social and material justice are, *The Argumentative Indian* and, to some extent, *The Idea of Justice.*[28]

Suffice it to say that the modern Indian society has always struggled to find the middle ground between its extreme inegalitarian practices, bequeathed from the ancient times, and modern egalitarian ideals, adopted and nurtured in post-independent era. B.K. Matilal points to the famous Jaina logic of 'multi-faceted value' of truth (*anekāntavāda)* which suggests that the 'truth' 'is ever elusive for a single individual (or a single creed) unless he happens to be omniscient. Or, following the Buddha, one might say that emphasis on the similarity and sameness will be another form of eternalism or *śāśvatavāda*, and emphasis on the ultimate difference of annihilationism (*ucchedavāda*).'[29] Therefore, it would be prudent to follow the 'Middle Path'. Terming as 'existentialist' Max Weber's analysis of Indian ethical predicaments, represented by two seemingly conflicting notions, *dharma* vs *svadharma,* Pratap Mehta says: '[T]he rational ethical imperatives of the world find themselves in complete tension with the irrationalities of the world. The world seems constantly off balance, spiralling out of control and not responsive to the effect of ethical action' and, therefore, 'all our choices of actions are contingent…in the sense that there is no inner necessity or transcendental grounding for one choice over another.'[30] However, Wendy Doniger has suggested that this 'ethical tension' gets resolved by a kind of 'moral Teflon' in the teaching of the *Bhagvadgītā*, by the inclusion of a third choice, *Bhakti* or devotion which acts as a mediator 'between the other two terms of dialectic.'[31]

Writing on the ethical, moral and social ideals, supposedly unbroken (*sanātana*) yet demonstrably often compromised, represented by the Sanskrit epics, the *Rāmāyaṇa* and the *Mahaabhārata*, Robert P Goldman insightfully remarked: 'Few of the nations that have emerged as independent in post-colonial period have a more elaborate set of egalitarian ideals and instruments at their foundation than does India. The constitution of the Republic of India…is the foundation for a secular, egalitarian, and democratic state based upon universal adult suffrage which is officially committed to the elimination of the traditional inequalities of class, caste, community, etc. At the same time many segments of the Indian society…still cherish these texts and their heroes and heroines deeply and are willing to see in them normative, emulable, and indeed exemplary models for the political, social, and religious life of the nation.'[32]

Humanism *vs* Dharma: Home and the World

So what is Humanism? The literal meaning of this term would suggest that it is a characteristic by which we identify ourselves as humans. But it is precisely this anxiety among some scholars of fixing the nature and propagation of certain characteristics of Humanism that causes confusion among many, which, perhaps, prompted Mahatma Gandhi to remind us of universal humanism, and this he did by invoking India's heritage of what he called Indian *dharma* the true spirit of which defines the diversity of Indian ethos, be that the Buddhist, Jaina, Sceptics, Sikh and Christian. He said that nobody has the moral right to appropriate the wisdom of what we call Indian dharma, i.e. universal Humanism; all these various faces of Indian tradition rest mainly on the fact that the discovery of what is true and what is false has to be constant and cannot at any given point be complete.[33] But this process of universalisation and appropriating others' cultural categories and/or identities may lead to what some have feared 'hybridization' or confusion of cultural identity. Pratap Mehta has suggested that the process of diversity, or appropriating and borrowing from the pool of universal values, will inevitably suffer from selectivity, for such borrowings are done 'in a way that does not put anything serious in one's culture at risk.'[34] Could this be one of the reasons that the ancient Indian ethics warns against the dangers of *varṇasaṃkara*, or mixing of diverse groups even within one culture? Or, is this analogy too far-fetched to be applied in the present context?[35]

As I have mentioned above, modern Indian thinkers have tried to analyse this vision of Indian religion scientifically, and Mahatma Gandhi and Radhakrishnan both tried to suggest that a religion becomes authoritarian when it is perceived or practised without analysis.[36] Because there is no room for authority or superiority in any analysis for it kindles the spirit of free inquiry and the right to think for oneself.[37] Radhakrishnan does not see much difference between the inquiry of science and that of religion, because both claim to get closer to the truth as time goes on; both envision the future: 'Why should we think that only in religion truth is something handed down from the past which we have to guard jealously lest we should stray further away from it? The golden age is in the future vision, not in the fabled past.'[38]

If we thus were to analyse the vision of Indian dharma, as proposed above, we would find that it refers to what some have called the true religion of mankind, i.e. (a constant, unbroken effort to seek) one's identity, the truth. There was this vision in mind when the seers of India called Indian religion the *Sanātana dharma*, a *dharma* that expects continuity not only in search of the truth but also in experiments with the paths to that search. However, Goldman has suggested that 'a close synchronic analysis' of the Indian *dharma* 'accompanied by the diachronic examination of the culture's shifting response' to the ethical predicaments the epics represent reveals that 'while epics and the culture in which they are embedded make frequent rhetorical appeals to *sanātana dharma*, a theoretically single, eternal, and immutable code of values, in reality the texts and their interpreters have always understood *dharma* to consist of a complex set of codes from which the justification for a variety of actions could be drawn.'[39]

The Vedic poets, too, stressed that the language in which they sing unifies all elements of the universe—humans, animal and nature – and not divides them: 'The first beginning of Speech was when wise men appeared engaged in giving names. From their love for the world they revealed their best, most perfectly guarded secret. With the sacrifice, they followed the path of Speech. They found her within the sages. They brought her out and divided her into diverse parts. Seven men join in singing her encomia. One man looks, but does not see 'Speech'; the other listens but does not hear 'Speech'' and so on (*Ṛg Veda* 10.71.1-4).[40] This description of universal unity is what has laid the foundation of humanity in ancient Indian texts and context and has thus beckoned the minds of great people in successive generations.[41] As Muzaffar Alam has explained in his paper in this volume, in an attempt to consolidate their power and to be able to rule in peace in an otherwise hostile atmosphere of the Hindu majority north India the early Sultans of Delhi recognised and patronized, the concept of 'unity in diversity', which was adopted, practised and preached by the Sufi Shaikhs, and thereby tried to legitimise their rule through *'waḥdat-al wujūd'* (or the 'Unity of Being'), the language and belief of the Sufis. Muzaffar Alam goes on to say that in an effort to make the atmosphere conducive for 'greater interaction between different sects and appreciation of their apparently divergent thoughts and practices, as all were believed to be one in the ultimate analysis.'[42] In fact, the idea of *waḥdat-al wujūd* gained greater prominence during the reign of the Mughal emperor Akbar when his minister and, later, biographer, Abu'l Fazl, organised with the full blessings of the emperor the translation project of important Sanskrit texts into Persian.[43] Thus through the doctrine of *waḥdat-al wujūd* the 'alignment of Rama with Rahim, Hari with Hazrat, Krishna with Karama, Muhammad with Mahadeva perhaps represented more than a mere verbal equation.'[44]

The story of Rāma, too, envisages an ideal, happy world, where 'no one had any fear from disease, nor from snake as far as Rāma's rule extends; the society was free of robbers, nobody ever faced adversity; every one emulated Rāma in observing righteousness and was always happy; nobody indulged in any violence with each other.'[45] This utopian view, Berlin (1990:20) has pointed out, has always occupied the human mind, beckoned individuals, both in the East and the West, for there remains a wish for a perfect society that 'lives in a state of pure harmony, in which all its members live in peace, love one another, are free from physical danger, from want of any kind, from insecurity, from degrading work, from envy, from frustration, experience no injustice or violence, live in perpetual, even light, in a temperate climate, in the midst of infinitely fruitful, generous nature.' Mahatma Gandhi did his best to emulate these values and made the ethical position of Rāma, the hero of the *Rāmāyaṇa,* his ideal,[46] for such an approach to life and the world will be, in the words of B.K. Matilal, a "humanizing process" and, therefore, 'what we may call human religion will teach us to regard nobody as sub-human; it will teach us to discard the peculiar, infantile, "strange-therefore-enemy" logic which unfortunately persists in human behaviour.'[47]

Notes and References

1. This is the revised version of the paper presented at the ICCR's 60th Anniversary Seminar on *Indian Culture in a Globalized World*, at the ICCR, New Delhi, November 11-12, 2010. I am grateful to Dr. Karan Singh, President, ICCR, Shri Suresh Goyal, DG, ICCR, Mr. Sunil Mehdiratta, Director, ICCR, my friend and colleague, Amitabh Mattoo for inviting me to participate in the seminar.
2. M.K. Gandhi (1961: 27), *Truth Called Them Differently* (*Tagore-Gandhi Controversy*), R.K. Prabhu and Ravindra Kelekar, editors, Navjivan Publishing House, Ahmedabad. See also Ramachandra Guha, "The Independent Journal of Opinion," www.india-seminar.com/1999.
3. Patañjali, *Paspaśāhnika,* I:1, 6-13. (All the translations from Sanskrit to English are mine, unless indicated otherwise.)
4. See Heeraman Tiwari, *From form to Universal: the Evolution of a Theory of Universals in Early Brahmanical Philosophy* (unpublished DPhil Thesis), Oxford University, Oxford,1993: Chapters 2 and 3.

5. J.N. Mohanty (1992: 58), *Reason and Tradition in Indian Thought: An Essay on Indian Philosophical Thinking*, Oxford: Oxford University Press.
6. V.S. Naipaul (2010: 212-213) *The Masque of Africa: Glimpses of African Belief*. London.
7. Ibid. 293-299.
8. S. Radhakrishnan (1932: 50-51), *An Idealist View of Life*, London: George Allen & Unwin.
9. *The Kiṣkindhā Kāṇḍa. Vālmīki Rāmāyaṇa:* 4.8.15. *Critical Edition*, Baroda: The Oriental Institute,1960-1975. For an insightful analysis on the ethical and moral predicaments in the two epics, particularly in the *Rāmāyaṇa*, see Robert P. Goldman (1997: 187-223), "*Eṣa Dharmaḥ Sanātanaḥ:* Shifting Moral Values and the Indian Epics," in the *Relativism, Suffering and Beyond: Essays in Memory of Bimal K. Matilal*, edited by P. Bilimoria and J.N. Mohanty, Delhi: Oxford University Press.
10. Johann Wolfgang von Goethe. *Sämtliche Werke*, Stuttgart, 1902-7, Vol. 4; p. 73. (Quoted from Gombrich, E H. 1993: 37. *Topics of Our Time: Twentieth-century issues in Learning and in Art*, Berkeley: University of California Press.)
11. See *The Yuddhakāṇḍa. Vālmīki Rāmāyaṇa: Critical Edition,* Baroda: The Oriental Institute, 1960-1975.
12. *The Bhagavadgītā*, 1.30: *gāṇḍīvaṃ sraṃsate hastāt tvak caiva paridahyate/ na ca śaknomy avasthātuṃ bhramtīva ca me manaḥ//*
13. *The Bhagavadgītā,* 15.6: *na tad bhāsayate sūryo na śaśāṅko na pāvakaḥ/ yad gatvā na nivartante tad dhāma paramaṃ mama//* See also, the *Kaṭhopaniṣad*, 2.2.15: *na tatra sūryo bhāti na candratārakaṃ, nemā vidyuto bhānti kuto 'yam agniḥ/ tam eva bhātam anubhāti sarvaṃ tasya bhāsā sarvam idam vibhāti,* 'There shines not the sun nor the moon, nor the stars. What to speak of the fire? Everything shines when That glow by which is illuminated the entire world.'
14. Cf. Isaiah Berlin (1990: 20): "The idea of a perfect society is a very old dream, whether because of the ills of the present, which lead men to conceive of what their world would be like without them – to imagine some ideal state in which there was no misery and no greed, no danger or poverty or fear or brutalising labour or insecurity – or because these Utopias are fictions deliberately constructed as satires, intended to criticise the actual world and to shame those who control the existing regimes, or those who suffer them too tamely; or perhaps they are social fantasies – simple exercises of the poetical imagination." *The Crooked Timber of Humanity*, ed. Henry Hardy, London: Fontana Press.
15. S. Gopal (1989: 18), *Radhakrishnan: A Biography*, London: Unwin Hyman Ltd.
16. S. Radhakrishnan (1932: 218), *An Idealist View of Life*, London: George Allen & Unwin.
17. Daniel H.H. Ingalls (1960: 191-197), "On the Study of the Past", in *Journal of the American Oriental Society*, Vol. 80, No. 3.
18. Ibid, p. 191.

19. Ramachandra Guha (2010: 522) *Makers of Modern India.* Edited and Introduced by Ramachandra Guha, Delhi: Penguin India. See also Ramachandra Guha. *The Sunday Times of India.* October 17, 2010: 10, New Delhi.
20. Ramachandra Guha (2010:518), *Makers of Modern India.* Edited and Introduced by Ramachandra Guha, Delhi: Penguin India.
21. Ibid. p. 520.
22. Sheldon Pollock, on the other hand, raised the question, recently: 'Why do we care about the past?'; he followed it up by answering that 'we care about the past because we care about the future. And we want to have a more human world, where we have better choices than we had in the past.' (Sheldon Pollock, "A Pre-colonial Language in Post-colonial World," interview in the *International Institute in Asian Studies* Newsletter No. 36, March 2005, Leiden: The Netherlands, pp. 1 & 4-5.)
23. See B.K. Matilal (1990: 106-132), *The Word and the World: India's Contribution to the Study of Language*, Delhi: Oxford University Press.
24. Daniel H.H. Ingalls (1960: 191-197), "On the Study of the Past", in *Journal of the American Oriental Society*, Vol. 80, No. 3. See Daniel H. H. Ingalls (1960: 194-212, "The Heritage of Asia and Asia Today," in *Both Human and Humane: the Humanities and Social Sciences in Graduate Education,* edited by Charles E Boewe and Roy Nichols. Philadelpia: University of Pennsylvania Press; Amartya Sen (2005), *The Argumentative Indian: Writings on Indian History, Culture and Identity.* London: Allen Lane.
25. Amartya Sen (2005), *The Argumentative Indian: Writings on Indian History, Culture and Identity*. London: Allen Lane.
26. Daniel H.H. Ingalls (1960: 191-197) 194-212), "The Heritage of Asia and Asia Today," in *Both Human and Humane: the Humanities and Social Sciences in Graduate Education,* edited by Charles E Boewe and Roy Nichols. Philadelpia: University of Pennsylvania Press.
27. Amartya Sen (1999: 13), *Development As Freedom.* New York: Alfred A. Knopf, Inc.
28. Amartya Sen, *The Argumentative Indian: Writings on Indian History, Culture and Identity*. London: Allen Lane, 2005; *The Idea of Justice.* London: Allen Lane, 2009. See also B.K. Matilal, *Perception: An Essay on Classical Indian Theories of Knowledge*, Oxford: Clarendon Press, 1986 (Paperback 1991): 69-93. Amartya Sen (2005) quotes the above work of Matilal's to make his point on the healthy practice of ancient debates in Indian philosophy. For a critique of Amartya Sen's *The Argumentative Indian*, see Jonardon Ganeri, "Intellectual India: Reason, Identity, Dissent," in *New Literary History*, Volume 40, Number 2, Spring 2009, pp. 247-263.
29. B.K Matilal (1977), *The Logical Illumination of Indian Mysticism: An Inaugural Lecture delivered before the University of Oxford on 5 May 1977.* Oxford: Clarendon Press, 1977: 30. See also B.K. Matilal (1981),

The Central Philosophy of Jainism (Anekāntavāda), L.D. Series 74. Ahmedabad: L.D. Institute of Indology, 1981.

30. Pratap Bhanu Mehta, "The Ethical Irrationality of the World: Weber and Hindu Ethics," in *Critical Horizons* 2:2 (2001), Leiden: K Brill NV, 2001: 203-225.
31. Discussing the *Dharma* of the *Mahābhārata,* Wendy Doniger says that within the text of the *Mahābhārata* 'the warrior with ethical misgivings has been persuaded to kill, just as the god kills, and outside the text, the reader or the hearer has been persuaded that since war is unreal, it is not evil. …The *Mahābhārata* as a whole is passionately against war, vividly aware of the tragedy of war, despite the many statements that violence is necessary. Nor, despite the way that Krishna persuades Arjuna to fight, is the *Gītā* used in India to justify war; it is generally taken out of context and used only for its philosophy, which can be used to support arguments for peace, as, notably, in the hands of Gandhi.' Wendy Doniger, *The Hindus: An Alternative History*, Delhi: Penguin/Viking, 2009, pp. 282-285.
32. Robert P Goldman (1997), "*Eṣa Dharmaḥ Sanātanaḥ:* Shifting Moral Values and the Indian Epics," in the *Relativism, Suffering and Beyond: Essays in Memory of Bimal K. Matilal,* edited by P. Bilimoria and J.N. Mohanty, Delhi: Oxford University Press, 1997: 199.
33. *The Collected Works of Mahatma Gandhi* (1960-1994), Ahmedabad: Navjivan Press. Volume 21, p. 256.
34. Pratap Bhanu Mehta (2000: 630), "Cosmopolitanism and the Circle of Reason," in *Political Theory*, Vol. 28 No. 5, October 2000: 619-639.
35. See *The Bhagavadgītā*, 1.41-44.
36. Mahatma Gandhi wrote in the *Young India* (12 May 1920): "Let me explain what I mean by religion. It is not the Hindu religion, which I certainly prize above all other religions, but the religion which transcends Hinduism, which changes one's very nature, which binds one indissolubly to the truth within and which ever purifies. It is the permanent element in human nature which leaves the soul restless until it has found itself."
37. S. Radhakrishnan (1932: 12), *An Idealist View of Life*, London: George Allen & Unwin. Quoting the famous European philosopher and psychoanalyst S. Freud, Radhakrishnan says that religion when understood in terms of 'certain dogmas, assertion about facts and conditions of external (or internal) reality which tell us something that one has not oneself discovered and which claim that one should give them credence,' then the religious doctrines become nothing more than "illusions".
38. Ibid. p. 13. For relationship between religion and humanism, see pp. 56-57.
39. Robert P Goldman (1997: 211), "*Eṣa Dharmaḥ Sanātanaḥ:* Shifting Moral Values and the Indian Epics," in the *Relativism, Suffering and Beyond: Essays in Memory of Bimal K. Matilal,* edited by P. Bilimoria and J.N. Mohanty, Delhi: Oxford University Press, 1997.

40. *Ṛg Veda* 10.71.1-4. Also, cf. tr. B. S. Miller, 1984: 28; *The Theater of Memory: Plays of Kālidāsa*, New York: Columbia University Press (Indian edition, Delhi 1999). I have largely borrowed Miller's translation with minor changes here and there.
41. The various mantras, verses and commentaries from the ancient Vedic, Buddhist and Jaina to the pre-modern texts, all espouse, without compromising the unbroken chain of wisdom, the freedom of choice for which a fellow human being must aspire.
42. Muzaffar Alam (2013: 145-76), "The Sufi Shaikhs and the Formation of the early Mughal Regime," in *Culture, People and Power: India and a Globalized World,* ed. A. Matto & H. Tiwari; Shipra Publications, 2013, Delhi.
43. See Jonardon Ganeri (2009: 247-263), "Intellectual India: Reason, Identity, Dissent," in *New Literary History*, Volume 40, Number 2, 2009: "In India… a long running process of religious isomorphism, pioneered by Akbar's minister Abu'l Fazl and orchestrated around Ibn al Arabi's idea of 'Unity in Being' (*waḥdat-al wujūd*) reached fulfilment n Dara Shukoh's grand project to translate fifty-two Upanishads into Persian… Dara believed that he could establish that the differences between Hinduism and Islam were largely terminological, and even that the Upanishads could be read as a sort of commentary on the Qur'an." (pp. 258-259)
44. Muzaffar Alam (2013: 145-76), "The Sufi Shaikhs and the Formation of the early Mughal Regime." in *Culture, People and Power: India and a Globalized World,* ed. A. Matto & H. Tiwari; Shipra Publication, 2013, Delhi.
45. *The Vālmīki Rāmāyaṇa: Critical Edition* (1960-1975); see the last chapter of the Book Seven, *Uttarakānda.*
46. Cf. Arshia Sattar, *The Vālmīki Rāmāyaṇa: Translated with an Introduction, Delhi: Oxford University Press,* 1996: 576-592: "Under Rāma's rule, no one ever heard the wailing of widows, nor was there any fear of disease or poisonous snakes. There was no cruelty or injustice and the old never had to do the work of the young. There was happiness everywhere and *dharma* flourished. People took their example from Rāma and were never violent towards each other. Everybody lived for a thousand years and had a thousand sons. They knew neither disease nor happiness. Trees yielded fruit and flowers all year, the rains always came at the right time and the touch of the wind was always pleasant. Everybody did their own work and happily lived the lives prescribed for them. Everyone abided by *dharma* and there was no unrighteousness. …A long time went by as mighty Rāma actively pursued dharma and ruled his kingdom wisely and well. The bears, monkeys and *rākṣasas* lived under his control and everyday the vassal kings did what would please Rāma. The rain god sent rain on time, and the people in the cities and in the countryside were happy and prosperous. Under Rāma's rule, no one died an untimely death, no calamities occurred and no one acted un-righteously."

47. B.K. Matilal (2004: 172). *Logical and Ethical Issues: An Essay on Indian Philosophy of Religion*, (revised second edition, Heeraman Tiwari, ed.) Delhi: Chronicle Books. Also, C. P. Bhambhri, has suggested that cultural, philosophical, political and social narratives articulated throughout the Indian history have helped "the issue of identity", because 'while identity is a relational position in society with others, an "exclusivist" identity can also be constructed while defining "self" in relation to others.' (C.P. Bhambhri, *The Idea of Identity: Foundation Day Lecture,* Number 1, Academic Staff College, Jawaharlal Nehru University, New Delhi, 2010, p. 12.)

Notes on Contributors

Amitabh Mattoo is the Director of the Australia India Institute, Professor of International Relations at the University of Melbourne, and Professor of Disarmament Studies at the Centre for International Politics, Organisation and Disarmament at Jawaharlal Nehru University, New Delhi. He was the Vice-Chancellor of the University of Jammu from 2002-2008. Professor Mattoo has been a Member of the National Knowledge Commission, a high-level advisory group to the Prime Minister of India and the National Security Council's Advisory Board. He received his Doctorate from the University of Oxford and has been a visiting Professor at Stanford University, the University of Notre Dame, the University of Illinois, and the Maison des Sciences de l'Homme in Paris. He was awarded the *Padma Shri* for his contribution to education and public life.

David Cortright is an American scholar and peace activist. He is the Director of Policy Studies at the Kroc Institute for International Peace Studies at the University of Notre Dame and Chair of the Board of the Fourth Freedom Forum, USA.

Heeraman Tiwari was educated at Lucknow (M.A.), Delhi (M.Phil. and Ph.D.) and at Balliol College, University of Oxford, England (D.Phil.). He teaches, intellectual history and philosophy of ancient India and Sanskrit language and literature, at the Centre for Historical Studies, Jawaharlal Nehru University, New Delhi. He was Heinrich Zimmer Professor of Indian Philosophy and Intellectual History, jointly at the Department of Philosophy and South Asia Institute, Heidelberg University, Heidelberg, Germany (2011-12). He has published several papers and edited volumes including *The Character of Logic in India* by B.K. Matilal (edited with J Ganeri, 1999) and *Six Systems of Indian Philosophy* by F. Max Mueller, New Abridged Edition (abridged and edited, 2004).

Jean-Luc Racine is Senior CNRS Fellow, Centre for South Asian Studies, School for Advanced Studies in Social Sciences, Paris and Director, Science Policy, Foundation Maison des Sciences de l'Homme, Paris.

Johannes Bronkhorst is one of the most famous Indologists and an Emeritus Professor of Sanskrit and Indian Studies, University of Lausanne, Switzerland. His many publications include *Buddhism in the Shadow of Brahmanism* (2011), *Language and Reality: On an episode in Indian thought* (2011), and *Greater Magadha: Studies in the Culture of Early India* (2007).

Muzaffar Alam is George V. Bobrinskoy Professor in South Asian Languages and Civilization at the University of Chicago. Previously, he was for many years Professor of History at the Centre of Historical Studies, Jawaharlal Nehru University, New Delhi. Professor Alam has held visiting positions in the Collège de France (Paris), Leiden University, University of Wisconsin (Madison), and the EHESS (Paris).

Muzaffar Ali is one of India's renowned film producers and directors.

Patrick Olivelle is Jacob and Frances Sanger Mossiker Chair in the Humanities and Professor of Sanskrit and Indian Religions, University of Texas at Austin, U.S.A. Among his many publications is his award-winning translation of the *Early Upaniṣads.*

Robert P. Goldman is Catherine and William L. Magistretti Distinguished Professor in South and Southeast Asian Studies at the University of California at Berkeley, U.S.A. Goldman has published many pioneering works on Sanskrit literature and Indian history and culture. He is the General Editor of the now famous *Rāmāyaṇa* Translation Project. Six of the Seven Books of *Vālmīki Rāmāyaṇa* have already been printed and the last Book (*Uttara*) of the translations is ready for publication.

Sally J. Sutherland Goldman is Lecturer at the Department of South and Southeast Asian Studies at the University of California at Berkeley. She has translated along with Robert P. Goldman several volumes of the *Vālmīki Rāmāyaṇa.* She is also the Co-editor of the *Rāmāyaṇa* Translation Project. Six of the Seven Books of *Vālmīki Rāmāyaṇa* have already been printed and the last Book (*Uttara*) of the translations is ready for publication.

Shashi Tharoor is an elected Member of Parliament (Lok Sabha) and Minister of State for Human Resource Development, Government of India; earlier, Dr Tharoor also served as Minister of States for External Affairs, Government of India. He was for many years at the United Nations, New York, and, before joining politics in India, Dr Shashi Tharoor was Under Secretary General of the United Nations, New York. He is also an award-winning author of over a dozen books (both fiction and non-fiction).

T.V. Paul is James McGill Professor of International Relations in the department of Political Science, and Founding Director of the Centre for International Peace and Security Studies, McGill University, Montreal, Canada.

Index